THE ORWELLIAN MOMENT

THE
ORWELLIAN
MOMENT

HINDSIGHT AND FORESIGHT

IN THE POST-1984 WORLD

EDITED BY
Robert L. Savage
James Combs
Dan Nimmo

The University of Arkansas Press
Fayetteville   London   1989

Manufactured in the United States of America
93 92 91 90 89   5 4 3 2 1
Designer: Brenda Zodrow
Typeface: Linotron 202 Granjon
Typesetter: G & S Typesetters, Inc.
Printer: Edwards Brothers, Inc.
Binder: Edwards Brothers, Inc.
The paper used in this publication meets the minimum requirements of the
American National Standard for Permanence of Paper for Printed Library
Materials Z39.48-1984. ⊗

LIBRARY OF CONGRESS CATALOGING-IN-PUBLICATION DATA

The Orwellian moment : hindsight and foresight in the post-1984 world
  / edited by Robert L. Savage, James Combs, and Dan Nimmo.
      p. cm.
    Includes bibliographies and index.
    Contents: Extending the Orwellian moment / by the editors—Orwell's po-
litical myths and ours / by John S. Nelson—Orwell's hopes, Orwell's fears / by
Michael P. Zuckert—Dark Utopia / by Mark E. Cory—Fictional 1984 and factual 1984 / by Thomas W. Cooper—Haigspeak, Secretary of State Haig, and
communication ethics / by Richard L. Johannesen—Manipulation and control of
people's responses to public opinion polls / by George F. Bishop—An Orwellian
Lasswell for today / by Hayward R. Alker, Jr.—Towards 2084 / by James Combs.
    ISBN 1-55728-027-4 (alk. paper)
    1. Orwell, George, 1903–1950. Nineteen eighty-four.   2. Politics in litera-
ture.   3. Future in literature.   4. United States—Politics and government—
1981-   I. Savage, Robert L.   II. Combs, James E.   III. Nimmo, Dan.
PR6029.R8N6455 1989
823'.912—dc19   88-18686
                                                                CIP

*To the wordsmiths anywhere, anywhen, whose language crafts
are devoted to the elevation of the human spirit.*

CONTENTS

The Orwellian Moment

EXTENDING THE ORWELLIAN MOMENT

AN INTRODUCTION

⟨ *The Editors*

In an essay penned in 1947, two years before publication in England of *1984* and three years before his death, George Orwell described the motivations for his craft. As might be expected, the essay—entitled "Why I Write"—was a highly personal account. He traced his interest in writing back to age "four or five" when he dictated his first poem to his mother, and knew shortly thereafter that "when I grew up I should be a writer."[1]

Orwell went on to say that he tried to abandon the idea of writing as a young adult, but returned to writing as a career and a passion by his mid-twenties, what was in fact to be the mid-point of his all too brief lifetime. And why did he settle on being a writer? Aside from the need to earn a living, he cited "four great motives for writing, at any rate for writing prose." First is what he labeled "sheer egoism," for he believed serious writers to be more vain and self-centered even than journalists, "though less interested in money." Second is a writer's aesthetic enthusiasm, the perception of beauty in the world and a desire to express it. Third is the motive of historical impulse, what today is captured in the phrase "tell it like it is" for posterity.

It is the fourth of Orwell's "great motives for writing" that serves in large measure as the rationale for this brief volume of essays about George Orwell and his enduring presence, a presence that has persisted well after his death in 1950 and in the renewed and heightened worldwide interest in Orwell that surrounded the year of 1984. For that fourth great motive is what Orwell designated "political purpose." By which he meant a broad sense of the notion "to push the world in a certain direction, to alter other people's idea of the kind of society that they should strive after." Orwell thought no book to be without political bias; in fact, even the view that art should have nothing to do with politics is itself, wrote Orwell, a political attitude.

This volume takes Orwell's fourth motive seriously. Most certainly Orwell himself took it seriously. Surely we must make such an assumption about a man who writes so directly that "what I have most wanted to do throughout the past ten years is to make political writing into an art." In fact, he wrote "my starting point is always a feeling of partisanship, a sense of injustice." Hence, he stressed "when I sit down to write a book, I do not say to myself, 'I am going to produce a work of art.'" Instead, he insisted, "I write it because there is some lie that I want to expose, some fact to which I want to draw attention, and my initial concern is to get a hearing."

We believe that the essays that constitute this anthology give Orwell a hearing by and among a group of people who only recently have taken much of his writing seriously. Certainly Orwell's work has been the subject of much commentary, assessment, and criticism by students of literature. His life, prose, poetry, and use of language have been the subjects for biography and detailed analyses.[2] But until recently—in fact a period coinciding with the approach of the year 1984 and popular concern with whether it would prove as "Orwellian" as he had allegedly prophesied—social scientists and particularly political scientists have given little attention to the relevance of Orwell's writings to politics in the modern world. Although Orwell himself thought *all* his prose to be politically motivated, by and large most social scientists did not.

There is no single reason why Orwell was so long ignored by social and political scientists. Perhaps one of the most overriding reasons is that so many of Orwell's essays are political in a broader sense of the term than most political scientists have been accustomed to using. More than eight decades ago, a founding father of political science as a separate discipline, Arthur F. Bentley, warned against "a dead political science" because it consisted of but "a formal study of the most external characteristics of governing institutions," and, when touching up "this barren formalism with a glow of humanity, an injection of metaphysics is used."[3] Bentley's warning went largely unheeded until recently; hence, Orwell's broader, nonformalistic definition of political went unappreciated as well. As Orwell put it in "Why I Write," essentially rejecting the "dead" political science of which Bentley warned, "and looking back through my work it is invariably where I lacked a *political* purpose that I wrote lifeless books and was betrayed by purple passages, sentences without meaning, decorative adjectives, and humbug generally."

To be sure, the more overtly "political" of Orwell's writing, that which conforms to the political science definition of "political," did attract the attention of political scholars. *Animal Farm* is a case in point, of which Orwell said that it was the "first book in which I tried, with full consciousness of what I was doing, to fuse political purpose and artistic purpose into one whole." And, certainly, *1984* is another example, although that work, too, was dismissed by most political scholars as only a political novel. That dismissal would not have come as a surprise to Orwell, for he had predicted that his next novel, which turned out to be *1984,* "was bound to be a failure, every book is a failure, but I do know with some clarity what kind of book I want to write."

Be that as it may, many politicians and political journalists accuse political science of ignoring the realities and trends of politics for esoteric and arcane analytical categories. Many social and behavioral scientists approach political writing as a science *qua* science, but Orwell by his own admission wished to make it into an art. Judging by many of the books and articles flowing from the word processors and laser printers of political scientists today, one can entertain the proposition that most of Orwell's political art remains as relevant and incisive as, if not more than, the contemporary products of the scientific discipline. Political art imitates, and sometimes stimulates, political life, even if much of political science does not. At least, that was Orwell's wish for political art. Thus this collection of essays is predicated on the view that Orwell's art deserves evaluation by scholars versed in various aspects of political and social relations with which the author dealt—political language, the totalitarian distribution of power, techniques of social control and manipulation, the ethical foundations of political communication, and related concerns at the heart of Orwell's writing.

In sum, a political assessment of Orwell's work, which certainly was stimulated by the interest in him surrounding the year of 1984, is appropriate and timely. Not only will such a political examination extend the Orwellian moment among political scientists provoked by *1984,* it will be of interest to lay audiences as well as scholars of mass communication, sociology, linguistics, futuristic studies, psychology, public administration, and related fields. The questions Orwell raised are urgent, especially to all who may find themselves living in the future he imagined. If, as Orwell prophesied, the human spirit can be destroyed by the demonic side of politics, then the nature and future of that demonic political power invites careful scrutiny.

Along with the motives that provoked his writing, there are aspects of Orwell and of what he wrote that prompt the publication of this series of essays.

George Orwell is the pen name for Eric Blair (1903–1950) who was born in Bengal, India, the son of an officer of the British Imperial forces. Orwell was educated at a prep school and at Eton, and later served with the Indian Imperial Police in Burma. "The Burmese experience," as he put it, only "increased my natural hatred of authority." Resentment of imperialism, the rise of Hitler and Nazi Germany, the Spanish Civil War—all turned Orwell toward the political left: "Every line of serious work that I have written since 1936 has been written, directly or indirectly, *against* totalitarianism and *for* democratic socialism as I understand it."

His personal experiences in Burma and Spain provided him with political orientation as did what he encountered as a young writer bumming around Paris and London. Soon there were novels and memoirs such as *Down and Out in Paris and London* and *The Road to Wigan Pier*. He lived in virtual poverty; nonetheless he acquired a literary reputation, writing essays for a wide variety of periodicals on politics, British life, popular culture, language, and writers such as Dickens and Kipling. Many of these essays are now classic examples of the form, widely reprinted, read and reread in literature courses.

Through his accumulated experience and reputation Orwell developed a unique political perspective. On the one hand, he was something of a political theorist of leftist persuasion. On the other, however, he was an incisive critic of the Left (a product, in part, of his participation in the Spanish Civil War). Hence, by the late 1940s Orwell was not only recognized as one of the major stylists and defenders of the English language, he was also the conscience of the British Left and a deeply committed political thinker-visionary of the era. *Animal Farm* (1945) and *1984* (1949) added worldwide fame to critical reputation and political notoriety. But a lifetime of poverty, overwork, and physical neglect could not be so easily assuaged by his success as a writer. In 1950 he died of a lung ailment.

Orwell's reputation has continued to grow since his death, partly because of the power of what he wrote and partly because of his personal example. As the world became increasingly threatened by totalitarianism and political reaction, his stubborn commitment to a benevolent socialism that avoided the totalitarian temptation yet realized the Enlightenment goals of liberty, equality, and fraternity survived. When he acquired a political purpose, a political maturity, his work began to come alive, to stir thought, and to enlarge our politial consciousness. For him, political writing became an art, and this wedding of politics and aesthetics led to Orwell's achievements as a political writer as yet unparalleled in this century.

His work survives, however, not only because of its inherent power but because the political conditions and trends he foresaw threaten the world now more than ever. Orwell said that he was "born, alas, in an evil time," and those evils he so honestly and persistently critiqued still beset us. The nature of his vision of the future continues to engage us because the horrible is now even more possible. We asked ourselves, as we neared 1984, were we nearing 1984 in Orwell's sense? Did we *want* the world of *1984?* What dark impulses in modern humankind, what social and political forces, seemed to impel us to create Orwell's nightmare?

Orwell's last novel depicts one of the two political nightmares of our time: The first is the possibility—many would now say the probability—that civilization will be destroyed by a nuclear holocaust, creating a nightmare of chaos; the second—Orwell's nightmare—is the possibility of a nightmare of control, an order that is "total" in its ability to regiment and manipulate the individual. Orwell's focus is on the individual, and how the last humane impulses—love, desire for freedom, the search for knowledge—can be controlled to the point of obliteration.

Both Orwell the man and Orwell the political writer, then, are worth consideration. As a man, he remains a model of political integrity, of the fearless pursuit of political truth, of the resolve of political commitment, of respect for and clear use of language, and of the belief that the pen is indeed mightier than the sword. Orwell the political writer, however, is our province. We want to look at the "age of Orwell" by evaluating the political import of *1984* in the light of the present, forty years after its publication. He raised, better than any writer of this century, important political questions which still haunt us. We want to ask those questions once again, as scholars impressed with the power and endurance of Orwell's accomplishments. As the world propels us toward the end of the twentieth century, those questions clearly need to be addressed. Orwell has been hitherto largely the province of the *literati.* As social scientists we believe that the symbolic figure of George Orwell deserves political scrutiny and may be used to explore some of the major political questions of our present and future. We frankly want to exploit the renewed interest that the passage of the year 1984 brought. But we also want to look at the world beyond 1984, for it is in that world that Orwell's vision of the future might become all too real. It is with the long-range political significance of *1984* with which we are concerned. We believe that the future may well bring an Orwellian world. But as we share his humane concern that the world's politics is truly bent in nightmarish directions, we also share his conviction that it is not a good thing. We may only hope that such an "evil time" will be averted and that this book will somehow contribute to the world not becoming Orwellian. In that sense, we share Orwell's purpose.

There is much controversy surrounding Orwell's intentions. What did he really intend as the message of *1984?* Intellectuals, journalists, and political hacks

have often asserted their interpretations of his profound intentions and thus justified their use of his works, especially *1984,* to promote whatever causes they
wanted to espouse. In a sense, the contributors to this volume are also asserting
something about Orwell's intentions. We feel, however, that the essays serve to
enlighten the reader about the larger values that Orwell espoused and that they
avoid the proselytising for narrow partisan causes characteristic of many of his
latter-day interpreters.

It should not be surprising, then, that no great surprises emerge in terms of
what those intentions were. Four broad themes generally characterize the essays:
the role and meaning of totalitarianism in the modern world, the dystopic vision
as a twentieth-century metaphysic, the prospects for social control through manipulative communication, and the maintenance of political integrity through
clear and systematic analysis of political language and beliefs. These do not exhaust the possibilities of what Orwell intended to address, nor are they mutually
exclusive. We simply hold that these are among the most plausible perspectives to
be taken in assessing what he really meant.

If there are no surprises in these thematic intentions, however, that is not to
say that there is nothing new here. Each contribution probes deeply into its chosen
theme to reveal new insights into its meaning for our lives today and to suggest
that the Orwellian vision continues to hold great significance for our future.

Just as Orwell assuredly did not intend to be a Nostradamus of the modern
age, neither should any of the following essays be taken as predictions nor blue-
prints for a revised vision of an "Orwellian world" at some future date. Rather,
the contributors hearken to that prophetic spirit which led Orwell to locate significant social and political tendencies and, without flinching or shirking, to ex-
trapolate their possible consequences as human alternatives. In the post–1984 era
we have the advantage of hindsight in looking at the present tendencies in the
light of Orwell's foresight.

The essays by John Nelson and Michael Zuckert, both political scientists,
focus on totalitarianism. Nelson examines that motif by addressing Orwell's role
in shaping our contemporary political myths. He points to Orwell's mythmaking
as the prophetic relevance of *1984* today, denying that Orwell sought to predict
some future time through futurological extrapolations. In shaping our expectations of Communistic totalitarianism, however, Nelson argues that Orwell by implication also shaped our conception of democracy simplistically as "non-totalitari-
anism." Ironically, the solution to the problems created by this mythmaking is the
creation of new myths more appropriate to our own time, myths that nonetheless
take account of the possibility of an Orwellian world. In a very real sense, then,
Nelson is asserting that Orwell's intention was not really the prediction of a totalitarian future but rather the opening of possibilities for a more democratic one.

Zuckert is less sanguine about that future. Certainly he recognizes that Orwell had his hopes for a better future. Yet Orwell's fears derived from squarely facing the dilemma of modern secular humankind. Rationalism has prevailed in the twentieth century, driving out both gods and demons of the old sacral order. But the exalted objectivity of this rationalistic worldview could not be sustained. The return to subjectivity, where human nature is essentially recognized as plastic, opened up frightful possibilities for a future where new human—all-too-human—gods and demons will structure new orders. Such, Zuckert finds, was Orwell's despair, providing the basis for his nightmare vision of a totalitarian future wherein the ruling demon-gods find their only justification in their seeming omnipotence. Zuckert's assessment does not directly contradict that of Nelson. While they come to different conclusions regarding the meaning of totalitarianism in Orwell's *1984,* their essays are genuinely complementary.

Since "totalitarianism" has such nightmarish connotations for those who write in the Western philosophic and political tradition, the corollary notion of "dystopia" also finds frequent treatment as a focus in examinations of *1984.* Mark Cory, a German-language scholar, engages us with an intriguing comparison of Orwell's novel with dystopic works of some of his German contemporaries. The German novels are not characterized by the same degree of pessimism noted in *1984,* perhaps, because they do not ascribe the same timelessness, the eternal present, of Orwell's totalitarian regime. Cory argues, moreover, that the German dystopias point to a transcendence, a religious experience, that is lacking in *1984.* He finds that recent German authors are less hopeful about human prospects, due in large part to the problems outlined in Zuckert's essay. One notable exception among these more recent German writers is Günter Grass whose works appeal to a spirit of revolt that, at least in terms of its consequences for the political regime, is not altogether unlike the transcendence suggested by the earlier German dystopists.

The totalitarian and dystopian themes focus upon the state and, in either instance, the emphasis is upon the exercise of power. While Orwell, like traditional political philosophers, recognizes that the state's ultimate distinction lies in its supreme capacity for coercion, he nonetheless emphasizes that control of the mind rather than control of the body is the ultimate exercise of power. Thus his concern with language and mediated communication follows rather naturally. Those who have subsequently focused upon "Orwellian communication" have not necessarily stressed the government's role in mediated social control. Instead, anyone who is in a position to structure the communication process may properly be examined for Orwellian tendencies. We present three such essays here, the first two by communication scholars and the other by a social psychologist.

The broadest focus on communication is taken by Thomas Cooper who treats those elements in *1984* that have perhaps stirred popular imagination—and public fear—more than others: technological developments in mass communication. More specifically, he is concerned with those developments as they relate to ethical concerns for mass mediated control of public consciousness. Cooper demonstrates that many aspects of such controls—only vaguely alluded to in *1984*—are with us now. He points primarily to the social-institutional forces that use and shape communication technologies as the likely, if sometimes unwitting, culprits. And these controllers are not always governmental regimes, totalitarian or otherwise. Cooper's primary contribution is to suggest that the cumulative impact of all these developments may have some results similar to the "soulless" population presented in *1984,* even without the singular center of governmental power represented by Big Brother and the Inner Party.

While Cooper raises ethical questions in a largely organizational context, Richard Johannesen does not overlook the implications of *1984* for the communication ethics of individuals such as a former high-ranking American government official. He examines the use of language by Alexander Haig during his tenure as U.S. Secretary of State, language designed to control his environment, particularly in his interactions with media representatives. Johannesen presents a penetrating case study of a power wielder who knowingly abused language to enhance his own power.

George Bishop offers a different kind of study in language manipulation. He demonstrates that the structure of questions in sample surveys can have a powerful effect on the answers of the respondents. While this is a sizeable step away from persuading people to follow up with action, the manipulation of verbal behavior through linguistic "trickery" conjures up the foreboding images of communication manipulation of the population in *1984.*

While many, if not most, of Orwell's readers since 1949 have been exposed only to *1984* and, perhaps, *Animal Farm,* these last two major fictional works flow from a much larger body of works and thought. Whatever logical "holes" one may find in the later works, the total written legacy of Orwell exhibits a penchant for clear, analytic language. Indeed, the author's frequent references to the need for such analysis heightens this theme as a compelling agent for the writing of *1984.* In any event, the political scientist Hayward Alker finds the locus of his essay here in a novel comparison between Orwell and an American contemporary of his, the great behavioral scientist Harold D. Lasswell. Like Orwell, Lasswell, albeit in the jargon of the social sciences, left a legacy of works filled with prophetic warnings based on extrapolations of tendencies he observed at the time. Not to presage Alker too much, one of these, Lasswell's depiction of the likely emergence of "garrison states," suffices here to show the parallel concerns of the two men. Lasswell, too, was a mythmaker, although his myths were not directed toward popular consumption. Still, his works beg to be reexamined by those who would continue the Orwellian tradition of bringing clear language to the study of politics.

James Combs concludes the volume by looking forward to still another mythic year, 2084. Just as Orwell made no pretense of predicting the state of affairs for 1984, Combs makes no specific assertions about what human civilization will be like a century from that date. Yet, through a succinct summary of the Orwellian vision presented in *1984*, he describes what remains a definite possibility, a world of death-cultures opposed to everything that George Orwell stood for in his life and work. Combs also points to the pertinence of a complimentary vision, just as chilling, first conjured up by Aldous Huxley, a brave new world indeed. The salient point in either case is that if we humans want a future offering honor, dignity, and integrity for individuals, we would do well to look to the example of George Orwell, the man and the writer.

Implicit in this final essay and, indeed, in this volume as a whole is the important distinction between an Orwellian vision or world and an Orwellian tradition. The former term derives from the pundits who would label the totalitarian, dystopian, manipulative aspects described in *1984* as a possible human future. The Orwellian tradition, on the other hand, points to the clear, unshrinking analysis of the human experience as it is, as it can be, and as it might be. Most of all it is, as is clear in the essays that follow, saying *no* to any and all forces that would enervate human consciousness. In that sense we want to extend the future of *1984*.

NOTES

[1] *The Collected Essays, Journalism and Letters of George Orwell,* Volume 1, Sonia Orwell and Ian Angus, editors (New York: Harcourt Brace Jovanovich, 1968), pp. 1–7. All quotations cited from this essay are from this source.

[2] See, as examples, Bernard Crick, *George Orwell: A Life* (Boston: Little, Brown, 1980) and W. F. Bolton, *The Language of 1984* (Knoxville: University of Tennessee Press, 1984).

[3] Arthur F. Bentley, *The Process of Government* (Chicago: University of Chicago Press, 1908), p. 162.

ORWELL'S POLITICAL MYTHS AND OURS*

≈ John S. Nelson

Myths are the realities of every civilization. "[E]very society must have a myth to live by, else it's a walking corpse that will soon fall to the ground."[1] "[E]very culture which has lost myth has lost, by the same token, its natural, healthy creativity. Only a horizon ringed about with myths can unify a culture."[2] In decay, defeat, or fragmentation, myths produce and express a profound unsettling of society. If "American myths are relatively new to human history," nonetheless "Americans frequently voice the fear that their world is falling apart. Certainly values and myths, beliefs and logics which we have held dear are being questioned by many. And the questions are serious."[3]

At least politically, myths are symbolic stories of the whole: the world, the community, the occurrence, the character, the environment, or some other entity. Because we ordinarily live as parts of mythic wholes, current myths remain mostly unremarked. For myths, this means that serious questions often signal serious troubles. Jeopardy to a mythos, to a complex of myths, is jeopardy to the culture that it helps to constitute. Recounted mythically, times of great jeopardy are times of terrible trouble.[4] Telling mythic-time can be tricky; still, for the last half of the twentieth century, Americans know that the time of terrible troubles is *1984*.

Americans know as well that the source of *1984* was George Orwell. Orwell saw himself as a political pamphleteer and polemicist for our times. If myths are "a common but neglected type of political argument,"[5] then surely Orwell was a political mythmaker—perhaps the greatest of our times. As collective imaginings, myths are never made wholly by a single person. Yet we may sometimes identify their main instigators as historical individuals. If the issue is mythic rather than literary excellence, then there is no doubt that Orwell's *1984* is our predominant tale of the nightmare society, that his classic allegory *Animal Farm* is our central story of revolution gone wrong, and that Orwell is the major author of our mythos of totalitarianism. Scores of scholars have articulated the mythos of totalitarianism into political theory, but again the crucial contributor is clearly Orwell.

Especially in *The Origins of Totalitarianism* and *Eichmann in Jerusalem,* but also through *The Human Condition, Men in Dark Times, On Revolution, Between Past and Future,* and *Crises of the Republic,* Hannah Arendt added telling detail to Orwell's outlines. She extended the stores of totalitarianism both historically and philosophically, and she shared Orwell's worry that democracy could atrophy into a shell for totalitarianism, especially as it stems from Orwell and Arendt.

In particular, let us explore a key irony from their mythmaking: how interaction with the mythos of totalitarianism has gradually leeched cultural and institutional vitality from the mythos of democracy. For I argue that current troubles of American political myth trace in important part to the genius of Orwell, Arendt, and their generation of political mythmakers. Much as the survival of democracy in the twentieth century has depended on their skill in making myths of totalitarianism, the revival of democracy in the twenty-first must rely on our will for remaking myths of politics. We must comprehend how the maladies in our mythos of democracy come from contrasting it to totalitarianism. But we must not lose the lessons propagated in our political myths of absolute power, ideology, and terror. Hence we need new stories to instruct our politics, new myths for democracy, including new tales of good mythmaking.

The Mythos of George Orwell

A mark of monumentally successful mythmaking is assimilation of the author to the myth as one of its main characters. Whether a historical personage or not, Homer became a major part of the great Greek myths of *The Iliad* and *The Odyssey.* So also has Orwell become a key character behind the great Anglo myths of *Animal Farm* and especially *1984.* In the apt terms of Lionel Trilling, Orwell became for our troubled times the archetype of the "virtuous man." As "a figure in our lives," Orwell is characterized as not merely by "moral goodness, but also fortitude and strength in goodness." To be sure, "he was not a genius, and this is one of the remarkable things about him. His not being a genius is an element of the quality that makes him . . . a figure." If we ask what Orwell "stands for, what he is the figure of, the answer is: the virtue of not being a genius, of confronting the world with nothing more than one's simple, direct, undeceived intelligence, and a respect for the powers one does have, and the work one undertakes to do."[6]

As a mythic character, Orwell epitomizes the indictment of our times—ourselves—for failing to face facts and fulfill responsibilities. He represents the alternative to mass men manipulated by totalitarian elites, just as he embodies the opposite of intellectuals dominated by abstract ideas. He characterizes the civic virtue of the full but humble democrat: determined to defend decency in an increasingly indecent world,[7] dedicated to declare truth and protect it by language plain and sincere,[8] devoted to traditional principles of right and wrong *because* the heavens may fall.[9]

In Orwell's own words, "Every line of serious work that I have written since 1936 has been written, directly or indirectly, *against* totalitarianism and *for* democratic socialism, as I understand it. . . . What I have most wanted to do throughout the past ten years is to make political writing into an art."[10] "[F]orced into becoming a sort of pamphleteer,"[11] Orwell's art of political writing became that of the mythmaker. Through memorable images and devices of fiction, he urged and helped us to respond realistically—even courageously—to the troubles of our times.[12]

Orwell was self-conscious and purposeful in his vocation as a mythmaker for our politics. He regarded literature as persuasion, insisting that, "Above a quite low level, literature is an attempt to influence the viewpoint of one's contemporaries by recording experience."[13] Thus, for Orwell, literature is a form of action, or at least of argument interjecting itself into the realms of action. The practice of this principle is evident in virtually every word that he wrote. "There is no such thing as genuinely non-political literature," he believed, "and least of all in an age like our own, where fears, hatreds, and loyalties of a directly political kind are near to the surface of everyone's consciousness."[14] Therefore, Orwell's preeminent realm of action is politics. "In our time," however, "political speech and writing are largely the defense of the indefensible."[15] Thus his mission became to tell truth and nurture imagination against the onslaughts of political propaganda, totalitarian ideology, and intellectual abstraction.

For various reasons, Americans in particular tend to treat *1984* as a set of predictions about what once was the near future, generating article after article about the accuracy of Orwell's warnings from the recent past. While not exactly wrong, this misses the main impetus of Orwell's project, confusing the extrapolations of futurologists with the prophecies of mythmakers. Orwell's prophecies, like his polemics,[16] always intended and usually effected a palpable sense of current travesties and perverse possibilities—urging us to face, rectify, and avoid them. Those who teach about pressing problems of the present or horrendous troubles in times ahead know well that statistical specifics and policy recommendations are no match for the immediate images and narrative interests of Orwell's dystopia.[17] In myriad ways Orwell's writings achieve the tangibility of potent mythmaking.

Orwell's mythmaking is apparent also from his use of fiction. The mythmaker's respect for the truth-telling faculties of fiction is plain not only in Orwell's allegory, dystopia, and other novels but also in his journalism. The mythic character of Orwell is directly evident in such works as *Shooting an Elephant, Down and Out in Paris and London, The Road to Wigan Pier,* and *Homage to Catalonia.*[18] There his famous prose, simple and flexible, is fully refined; and there his mythic themes, known to us as Orwellian, are amply present.

Lionel Trilling likened Orwell's temperament and interests to those of Peguy, G. K. Chesterton, Cobbett, and Hazlitt.[19] With *Animal Farm* and especially *1984* in mind, Orwell's themes are more often compared to the satires of Jonathan Swift, the dystopias of Eugene Zamiatin and Aldous Huxley, or Arthur Koestler's tomes of disillusionment. In complete compass, however, Orwell's concerns range far beyond totalitarianism and democracy. "Specific themes recurred throughout his journalism and essays: love of nature, love of books and literature, dislike of mass production, distrust of intellectuals, suspicion of government, contempt for and warnings against totalitarianism, advice on making, mending or growing things for yourself, anti-imperialism and anti-racialism, detestation of censorship, and praise of plain language, plain speaking, the good in the past, decency, fraternity, individuality, liberty, egalitarianism and patriotism."[20] If not a man for all seasons, Orwell was a man for many. Although he began with many interests, however, he harkened well to the peculiar "season in hell" that has been his and ours alike.[21]

Orwell's themes form five frames of argument that configure his contribution to the mythoi of totalitarianism and democracy:

RATIONALITY	TROUBLES	TRADITION	NATURE	DEMOCRACY
intellect	racism	decency	countryside	liberty
feeling	imperialism	history	environment	equality
imagination	monopoly	literature	sexuality	fraternity
language	bureaucracy	religion	privacy	personality
truth	totalitarianism	patriotism	independence	equity

By telling how Orwell's work coordinates these themes, we can account for his complex of political positions. But we can also begin to explain larger developments in the mythic dialogue between totalitarianism and democracy: how it has helped to save democracies by enlightening them about dangers of totalitarianism, and how it has started to distort ideals and practices of democracy by comparing them to features of totalitarianism. Let us look at the first column of the chart.

Orwell appreciated rationality as a requirement for human dignity, liberty, and responsibility. He associated rationality with prose and the capacity for making individual distinctions—and thus decisions—independent of the communal but easily overriding rhythms of poetry. Still, he worried about the modern inclination to reduce ratiocination to mere intellection, largely bereft of feeling and therefore impotent in imagination.[22] Especially as taught and practiced by intellectuals, this removes rationality from the common sense of ordinary people. Hence it robs rationality of the resources of everyday experience even as it reinforces the arrogance and ignorance of intellectuals. Eventually, this surely must corrupt thinking, which corrupts language, which in turn aggravates the corruption of thought.[23] Corrupted rationality often cannot and seldom cares to distinguish fantasy from reality. Accordingly, with intellectuals leading the way, we gradually lose our capacity for truth, especially in politics, where the motivations for distortion are as manifold as the failings which need be camouflaged and the people who need be fooled.[24]

On Orwell's account, then, the travails of our times trace to perversions of reality, which themselves stem from our incapacities for truth. Corrupted, our rationality is unable to recognize injustice. Even though art was the overarching ambition and sustaining skill of Orwell's political writing,[25] every particular work arose from his conjoint commitments to truth, rationality, and justice. "My starting point is always a feeling of partisanship, a sense of injustice. When I sit down to write a book, I do not say to myself, 'I am going to produce a work of art.' I write it because there is some lie that I want to expose, some fact to which I want to draw attention, and my initial concern is to get a hearing."[26]

Initially Orwell wrote against racism and imperialism. In *Burmese Days,* "A Hanging," and even *The Lion and the Unicorn,* he lambasted racists and imperialists not only for exploitation and a multitude of other injustices, but also for falsification of history and human interests, both abroad and at home. Through later events and experiences, Orwell discerned that our roster of troubles had increased to include three new sins of collectivism. "In our age, the idea of intellectual liberty is under attack from two directions. On the one side are its theoretical enemies, the apologists of totalitarianism, and on the other its immediate, practical enemies, monopoly and bureaucracy."[27] These travesties, too, he tied to disorders of rationality and truth.

It is especially plain in Orwell's treatment of totalitarianism that abstraction of intellect from feeling interrupts imagination, corrupts language, and disrupts truth. He accounts it to be the ultimate perversion that results from the intellectual and political debasement of language. It completely severs ties between rationality and reality. "The essential point of *Nineteen Eighty-Four* is just this, the danger of the ultimate and absolute power which mind can develop when it frees itself from conditions, from the bondage of things and history. But this . . . is a late aspect of Orwell's criticism of intellectuality. Through the greater part of his literary career his criticism was simpler and less extreme . . . : that the contemporary intellectual class did not think and did not really love the truth."[28] He observed that "The enemies of intellectual liberty always try to present their case as a plea for discipline versus individualism. The issue of truth-versus-untruth is as far as possible kept in the background."[29] By contrast, Orwell's mythmaking talents were devoted to pushing it as far as possible into the foreground. His mythos did not count the destruction of truth as the only source or instrument of totalitarianism but did make it preeminent, particularly through the brilliant construct of "newspeak."[30]

Orwell connected our worst troubles not only to depredations of rationality but also to degradations of tradition and nature. For Orwell, these subtler troubles of our times point to the elements needed if we aspire to adequate democracy. His writings sound almost conservative as they celebrate the traditional and natural aspects of ourselves which he regarded as dearest to the ordinary people who configure his vision of just societies. He encouraged us to combat twentieth-century troubles not only by taking personal responsibility for truth and language but also by cultivating decency, history, literature, patriotism, and perhaps even religion. Similarly, he urged us to revitalize our mythos of democracy by nurturing the countryside, the environment, sexuality, privacy, and personal independence.

The evident decline of the celebrated British sense of civility and decency upset Orwell deeply. He associated the atrophy of former senses of fair play with declining senses of justice, impaired faculties of judgment, and the spreading anomie which too often engenders mass and totalitarian movements. Moreover, respect for traditions of decency led him to recognize the dependence of decency on traditions. Hence he valued also the obstinate otherness and enduring variety of traditions, the past, and history as the source and protector of truth. He excoriated "the totalitarian point of view [that] history is something to be created rather than learned."[31] Instead of prizing the past, "Totalitarianism demands . . . the continuous alteration of the past, and in the long run probably demands a disbelief in the very existence of objective truth."[32] Relatedly, Orwell loved and lauded literature as our main repository of history. All life long, he read voraciously; and he wrote partly out of a "Historical impulse," a "Desire to see things as they are, to find out true facts and store them up for the use of posterity."[33]

Arendt argued that tradition, religion, and authority support each other in a classical trinity of commitments: when any one is impugned or diminished, the others will soon follow.[34] But even though Orwell venerated tradition, he usually disliked and disputed authority. Aside from his populist suspicion of government and intellectuals, this is most apparent from his castigation of religious authorities, especially those of the Roman Catholic Church. Nonetheless, there is something about religion which he instinctively respected; and he sometimes diagnosed modern troubles as symptoms of religious malaise, somehow in need of religious response. "The real problem is how to restore the religious attitude while accepting death as final."[35] Yet he said little specific about our religious requirements and how to meet them. "The major problem of our time is the decay of the belief in personal immortality," he maintained, but "it cannot be dealt with while the average human being is either drudging like an ox or shivering in fear of the secret police."[36]

Patriotism, on the other hand, received extensive and sympathetic attention from Orwell, who resisted its sneering desecration by fellow intellectuals of the left. "Orwell was careful, amid all his diatribes, to distinguish between *patriotism,* as love of one's own native land (so that anyone who grows into that love can be a patriot), and *nationalism,* as a claim to natural superiority over others (so that States must naturally consist of one nation and seek to exclude others)."[37] Orwell scored those who practiced or taught strict self-interest and hedonism.[38] He shared and treasured the affection of average citizens for their homeland, as he did the sacrifices that they were sometimes called to make for their country. In Orwell, this became "The Limit to Pessimism,"[39] the prime source of a hope even deeper and stronger than the despair apparent in *1984.* He believed that "the high sentiments always win in the end, the leaders who offer blood, toil, tears and sweat always get more out of their followers than those who offer safety and a good time. When it comes to the pinch, human beings are heroic."[40] Orwell was not naive about the exploitation and perversion of patriotism by many politicians. Still he held with Michael Walzer that "Patriotism may be the last refuge of scoundrels, but it is also the ordinary refuge of ordinary men and women."[41]

These paeans to love of country echo Orwell's fondness for the countryside, especially for the rural life and localities of England. Mythically harmonized, these became his eulogies of "the Golden Country,"[42] too likely passing away with the approach of "the Iron Haven" of *1984.*[43] Wonders of nature and worries of pollution made Orwell an early environmentalist.[44] Similarly, his concern for "the Golden Country" counterpoints a reverence for human nature which accounts for his interest in encouraging more relaxed but intense love and sexuality among people.[45] Moreover, the intimacies recommended by Orwell required vigorous protection of privacy, as does development of the right kind of individual rationality.[46] He associated that with providing natural, undeveloped spaces for visits by an increasingly urban humanity. Finally, he wrote so much about "making, mending or growing things for yourself" because he valued the human wholeness which self-reliance and a wealth of skills can bestow. He was too devoted to community and fraternity to promote full self-sufficiency of individuals. Yet he did prize and praise the personal independence that stems from a self-confident ability to meet natural exigencies as an experienced hand.

This independence was regarded by Orwell as the chief value and virtue of true democracy. Independent people are not just free but able to criticize themselves and their conditions; hence they are able to improve both.[47] Of course, Orwell has long been accounted the archetype of such independence in our times. In his ears the peals of such liberty do not dampen or drown out but instead accentuate the pleas of equality. As a democratic socialist, Orwell preached that full liberty requires ample equality: for freedom is as much fraternity as independence, and fraternity fails without considerable equality. Better than most, Orwell understood that equality cannot slide into sameness if independence and democracy are to endure. So he celebrated personality as the purpose and prerequisite of democracies. They depend on individuality for their existence, and they must be measured by their success in protecting it on the part of every person.

To defend independence and individuality while facilitating equality and fraternity, democracy requires a good sense of justice. To distinguish among individuals respectfully rather than invidiously, democracy needs decent standards and sound judgement. The resulting sense of justice is a rationality at once truthful, compassionate, and imaginative. It is a rationality duly disciplined by the concerns of nature and tradition articulated by Orwell, so that they individualize but do not homogenize or tyrannize. It is a rationality able to equalize, fraternize, and liberalize at the same time. In a word, it is what English legal theory has long recognized as a sense of *equity*. More than anything else, equity is for Orwell the mythic meaning of democracy. It is what democracy must have and what totalitarianism may not.

In mythic substance and sensibility, these themes tie Orwell's work closely to Arendt's.[48] Their projects share at least ten features crucial to creating the mythos of totalitarianism:

1. Both cultivated political sympathies primarily but loosely on the political left, although their common themes reveal how neither fits comfortably into modern classifications of left and right.
2. Both portrayed totalitarianism and bureaucracy as the most distinctive and terrible troubles of the twentieth century, even

as both decried the conventional alternatives of capitalism and liberalism.

3. Both characterized totalitarianism as bureaucracy run wild and made total, while both attacked bureaucracy as incipient or creeping totalitarianism.

4. Both insisted that totalitarian movements and regimes could happen here—virtually anywhere in the West, anywhere in the world.

5. Both indicted totalitarianism above all for destroying truth, which both regarded as the essential requirement for human dignity, liberty, morality, and rationality.

6. Both took totalitarianism as a radical challenge to our capacities for political mythmaking—stressing its irrationality, even by degenerate standards of Western politics.

7. Both indicted the commitments and concepts of contemporary intellectuals for contributing to the conditions, confusions, and contrivances of totalitarianism—rather than becoming effective critics of it.

8. Both implicated the gradual lapse of religion in modern times as a source of such political monstrosities as bureaucracy and totalitarianism, even though neither was conventionally nor actively religious.

9. Both characterized totalitarianism as political hell on earth—in order to warn us away from its lures and especially in order to reestablish decent standards for ordinary conduct in social and political affairs.

10. Both characterized democracy as the best possible approximation to political heaven on earth, and both made democracy the mythic opposite of totalitarianism, yet both disclosed and even contributed to significant troubles in the mythos of democracy.

As much by mythic implication as by express argument, the writings of Orwell and Arendt also hint at an eleventh theme in common:

11. The mythic confrontation between democracy and totalitarianism has ceased to serve us well, so that we need new political myths more adequate to the transformed circumstances of life late in the twentieth century.

From this point on, I continue to emphasize Orwell's mythmaking, but complement it with Arendt's. Since they stem from significantly different intellectual and political traditions, their agreements can increase our confidence in their myths. Moreover, their claims in common outline the rest of my argument for taking seriously their last, largely implicit theme: we need new myths of politics. To tell why, let us consider in turn the mythoi of totalitarianism and democracy.

THE MYTHOS OF TOTALITARIANISM

Originally, the mythos of totalitarianism was the work of several generations of scholars, journalists, and statesmen: Arendt, Franz Borkenau, Zbigniew Brzezinski, Winston Churchill, Erik Erikson, Carl Friedrich, Arthur Koestler, Herbert Marcuse, Franz Neumann, Orwell, Ignazio Silone, J. L. Talmon, Harry S Truman, and many others. Orwell was preeminent among them, particularly in shaping popular opinion. This is the testimony of supporters such as Irving Howe: "In the vast literature concerning totalitarianism, George Orwell's fictional *1984* occupies a central place."[49] "[I]t is a classic of our age."[50] But it is also the testimony of critics such as Isaac Deutscher: "Few novels written in this generation have obtained a popularity as great as that of George Orwell's *1984*. Few, if any, have made a similar impact on politics. . . . The novel has served as a sort of an ideological super-weapon in the cold war. As in no other book or document, the convulsive fear of communism, which has swept the West since the end of the Second World War, has been reflected and focused in *1984*."[51] In the words of another critic, Raymond Williams, Orwell become "the name for the change of mind of this generation [of leftist adults in the 1930s]: a change of mind that was seen as a hard-won and necessary truth, which must be passed on intact to its successors."[52]

Arendt was the academic equivalent of Orwell. Especially in *The Origins of Totalitarianism,* she told a story of the sources and courses of totalitarianism so vivid that supporters consider it to be "the most convincing single effort to grasp the meaning of the German and Russian regimes of the 1930s and 1940s,"[53] while critics condemn its comparison of Hitler's nazism and Stalin's communism for becoming a mythic juggernaut in cold-war politics.[54] To elaborate the mythos of totalitarianism, Arendt's elements make a fine complement to Orwell's.

Like Orwell, Arendt identified racism (in particular, anti-Semitism) and imperialism as origins of totalitarianism—but more as antecedents than causes. In them, she discerned the breakdown of the Western tradition of political thought and action and its replacement by mass society, making conditions ripe for totalitarian movements.[55]

END OF THE TRADITION	MASS SOCIETY
world alienation	atomization
radical doubting	superfluousness
radical sincerity	roles
radical mortality	stoicism

Again like Orwell, but in much greater detail, Arendt linked totalitarianism to bureaucracy and concentration camps. Bureaucracies are relatively partial and moderate embodiments of totalitarianism, while concentration camps are the most complete and extreme instances of totalitarianism yet achieved.[56]

BUREAUCRACY	TOTALITARIANISM	CONCENTRATION CAMPS
rationalism	ideology	extreme subjectivizations
efficiency	terror	gullibility and cynicism
mysticism	movement	truth as sincerity
endlessness	mass paranoia	amnesia and oblivion
self-protection	systematic mendacity	systematic self-deception
image-making	propaganda	lying the truth
banal evil	radical evil	new nihilism
rule by nobody	union	three circles of hell

Overall, the similarity of Orwell's and Arendt's accounts is so great that Arendt's silence on *1984* as a possible inspiration of her work is odd.

The mythos of totalitarianism began partly as a denial of differences said to separate Hitler's Germany decisively from Stalin's Russia. Among intellectuals, at least, the differences were usually claimed to the advantage of the Soviet Union, by partisans or sympathizers of communism. Insistence on a "fearful symmetry" between nazism and communism has been a basic component of almost all avowedly middle positions in politics since the Second World War.[57] Mythically, this was extended and diffused into a conviction of the fundamental identity of extremes, whether left or right. Rather than modern categories of left, middle, and right, politics became bifurcated into moderates and radicals. While Orwell and Arendt began (and remained, in a way) loosely on the political left, their mythic arguments denied deep significance to political spectra from left to right. Instead, they characterized the overriding requirement of our times as standing against totalitarianism, the radical evil that threatens to destroy the dignity of all humanity as it kills millions of people.

Orwell and Arendt made sharp criticisms of capitalism, individualism, liberalism, and other alternatives to leftist politics. Fascism and nazism were treated as so obviously vile that they hardly needed criticism—sheer exposure would suffice to discredit them; and conservatism seldom seemed to manage enough substance or significance to merit criticism. But despite the two mythmakers' ties to the left, their criticisms of it proved just as telling. In fact, the mythos of totalitarianism disclosed how incoherent the compass of right and left had become. Thinking only of the urgent need to resist totalitarianism, Orwell and Arendt in effect replaced the old compass with a new one of right and wrong. Contrary to their personal positions, however, the mythos of totalitarianism (in tandem with the mythos of democracy) soon grew into a fairly comprehensive vision of politics. It abstracted the new mythic compass into a simple map for virtually all politics as a war of freedom versus oppression, individualism versus collectivism, competition versus planning, independence versus bureaucracy, liberalism versus socialism, capitalism versus communism—in short, as a war of democracy versus totalitarianism.

Thus on the other side, the mythos of totalitarianism targeted communist, leftist, and other myths of the Soviet Union. "One ought not to exaggerate the direct influence of the small English Communist Party," Orwell wrote, "but there can be no question about the poisonous effect of the Russian *mythos* on English intellectual life. Because of it, known facts are suppressed and distorted to such an extent as to make it doubtful whether a true history of our times can ever be written."[58]

One result is that the mythos of totalitarianism aims at two different audiences: elites and masses. Arendt's work primarily addressed intellectuals. It is full of references to crowds and masses, sometimes disparaging the capacites (more than the intentions) of ordinary people. But Orwell concentrated more on average citizens as an audience. He took elites generally but intellectuals especially to be so removed from reality that they could seldom do better than irrelevance and often contributed mythically to our worst troubles. He believed that "totalitarian ideas have taken root in the minds of intellectuals everywhere,"[59] and he sought to scourge their influence over the public. His lifelong celebration of ordinary people as the greatest hope of humankind separates him decisively from the other "Menippean satirists" to whom he is often compared: Jonathan Swift and Mark Twain. He repeatedly reports about the lives of ordinary people, especially under oppressing and degrading conditions. This culminates in a mostly sympathetic portrait of the roles in Oceania. For brutal realism and unflagging respect, that appreciation of humanity in extremity is matched in my reading only by diaries from concentration camps and Aleksander Solzhenitsyn's stories of the Gulag.

Opposing the myths of the *Volk* and the Soviet Union, addressing intellectuals and ordinary people, the creators of the concept of totalitarianism meant to convey three main messages:

1. It is radically evil over there.
2. It can happen here.
3. It must be opposed at (almost?) any cost.

Confronting horrendous realities and combatting seductive myths, the counter-mythos depicted totalitarianism as the starkest and most absolute evil known to humanity: an irrational threat to the very soul of every living person and to the merest memory of every moment past.

In several essays, Arendt puzzled over the political implications of modern secularization. She wanted "to consider secularism in its political, non-spiritual aspect only and ask, which was the religious element in the past so politically relevant that its loss had an immediate impact on our political life? Or, to put the same question in another way, which was the specifically political element in traditional religion?"[60] Arendt argued that the answer is clear: "there is one powerful element in traditional religion whose usefulness for the support of authority is self-evident, and whose origin is probably not of a religious nature; at least not primarily—the medieval doctrine of Hell."[61] The roots of this doctrine reach past the Middle Ages to at least one source that is not primarily religious at all. And the really important point for Arendt was that "the doctrine of Hell in Plato is clearly a political instrument invented for political purposes."[62]

Secular societies cease to believe (deeply) in hell, with disastrous consequences for recent politics. For it is the one belief vouchsafed by the Western tradition that might withstand totalitarianism. Masses lack the sophistication required for other means to resist mobilization by totalitarian elites. Only a "noble myth" like Plato's portrait of hell as ultimate punishment after death could contest the lures and terrors of totalitarianism. But "the outstanding political characteristic of our modern secular world seems to be that more and more people are losing the belief in reward and punishment after death, while the functioning of individual consciences or the multitude's capacity to perceive invisible truth has remained politically as unreliable as ever."[63]

In this light, the mythos of totalitarianism plainly represents an attempt to fill the void left by the political impotence of religious hell. Orwell and Arendt led this effort. Their treatments of totalitarianism are among the richest mythically and clearest conceptually. The factual accuracy of their accounts is sometimes contested vigorously, but always they aimed at larger implications. Whether they decided consciously to display totalitarianism as the political equivalent of hell may be doubted. Whether their writings have had this effect may not. Arendt argued that totalitarian systems engage in "the almost deliberate attempt to build, in concentration camps and torture cellars, a kind of earthly hell whose chief difference from medieval hell-images lies in technical improvement and bureaucratic administration, but also in its lack of eternity."[64] Both Orwell and Arendt used images of hell to tell tales of totalitarianism as stories of utter, even ultimate evil. Striving to warn people away from totalitarian forms and temptations, both contributed to stories and symbols of consummate calumny and catastrophe in politics.

Neither meant to encourage despair, yet the mythic figures of inferno imported into their political hells evoke the gate that stood in Dante's vision, inscribed "Abandon Hope All Ye Who Enter Here!" Both favored apocalyptic terminology, images, and comparisons. Orwell depicted totalitarian progress as a path to ever greater pain and suffering. Arendt wrote that the trajectory of totalitarianism culminates in concentration camps where the morality, individuality, and humanity of inmates are destroyed before their bodies. Totalitarianism is a realm of the walking dead; its mythos is a pattern of apocalypse.

Totalitarianism is not mere tyranny or dictatorship but something worse invented in this century. As the junior Arthur Schlesinger says, *1984* "is about . . . a shattering discontinuity, a qualitative transformation, an ultimate change of phase. . . . Orwell's act of creative daring was to carry the logic of Nazism and Stalinism to the end of night." Thus "he helped shape for a season the theory of totalitarianism as unitary and irreversible, obliterating all autonomous institutions in society and reconstructing the human personality. This theory gained new authority with Hannah Arendt's *The Origins of Totalitarianism,* published two years later; for Arendt claimed as historical actuality what Orwell had advanced as admonitory fantasy."[65]

Orwell and Arendt were not alone in characterizing totalitarianism as an absolute and unprecedented evil. It is less a form of government than a new nihilism in which everything horrible is not only permitted but possible, at least in the concentration camps. Instead of fear to push citizens in certain directions, it deploys terror to panic and incapacitate them. Instead of rational calculation of means to individual ends, it moves masses through iron irrationalities of ideology and propaganda in an endless and uninstrumental worship of power. Instead of exploiting underclasses for a despot or overclass, it atomizes classes into one-dimensional masses which (for they are hardly *who's* anymore) await inspiration by a leader, discipline by a vanguard, and education by a new class of bureaucrats. Whereas tyranny takes away particular freedoms, totalitarianism destroys the very individuality which makes any freedom or humanity possible. Whereas tyranny turns the world upside down, debasing the best and exalting the worst, totalitarianism levels everything. In the memorable chant of Mark Crispin Miller, totalitarianism "makes no difference."[66]

The mythos of totalitarianism implies that it can happen here, in the West or elsewhere in the world. To early readers of *1984*, Orwell's Oceania seemed only a short time away from the London of World War II. Arguing that the Western tradition is failing, that civil societies are devolving into mass societies suited to bureaucracy and vulnerable to even worse totalitarianism, Arendt too implied that it can happen here. Others warned that it is already here, but only in limited terms. This may "contradict" an apparent requirement for *total*itarianism (in a way common among mythos), yet it lent urgency to calls for containment and vigilance. Thus Erik Erikson, Erich Fromm, Robert Jay Lifton, and others studied "totalism" as a psychological pathology already among us in important if still small respects. Similarly, Erving Goffman explored the logic of "total institutions" such as asylums and prisons. More daringly, Robert Nisbett argues that "the first twentieth-century preview of the totalitarian state was provided by the United States in 1917–18" under Woodrow Wilson.[67] Various writers suspect totalitarianism in "the corporate economy, the microchip society, or the welfare state."[68] Herbert Marcuse maintained that America and probably the other advanced industrial societies of the West have become subtly totalitarian dominions of Madison Avenue, manipulating us into one-dimensionality. In fact, it has become strangely common for intellectuals, at least, to take "*1984* as an allegory for America."[69]

Mostly, totalitarianism can happen here because it thrives on troubles for truth. Fully and firmly established, totalitarianism attacks the very possibility of truth. But by the accounts of Orwell and Arendt, it begins to ooze into our lives almost any time that lying becomes large-scale and systematic in the conduct of daily affairs. (The ordinary but distant lies of foreign affairs and moderate politics seldom threaten the fabric of everyday reality.) According to the mythos of totalitarianism, to control truth is to control reality, and to control language is to control truth. Primarily, this is the path of soft and subtle totalitarianism—by contrast with the hard and crude kind which violently rearranges reality to suit itself, coercing all and killing many. Yet even the hardest totalitarianism seeks to control language and truth; for ultimately, it seeks to control all reality, unto the few human souls it does not destroy. And how many souls be swayed except through thought that seeks the shape of language? Hence the mythos of totalitarianism condemns it above all for destroying truth, conceived as the key requirement for human dignity, liberty, morality, and rationality.

To attempt the destruction of all truth is to flirt with the destruction of all reality. Totalitarianism is not the purposeful or despairing nihilism of nineteenth-century politics but an experimental, sadistic, yet frivolous fury that makes no sense. Orwell and Arendt emphasized that totalitarianism could not be comprehended in Western terms. It is neither a Machiavellian nor a Hobbesian politics of power. It is not a miscalculation of means to ends. At the core it is not rational at all. Orwell saw it as an awful obsession of power. Arendt saw it as a radical evil that defies reason. Totalitarian irrationality demands mythical accounting even more than theoretical explaining, since only by telling its particular stories can its qualities be reckoned well.

The least persuasive part of *1984* is its attempt to account for totalitarianism as an idolatry of pure power. In comparing Evgeny Zamiatin's *We* and Aldous Huxley's *Brave New World,* the two main precursors of *1984,* Orwell contended that "It is this intuitive grasp of the irrational side of totalitarianism—human sacrifice, cruelty as an end in itself, the worship of a Leader who is credited with divine attributes—that makes Zamiatin's book superior to Huxley's."[70] But Orwell may have gone most astray in *1984* when he put this theory of totalitarianism into the preachings of O'Brien. They disrupt the spell of his story in ways not suffered by *Animal Farm,* and the parts of power feed the misguided fascination of intellectuals with airy abstractions.

Among intellectuals, one of the most famous passages in *1984* is O'Brien's perverse paean to totalitarians as "priests of power," the one that ends in a sadistic image of the totalitarian future as "a boot stamping on a human face—forever."[71] Yet as Isaac Deutscher wrote, this "mysticism of cruelty" is "the oldest, the most banal, the most abstract, the most metaphysical, and the most barren of all generalizations: all *their* conspiracies and plots and purges and diplomatic deals had one source and one source only—'sadistic power-hunger.'"[72] Orwell meant O'Brien's speech to convey the secret of totalitarian irrationality, but what he produced is the rhetoric of intellectuals at the pessimistic pole of their love-hate relationship to power. Then they want to despise power in all respects, in order to escape the ethical complications of facing it skillfully. At other points, Orwell knew better than this theory, recognizing in such reductions (of power as well as totalitarianism) what he regarded as the intellectual's typical fall into empty abstractions and perverse absolutes. I find it easy to believe that, had he lived another decade, he would have recanted on this point.

Arendt later produced a much better account of power, but her early tales of totalitarianism mystified it in much the same manner as Orwell. Indeed, the mythos of totalitarianism has come to rely most on mystification of power to warn us away from totalitarian terrors, ideologies, and institutions.[73] Thus the mythos impedes our ability to understand totalitarian politics of power; and when we do despite the mythos, it impedes our continuing to combat regimes as totalitarian. The result is to deprive our democratic politics of an exceptionally valuable, and perhaps rhetorically necessary, resource.

Beyond irrationalism, the mythos reckoned totalitarianism radically evil because of its totalism.[74] Totalitarianism seeks complete control of its inhabitants and their environments. This involves at least three objects or projects of control: the soul, the world, and the clock.

According to the mythos, the ultimate aim of totalitarianism is total control of the human soul. Once we describe a society, regime, movement, or cult as totalitarian, we acknowledge such basic violations of the human rights recognized by democracies that we imply a pressing need for action. The impulsion may be overridden by excessive dangers or undermined by insufficient means, but it remains an imperative for later times. The mythos may exaggerate the severity of conditions in organizations termed totalitarian on grounds other than jeopardy to the human soul. But even without the absolutism, what we have learned to term "totalitarian" remains qualitatively worse than what we call "authoritarian" or "dictatorial." If the mythos of totalitarianism were discredited, instead of revised or transcended, we would lose political distinctions not just valid but virtually imperative. Reconceiving totalitarianism could serve the needs of a prudent and tolerant but also principled democracy. Among departures from democratic policies, a good democracy must distinguish differences that are acceptable, those that are unacceptable but not so serious as to require intervention, and those that are so obnoxious that they must be contested actively and directly (except in the worst of circumstances).

Similar alterations seemed warranted for the second object of totalitarian control. Mythically, the totalitarian ambition to dominate the entire world follows not only from an irrational pursuit of unlimited power but also from an instrumental link between the scope and success of total control. How can control of some be complete unless they are severed from any contact whatever with others? Yet how can this be insured unless the others are completely controlled as well? The political rhetoric of world socialism is that none can be fully free until all are liberated. The mythic logic of world communism is that none can be totally controlled until all are dominated. When there is any totalitarianism, the rest of the world is made of dominoes. As radically evil, totalitarianism must be radically expansionist, radically imperial. Thus the Soviet Union is not merely an empire but, in the fine mythic phrase of Ronald Reagan, "an evil empire." Moreover, the mythos attributes to totalitarianism two special means of expansion: subversion through fifth columns and guerrilla wars—although neither Orwell nor Arendt did much to add these elements to the mythos.

By now, we have reason to know that the mythos is not utterly wrong in this respect and that many countries termed "totalitarian" are unusually devoted to expansion or at least agitation beyond their borders. (The latter seems true as well of some countries called "democratic.") But we have also seen enough to know how the mythos exaggerates the dedication of totalitarian regimes to expansion, their reliance on fifth columns, and the limitation of guerrilla tactics to totalitarian fighters. Moreover, we should by now be able to tell how most of the "expansions" are less a spread of totalitarianism than an imposition of imperialism by military force. So again, democrats need to tone down their treatments of totalitarianism in order to make distinctions important for foreign policy. By extension, the same could be said of the domestic need to come to terms with cults or other occurrences that tend toward totalitarian effects.

Mythically, the third object of totalitarian control is time. Through totalizing internal and external space, the intent of totalitarianism is to endure forever—essentially to escape any impediments of time. *1984* starts with the clock striking thirteen, indicating not only the suspension of normal time characteristic of nightmares but also a breaking beyond the restricted cycles of clock time into an eternal future. Not only is this the mythic ambition of totalitarianism, but it is also the mythic result. The mythos discovers no internal source of breakdown or decay. Should an external source intervene, then the totalitarianism evaporates suddenly and entirely, as swiftly as our dreams depart in day and as fully as the disintegration of Oliver Wendell Holmes' wonderful one-hoss shay.[75] But in that event, the totalitarianism had not become perfected—that is, total—in extent. Were it perfected in scope and intensity, then its monotonous moment would monopolize the entire future, irreversibly. Such dominations of time, such foreclosing of future change is why democrats could declaim of themselves and others: "Better dead than Red!"

Because we must now know mythically that nothing on this earth—not even totalitarianism—can reach full perfection or otherwise transcend time, we are ready to revise this element of the mythos as well. In fact, for all his final pessimism, Orwell did not endow *1984* with unambiguous features of totalized time. The ending defeat for freedom in *1984* is nearly necessary to the fictional form of the dystopia; with any happier ending, *1984, We, Brave New World,* or any other nightmare work would be in danger of transformation into heroic romance. Hence there is reason to wonder whether total control of time is as central to the mythos as some have assumed. Arendt, who lived and wrote late enough to know better, accounted particular totalitarianisms to be peculiarly transient, although she did reckon the reoccurrence of totalitarianism to be a continuing threat.

In alerting us to atrocities, steeling us to terrorisms, and sensitizing us to the significantly new travesties of twentieth-century existence, the mythos of totalitarianism is a real achievement of our politics. But now, toward the end of the twentieth century, it needs major modifications. Their urgency is most evident in the mythos of democracy: our counterpoint to the mythos of totalitarianism.

THE MYTHOS OF DEMOCRACY

As Senator J. William Fulbright observed, "The master myth of the cold war is that the Communist bloc is a monolith, composed of governments which are not really governments at all, but organized conspiracies . . . all equally resolute and implacable in their determination to destroy the free world." [76] The master myth of the cold war is part of the place where the mythoi of totalitarianism and democracy meet. Whether or not all major elements of myths come as pairs of opposites, as Claude Levi-Strauss contends, [77] the opposition of totalitarianism and democracy is a commonplace of our times. This explains the striking extent to which each mythos defines the other. In this respect, the logic of myth is dramatic and ironic: "what goes forth as A returns as non-A." [78] "In myths things always turn into their opposites as one version supersedes the next." [79]

The opposition between the free world of democracy and the iron curtain of totalitarianism has done more to define the mythos of democracy than anything else in the twentieth century. To be sure, that mythos has much earlier roots in ancient Greece, Atlantic republicanism, and evolutionary socialism. Yet our sense of democracy as the single worthy standard of political legitimacy (if not always excellence) traces back no further than the nineteenth century of Andrew Jackson and Alexis de Tocqueville. Nor did it become accepted around the world until well into the twentieth century. To an extent that we are apt to find surprising, the mythos of democracy is a creation of relatively recent times. And to a degree that we are apt to find astounding, the mythos of democracy owes as much to the cold war as to any other occurrence in this period.

Mythically, democracy is for us the mirror of totalitarianism. On the surface, it reverses and opposes everything totalitarian. To be sure, the same thing may be said the other way around: totalitarianism is the mythic mirror of democracy. Mythically, these opponents need one another too much for either to claim clear precedence. Insofar as we are surprised by the mythic interdependence of democracy and totalitarianism, our forgetting is motivated mythically by a political compulsion to portray the two as implacable foes. The main virtue of democracy becomes its differences from totalitarianism, since they form our decisive choice. But for us this means that the character of democracy is determined as much by its new opposition to totalitarianism as by any independent history and principles. This occurs in at least three ways.

First, mythic contrasts between democracy and totalitarianism are so stark that they invite democrats to do some things differently from totalitarians primarily for the sake of being different. Of course, the substantive implications depend on the notion of totalitarianism. As long as its overriding opposition to democracy remains intact, the more insecure democrats become in their identity as democrats, the more that they think and act mainly to differ from totalitarians. Recent rhetoric in American politics sometimes expresses this dynamic by condemning courses of action as "too much like how they do it over there." But for the most part, Americans are too secure (or arrogant) in their identity as democrats to follow the first dynamic frequently.

Second, interactions between the mythoi of democracy and totalitarianism encourages democrats to do what totalitarians do primarily in order to avoid competitive disadvantages. If totalitarians increase military spending, then so should democrats. If totalitarians conduct covert operations, then so should democrats. If totalitarians intervene in Southeast Asia, then so should democrats. Again the substantive implications depend on how the totalitarian opposition is identified and characterized. The more confident that the democrats are as democrats, the greater the mythic impulse to think and act in this second way. (Utter desperation can sometimes have the same effect, since dire necessity can sometimes invert mythic logics.) Thus Senator Fulbright devoted many years to warning Americans against their inclination to fight fire with fire where tactics of totalitarian expansion are discerned.

These two dynamics are familiar as mirror opposites. Their dangers are obvious, and thus we may hope that they tend to cancel each other before either danger develops far. When thinking of totalitarian regimes, we even hope that the second dynamic somehow leads to "liberalization" in the long run. As democrats, we draw encouragement for this hope from the fact that democracy is the twentieth-century term for all that is good in politics, to the point where our totalitarian opponents must call themselves democrats and may gradually come to mimic commitments of democracy. But our realism is too great to miss how the second dynamic of arrogance can, in combination with totalitarian trashing of truth, lead our opponents to believe themselves democrats—without becoming a whit more democratic than before. We recognize also how the first dynamic of insecurity can, in concert with totalitarian terror, lead our opponents to eliminate the dissidents and adjustments that might mark even the most minor democratization. In a limited sense, then, we have known all along that the mythoi of democracy and totalitarianism interact, because their first two dynamics of mutual dependence appear on the surface of our politics. Yet we seldom understand the significance of such dependence.

Rarely do we recognize the first two dynamics directly and in themselves as continuing dynamics of myths. Instead, we perceive them only indirectly, intermittently, and therefore incompletely as mistakes. When either dynamic becomes dangerous in a particular context, someone decries that particular danger and attributes it to some "myth" of our politics: a sustained mistake of perception and conception. The rhetorical strategy is to pit "myths" against "realities" in hopes of defeating the "myths," overcoming the mistakes, and avoiding the dangers said to impend. Thus Senator Fulbright addressed *Old Myths and New Realities* of American foreign policy in order to identify errors, characterize their sources, and project needed improvements.[80] But not even when we acknowledge patterns of mistakes as continuing myths do we appreciate their roots in the mythic interdependence of democracy and totalitarianism. We fail to discern in them the dynamics of repulsion and attraction of mythic opposites. How could this happen?

Since the substantive implication of these dynamics depends on how the opposition is identified and characterized, their impact might be small. They could be overwhelmed by the effect of projecting onto opponents whatever features allow us to be and do what we want, while preserving our opposition to the other side. Uninfluenced by totalitarians, democrats may choose their principles independently but keep the mythic contrast intact by attributing opposite principles to their foes. Suppose that we democrats decide apart from cold-war considerations that we need a civil service or that the one which we have is good. Then if we are insecure, we can contrast it with an uncivil bureaucracy, in order to reinforce the mythic opposition between democracy and totalitarianism. Or if we are confident, we can invent secondary arguments about how a civil service helps us to (over)match the administrative means of the totalitarians, again so as to fortify our mythic opposition to them.

Insofar as a contrast between bureaucracy and civil service is fitting, it supports and thus strengthens mythic contrasts between totalitarianism and democracy. Insofar as it is not, it confuses and thus weakens them. If myths were mere mistakes, mere errors about reality, then the converse would be the case. The mythoi of democracy and totalitarianism are neither mere nor systematic mistakes about reality but significant aspects of it. Insofar as mythic projections enter into political interactions (through what psychologists call enactments and ordinary people term self-fulfilling prophecies), their aspects of reality remake other aspects of reality. Thus in both image and interaction, dynamics of identifying and characterizing opponents may reduce the political effect of the first two dynamics of mythic opposition.

Yet the same dependence might give the two dynamics a large impact. If few details independent of the mythoi remain to characterize the opposites, then the two dynamics of opposition may operate without restraint. This is what happens when our senses of democracy and totalitarianism come almost exclusively from the intertwined mythoi of democracy and totalitarianism. Since totalitarianism is by definition a new phenomenon, delimited almost wholly by its current mythos, it meets this condition. But democracy is much older; and therefore we might suppose it to be a much richer construct, with far too much content independent of cold-war mythmaking for that to dominate its meaning. Unfortunately, the third dynamic calls any such supposition into question.

The third dynamic occurs when one side of a mythic opposition is absolutized or radicalized. For mythic balance to be maintained, for the opposition to remain a contrast of two sides roughly the same in mythic level and significance, the other side must also be absolutized. Otherwise it is either subsumed and defined fully by the absolutized side, or it is severed from that complex of myth. Once totalitarianism is absolutized (as utter irrationality, total control, or political hell on earth), then democracy must be absolutized (as true rationality, full freedom, or political heaven on earth). Otherwise, totalitarianism subsumes democracy (as a pre- or post-totalitarian form of government, for instance). Or democracy loses relevance to the myths at issue (so that it might, for example, be taken as a kind of movement in contrast to totalitarianism as a form of government— or vice versa). As long as a major meaning of "totalitarian" is "anti-democratic" and a major meaning of "democratic" is "anti-totalitarian," to absolutize or radicalize one mythos is slowly to do the same to the other.

From its mythic inception, totalitarianism has been directly and radically anti-democratic. Through some fourth dynamic, the mythos of democracy might have declined the compliment of defining its central foe as totalitarianism; it might have refused the opposition claimed in the mythos of totalitarianism. But it did not. Or the mythos of democracy might have tried to prevent or reverse the absolutizing of totalitarianism. But it has not. As a result, the mythos of democracy is being radicalized by implication. It is putting down new roots; and they are rapidly becoming its main ones, while the old roots in long-ago Greece, France, and the like are swiftly withering away. The mythic absolutism of totalitarianism permits not less.

The effect is to empty the mythos of democracy of previous content. Elements in conflict with a newly absolutized sense of cold-war democracy, directed against totalitarianism, fade away or find another complex of myth. Since strong myths are vividly detailed, this weakens the mythos of democracy greatly—unless it develops new details, new content. Yet the mythic opposition with totalitarianism provides few telling details and little new content, because absolutized ideas are highly abstracted ideas: they lack the usual tangibility of myths. Thus the mythos of totalitarianism transmits its defects to the mythos of democracy.

No myths express this better than the myths of the cold war. Take the myth of monolithic communism decried by Senator Fulbright. Its democratic equivalent is less recognized but no less significant. The myth of monolithic democracy is that there is a single form of good government chosen by free people, just as there is a single phalanx of free nations united in opposition to totalitarianism. Democracy becomes the sole standard of political justice and legitimacy only by becoming too diffuse to retain much mythic detail (or political acumen).

Yet the mythos of democracy is not a passive victim in this plot. In fact, it has helped to generate the mythos of totalitarianism. The high-minded (that is, abstract) militancy of Wilsonian democracy moved toward its own absolutism and radicalization. It turned the humanist universalism of modern times into crusades for democracy. Thus it betrays the beginnings of what Garry Wills decries as a foolish foreign policy based on causes rather than interests.[81] Wills might be wrong to ban all causes from foreign affairs, but he is right to insist that they have inclined democracies toward an intense moral concern with the internal affairs of other countries that finds little precedent in international relations before the twentieth century. At the same time, and from many of the same sources, communism makes a concern with the domestic politics of other polities into a doctrine of world revolution. The resulting confrontations of communism and liberal democracy called forth the mythos of totalitarianism. Thus the mythic interaction of democracy with totalitarianism aggravates rather than creates the dynamic of abstraction and absolutism that now bedevils the mythos of democracy. When totalitarianism is tied to the leveling and terror that some see as the French Revolution's unfortunate donation to the mythos of democracy, then the process by which the mythos of totalitarianism troubles our mythos of democracy could even be termed a mythic return (and revenge) of the repressed.

Alexis de Tocqueville cautioned that "Foreign policy demands scarcely any of those qualities which are peculiar to a democracy" and observed as a rule that "democracies have very confused or erroneous ideas on external affairs, and generally solve outside questions only for internal reasons."[82] As Fulbright's arguments imply, though, these defects are gravely aggravated by the three dynamics of mythic opposition between democracy and totalitarianism. They make would-be democrats highly unsure how to address possible totalitarians in international relations, especially in a world with nuclear weapons.

Related troubles arise in domestic definitions and practices of democracy. In mythic tension with totalitarianism, democracy simultaneously becomes more in demand and yet more in need of new mythmaking to legitimize its actual institutions. This is partly because appreciation for traditions of democracy must withstand the increasingly absolute and abstract standards of democracy evolved in tandem with ideas of totalitarianism. It is also due to the mythic tendency for the specific contents of democracy to fall into inconsistency by reversing the impossible combinations of features attributed to radical instances of totalitarianism. Thus democracies become caught in dilemmas of individualism versus collectivism, freedom or welfare, and rights against justice that imperil their legitimacy.[83] Since some analyze myths in terms of oppositions posed, tensions sustained, or contradictions reconciled,[84] let me emphasize that these are real *dilemmas* or *confusions* that signal increasing *incoherence* in the mythos of democracy.

These troubles appear in recent political theory.[85] Despite conventional allegiance to democracy, political scientists repeatedly find that present paradigms of "democratic representation" make little sense of politics in the United States or other putative democracies. Moreover, they virtually prove that their paradigms—drawn directly from our mythos of democracy—are either abysmally vague or internally incoherent. Hence they fumble with possible replacements for straightforward democracy: pluralism, legalism, corporatism, constitutionalism, republicanism, and participism. But so far, their efforts founder on the continuing appeal of radical standards of democracy that trace more to mythical contests with totalitarianism than to historical developments of policies and practices.

The twentieth century shows an urgent interest in similarities of structure between political heavens and hells.[86] Emptied of mythic detail, they differ mostly in diffuse (if strongly felt) tonality; formally they are identical. For example, Arendt uses the same abstract architecture to characterize totalitarianism and democracy as forms of government.[87] The radical visions of democracy proclaimed by American populists routinely attract accusations of demagoguery and totalitarian tendencies. Others suffer the same: witness the commonality of complaints that one person's "democracy" is another's tacit or incipient "totalitarianism."

Mythic incoherence perplexes even democratic ideals of citizenship. For example, practices of political participation develop both rhetorical and institutional troubles. On one side, minimalists push democracy as far as possible toward forms of elitism. Minimalists profess themselves too "realistic" to tie democracy to "the classical model" that demands impossibly high levels of political participation and skill from ordinary citizens.[88] In fact, however, this model is a more recent invention, since the ancients knew that large polities could not sustain intensive politicking by such an extensive membership. The unrealistic standards of "the classical model" actually come from hollowing out real democratic traditions in order to assimilate them to a mythic bulwark against totalitarianism. Prior to that twentieth-century exercise, almost no one had considered high extremes of public action compatible with government of any kind. Thus their advocates in the nineteenth century promoted them as revolution or anarchism, but not as democracy.

Reacting against absolutisms of participation produced by contrasting democracy to totalitarianism, minimalists collapse standards into alleged realities. Democracy *is* as any country that we call a "democracy" *does*. Such elitists eliminate from their definitions of democracy almost every kind of active involvement by citizens in politics. As critics have been quick to show, this eradicates democracy as a political ideal. It defines away any significant assumption of responsibility by ordinary members of a democracy, even though that has long been crucial to the mythos of democracy. Moreover, it leads minimalists to ignore many of the real—if historically quirky—institutions of citizen engagement created by actual democracies. Mesmerized by elections and interest groups, two of the most minimal forms of citizen politics, the minimalists produce a political science and a civic education that threaten to omit most of the meat of democracy.

Little better can be said of the maximalists. They seem determined to leave behind the actual accomplishments of democratic traditions in favor of exaggerated expectations of democratic participation that make sense only in antithesis to abolutized totalitarianism. Notwithstanding their fine criticisms of minimalism in democracy, populists such as Carole Pateman and Benjamin Barber often push democracy too far toward public-spirited anarchism or participation-mandated paternalism.[89] In fact, some maximalists even embrace the very model of "classical" democracy invented in the mythos of totalitarianism and appropriated by minimalists as the foil for their elitist argument. Like the minimalists, these maximalists lose track of the real alternatives and mythic specifics of democracy.

In debates between minimalists and maximalists, the weakness of our mythos of democracy usually gives the former an advantage. Emptied of telling details, the mythos of democracy is liable to identification with current practices in whatever are called democracies. Since those are usually far less participist than the populists propose, the mythos of democracy gravitates toward elitism. As Senator Fulbright said, "We are inclined to confuse freedom and democracy, which we regard as moral principles, with the way in which these are practiced in America—with capitalism, federalism and the two-party system, which are not moral principles but simply the accepted practices of the American people."[90]

Still, Fulbright's declaration betrays a tendency to confine democracy to a realm of moral abstractions divorced from historical practices. And this, too, shows the mythic degeneration suffered by democracy. The result is to separate ideals of democracy from specific practices and telling images. How airy democracy can become when celebrated as the absolute alternative to political evil is plain from a respected definition published in 1940:

> "Democracy—the essential thing as distinguished from this or that government—was primarily an attitude of mind, a spiritual testament, and not an economic structure or a political machine. The testament involved certain basic beliefs—that the personality was sacrosanct, which was the meaning of liberty; that policy should be settled by free discussion; that normally a minority should be ready to yield to a majority, which in turn should respect a minority's sacred things."[91]

When the mythos becomes so diffuse that democracy reduces to a continuing conversation among enlightened liberals, it is in big trouble.

Even our humble versions of democracy tend to lack practical content apart from contrasts to totalitarianism. Winston Churchill is widely approved for saying that "Many forms of government have been tried, and will be tried in this world of sin and woe. No one pretends that democracy is perfect or all-wise. Indeed, it has been said that democracy is the worst form of Government except all those other forms that have been tried from time to time."[92] Such observations early in the Cold War helped to focus the mythic contrast between totalitarianism and democracy, to which Churchill contributed many stirring images. But notice how little direction for political action such a vague conception of democracy can give us now. What was then good political mythmaking, required to resist the initial threats of several totalitarianisms, has deprived the democratic mythos of the telling detail needed to direct present politics.

THE NEED FOR NEW MYTHS

Should we simply abandon the mythos of totalitarianism? If should implies could, then we must first wonder whether abandonment is truly possible. Proposals to turn our backs on a major mythos are always suspect, although not always wrong, because they tend to underrate the tenacity of any mythos deeply ingrained in our politics, as surely the mythos of totalitarianism has become. This may make mere elimination of the mythos an impossibility in the short or middle run. Old myths seldom die; they often fade away to return substantially intact, if significantly reversed. As feasible, we would do well to work directly for our own reversals. Otherwise we must suffer whatever the mythmaking of different principles than ours is able to produce. By itself, that probably renders sheer renunciation of the mythos of totalitarianism a mistake.

But more than that, troubles of totalitarianism are yet to disappear. For all the urgency of its failings, the mythos of totalitarianism continues to serve important political needs. Furthermore, no apparent replacement promises to meet them more than a small fraction as well. Finally, we would be unwise to oppose an entire mythos without first exploring its potential for revision.

Due to their intertwined troubles the counterposed mythoi of democracy and totalitarianism need modification. Some needs can be gleaned from recent criticisms of the very concept of totalitarianism. Although the critics often intend to dispel the mythos entirely, their arguments give reasons to retain and revise it instead. Since many troubles suffered by myths of democracy and totalitarianism alike come from absolutizing them, a major target of change should be the attribution of utter irrationality and totalization to totalitarian systems. Here critics imply at least four revisions that could deradicalize the mythos of totalitarianism.

Robert Tucker criticizes Orwell for slighting the significance of flesh and blood Big Brothers, since Orwell hinted that Big Brother might exist only as a ploy of totalitarian manipulation. Thus "Orwell accepted the idea of totalitarianism's impersonality."[93] But the "failure was not his alone; it was the failure of a generation of powerful uncomprehending theorists who influenced his thinking about the elusive phenomenon" of totalitarianism.[94] Tucker argues persuasively that flesh and blood leaders are crucial to totalitarianism. They focus the cults of personality that are almost a necessary condition for it. While the cults could be called "irrational," they are not radically—that is, incomprehensively—so. The effect of Tucker's revision is to remove the "mysticism of cruelty" from the mythos of totalitarianism, substituting psychologically accessible dynamics of public relations in totalitarian circumstances. Further improvement in the mythoi of democracy and totalitarianism could come from taking greater account of their systems of communication and symbolism.

Milovan Djilas tackles another aspect of absolutism in the mythos of totalitarianism: the claim that totalitarian revolutions and regimes eliminate classes. In *The New Class,* Djilas gives momentum to the study of totalitarian structures by showing that they produce a special ruling elite of *apparatchiks* or bureaucrats.[95] This contests extreme versions of the claim that totalitarianism "makes no difference." It also disputes images of complete irrationality and total control. Through its potential for articulation into an account of bureaucratic limits on totalitarian domination, this line of investigation again tends to deradicalize the mythos.

More profoundly, Jacobo Timerman insists that "There is nothing more nationalistic than a specific totalitarianism. Its ideas, its methods, and its psychology are always profoundly national. It endures because of its nationalism."[96] To work through this modification, to work it into the mythos of totalitarianism, is to challenge the universalism implicit in the mythos. It would depart so dramatically from the usual tales of totalitarianism that some of its new stories would need to be told in detail before its specific implications could be extrapolated. Nonetheless, it could be expected to refigure the three projects of total control in subtle but significant respects. Hence it, too, would improve the mythos by reducing its radicalism.

Summarizing many criticisims already mentioned or implied, Michael Walzer maintains that strictly (that is, absolutely) totalitarian projects must fail. The perfection of total control is unavailable to human beings, and the historical record testifies that no attempted totalitarianism has lasted in anything approaching strict totalitarian terms. Yet attempts do occur. Moreover, the aspiration to total control is such a monumental perversion of politics that we need a name for it. Therefore, Walzer proposes to call it "failed totalitarianism."[97] He argues that makers of foreign policy should no longer think or talk in terms of totalitarianism, because it poses a practically misleading contrast with authoritarianism as a less evil and dangerous form of rule. In fact, he suggests a foreign policy so averse to the category that it might not speak even of "failed totalitarianism."[98]

Walzer is right to deny that would-be totalitarianisms could achieve absolute control, even through concentration camps or torture chambers. But for this reason, his phrase obstructs the kind of common sense that we ought to cultivate: one that readily recognizes the necessary imperfection of any attempted totalitarianism. Why not keep the shorter name for identifying the distinctive ambition and perversion of what we have termed totalitarian? This could combat our penchant to absolutize the mythos, without imperiling our recognition that something importantly new and qualitatively worse than old dictatorships has materialized in the twentieth century.

Of course Walzer might object that Jeane Kirkpatrick and other apologists for authoritarian regimes could invoke the revised mythos to defend their bad policies. This is a problem but it pales beside the costs of an inability to recognize, name, and explain the major differences between Hitler's Germany, Stalin's Soviet Union, Mao's China, or Pot's Kampuchea and Franco's Spain, Somosa's Nicaragua, Sadat's Egypt, or the like. Even for combatting the politics of Kirkpatrick, to improve the category of totalitarianism by revising its mythos is a better bet than any attempt to wish away a term so deeply embedded in our lives since the Second World War. Lands of death squads, police oppression, and random terrorism might not be fully totalitarian, even in a well modified sense. But Kirkpatrick and company to the contrary notwithstanding, such regimes are typically much closer to totalitarianism than to authoritarianism, even by the old mythos.

One of our main political needs is a better mythos of political evil. Another is a richer mythos of political virtue and participation. Without them, democrats (especially) will continue to experience trouble in trying to engage public affairs more ethically and effectively than before. "To construct, through diligent thought, a true background against which events of this moment might be juxtaposed is the work of art now."[99] This public art is the political mythmaking practiced with excellence by Orwell and Arendt. Yet no work of politics stands alone and none can endure well without ample revision along the way. Their myths of totalitarianism and democracy require repair. We must become the political mythmakers to do it.

NOTES

*I thank the University of Iowa for a University House Interdisciplinary Research Grant that provided time and conversation for revising this essay, originally presented at the Annual Meeting of the American Political Science Association, Washington, D.C., September, 1984.

[1] Poul Anderson, *Orion Shall Rise* (New York: Simon and Schuster, 1983), p. 58.

[2] Friedrich Nietzsche, *The Birth of Tragedy,* Francis Golffing, trans. (Garden City, NY: Doubleday, 1956) Section XXIII, p. 136.

[3] James Oliver Robertson, *American Myth, American Reality* (New York, Hill and Wang, 1980), pp. 345 and 349–350.

[4] *See* John S. Nelson, "Stands in Politics," *Journal of Politics,* 46 (February, 1984): pp. 106–131, especially pp. 109–112.

[5] *See* Henry Tudor, *Political Myths* (New York: Praeger, 1972), especially pp. 11–64.

[6] Lionel Trilling, "George Orwell and the Politics of Truth," *Orwell's Nineteen Eighty-Four,* Second Edition, Irving Howe, editor (New York: Harcourt Brace Jovanovich, 1982), pp. 346–347.

[7] *See* John Atkins, *George Orwell: A Literary Study* (London: John Calder, 1954), pp. 1–30.

[8] *See* George Orwell, "Politics and the English Language," *Orwell's Nineteen Eighty-Four,* pp. 248–259.

[9] *See* Trilling, "George Orwell and the Politics of Truth," p. 347.

[10] *See* Orwell, "Why I Write," *Orwell's Nineteen Eighty-Four,* p. 247.

[11] Orwell, "Why I Write," pp. 245–246.

[12] On the relationship between Orwell's courage and his admirable prose, *see* John Wain, "George Orwell," *Orwell's Nineteen Eighty-Four,* p. 363.

[13] George Orwell, "The Prevention of Literature," *Orwell's Nineteen Eighty-Four,* p. 268.

[14] Ibid., p. 268.

[15] Orwell, "Politics and the English Language," p. 256.

[16] *See* Wain, "George Orwell," pp. 357–358.

[17] *See* Richard Lamm, "1994: A Prediction," *Playboy*, 31, (August, 1984): 83–84, 94, 144–145; Robert L. Heilbroner, *An Inquiry into the Human Prospect*, Second Edition (New York: Norton, 1975). My students have responded to *1984* far more enthusiastically than have those of Luther P. Carpenter, see his "*1984* on Staten Island," *1984 Revisited: Totalitarianism in Our Century*, Irving Howe, editor (New York: Harper and Row, 1983), pp. 72–85.

[18] On *Down and Out in Paris and London, see* Bernard Crick, *George Orwell: A Life* (New York: Penguin Books, 1980), pp. 187–188. Crick makes similar comments about Orwell's other works of reportage and reflection.

[19] Trilling, "George Orwell and the Politics of Truth," pp. 348–349.

[20] Crick, *George Orwell*, p. 21.

[21] *See* George Steiner, *In Bluebeard's Castle* (New Haven: Yale University Press, 1971), pp. 27–56.

[22] *See* Orwell, "The Prevention of Literature," pp. 269–273.

[23] *See* Orwell, "Politics and the English Language," pp. 256–257; John S. Nelson, "Toltechs, Aztechs, and the Art of the Possible: Parenthetic Comments on the Political through Language and Aesthetics," *Polity*, 8 (Fall, 1975): 80–116.

[24] *See* Orwell, "Politics and the English Language," p. 255.

[25] *See* Orwell, "Why I Write," p. 247: "I could not do the work of writing a book, or even a long magazine article, if it were not also an aesthetic experience."

[26] Orwell, "Why I Write," p. 247.

[27] Orwell, "The Prevention of Literature," p. 263.

[28] Trilling, "George Orwell and the Politics of Truth," p. 353.

[29] Orwell, "The Prevention of Literature," p. 264.

[30] George Orwell, "The Principle of Newspeak," *Orwell's Nineteen Eighty-Four*, pp. 198–205.

[31] Orwell, "The Prevention of Literature," p. 266.

[32] Ibid., p. 266.

[33] Orwell, "Why I Write," p. 245.

[34] Hannah Arendt, "What Is Authority?" *Between Past and Future*, Enlarged Edition (New York: Viking Press, 1968), pp. 91–141.

[35] George Orwell, "Arthur Koestler," *As I Please: The Collected Essays, Journalism and Letters of George Orwell, Volume 3, 1943–1945*, Sonia Orwell and Ian Angus, editors (New York: Harcourt Brace Jovanovich, 1968), pp. 243–244.

[36] George Orwell, "Looking Back on the Spanish War," *My Country Right or Left: The Collected Essays, Journalism and Letters of George Orwell, Volume 2, 1940–1943*, Sonia Orwell and Ian Angus, editors (New York: Harcourt Brace Jovanovich, 1968), pp. 265–266. Also see Wain, "George Orwell," p. 367.

[37] Crick, *George Orwell*, p. 22. See Christopher Hollis, "Nationalism," *A Study of George Orwell* (London: Hollis and Carter, 1956), pp. 168–181; Gregory Claeys, "The Lion and the Unicorn, Patriotism, and Orwell's Politics," *Review of Politics*, 47 (April, 1985): 186–211.

[38] *See* George Orwell, "Prophecies of Fascism," *My Country Right or Left*, pp. 30–31; Crick, *George Orwell*, p. 467.

[39] George Orwell, "The Limit to Pessimism," *An Age Like This: The Collected Essays, Journalism and Letters of George Orwell, Volume 1, 1920–1940*, Sonia Orwell and Ian Angus, editors (New York: Harcourt Brace Jovanovich, 1968), pp. 533–535.

[40] George Orwell, "The Art of Donald McGill," *My Country Right or Left*, p. 164.

[41] Michael Walzer, *Just and Unjust Wars* (New York: Basic Books, 1977), pp. 299–300, footnote.

[42] *See* Ruth Ann Lief, "The Golden Country," *Homage to Oceania* (Columbus: Ohio State University Press, 1969) pp. 103–125; Richard I. Smyer, "The Golden Country," *Primal Dream and Primal Crime* (Columbia: University of Missouri Press, 1979), pp. 136–159.

[43] *See* Christopher Small, "The Iron Haven," *The Road to Miniluv* (Pittsburgh: University of Pittsburgh Press, 1975), pp. 136–173.

[44] *See* Crick, *George Orwell*, pp. 106, 242.

[45] *See* Elaine Hoffman Baruch, "'The Golden Country': Sex and Love in *1984*," *1984 Revisited*, pp. 47–56.

[46] *See* Orwell, "The Prevention of Literature," p. 270.

[47] *See* George Orwell, "Letter to H. J. Willmett," *As I Please*, p. 150.

[48] *See* John S. Nelson, "Pure Praxis: Aspects of Ironism in Arendt's Political Theory," *Ironic Politics*, Ph.D. dissertation, University of North Carolina, Chapel Hill, 1977, pp. 459–752, especially on pp. 520–660; Nelson, "Politics and Truth: Arendt's Problematic," *American Journal of Political Science*, 22 (May, 1978): 270–301; Stephen J. Whitfield, *Into the Dark* (Philadelphia: Temple University Press, 1980), p. 113; Taylor Branch, "America's Errant Philosopher," *Washington Monthly*, 15, 2 (April, 1983): 48–57.

[49] Irving Howe, "Preface," *1984 Revisited*, p. ix.

[50] Howe, "1984: Enigmas of Power," *1984 Revisited*, p. 3.

[51] Isaac Deutscher, "*1984*—The Mysticism of Cruelty," *Orwell's Nineteen Eighty-Four*, p. 333.

[52] Raymond Williams, "Introduction," *George Orwell: A Collection of Critical Essays* (Englewood Cliffs, NJ: Prentice-Hall, 1974) p. 4.

[53] Whitfield, *Into the Dark*, p. ix.

[54] *See* Herbert Spiro, "Totalitarianism," *International Encyclopedia of the Social Sciences*, David L. Sills, editor (New York: Macmillan, 1968), Volume 16, p. 112; Robert Burrowes, "Totalitarianism: The Revised Standard Version," *World Politics*, 21 (January, 1969): 272–294; N. K. O'Sullivan, "Politics, Totalitarianism and Freedom: The Political Thought of Hannah Arendt," *Political Studies*, 21 (June, 1973): 183–198; Whitfield, *Into the Dark*, pp. 25–131.

[55] *See* Nelson, "Pure Praxis," pp. 483–520.

[56] Ibid., pp. 520–658.

[57] *See* Whitfield, "Fearful Symmetry," *Into the Dark*, pp. 25–52.

[58] Orwell, "The Prevention of Literature," p. 265.

[59] George Orwell, "Letter to Francis A. Henson," *In Front of Your Nose: The Collected Essays, Journalism and Letters of George Orwell, Volume 4, 1945–1950*, Sonia Orwell and Ian Angus, editors (New York: Harcourt Brace Jovanovich, 1968), p. 502. Also *see* Orwell, "The Prevention of Literature," pp. 272–273.

[60] Hannah Arendt, "Religion and Politics," *Confluence*, 2 (September, 1953): p. 120. On totalitarianism as political hell on earth, *see* Steiner, "A Season in Hell," *In Bluebeard's Castle*, pp. 27–56.

[61] Arendt, "Religion and Politics," p. 121.

[62] Ibid., p. 124.

[63] Ibid., p. 125.

[64] Ibid., p. 125.

[65] Arthur Schlesinger, Jr., "Familiar Barbarities," *New York Times Book Review*, 88 (September 25, 1983): 24.

[66] *See* Mark Crispin Miller, "The Fate of *1984*," *1984 Revisited*, pp. 19–46.

[67] Robert Nisbet, "*1984* and the Conservative Imagination," *1984 Revisited*, p. 188.

[68] Schlesinger, "Familiar Barbarities," p. 24. *See* Johanno Strasser, "*1984:* Decades of the Expert?" John E. Woods, trans., *1984 Revisited*, pp. 149–165; James B. Rule, "*1984:* The Ingredients of Totalitarianism," *1984 Revisited*, pp. 166–179; Nisbet, "*1984* and the Conservative Imagination."

[69] A. M. Eckstein, "An Orwellian Nightmare Fulfilled: An Eyewitness Account," *Chronicle of Higher Education* (October 17, 1984): 72.

[70] George Orwell, "Freedom and Happiness," *Orwell's Nineteen Eighty-Four*, p. 152.

[71] George Orwell, "1984," *Orwell's Nineteen Eighty-Four*, pp. 175–178.

[72] Deutscher, "The Mysticism of Cruelty," p. 341.'

[73] *See* Irving Howe, "*1984:* History as Nightmare," *Orwell's Nineteen Eighty-Four*, pp. 330–331; Philip Rahv, "The Unfuture of Utopia," *Orwell's Nineteen Eighty-Four*, pp. 313–315.

[74] Michael Walzer, "On 'Failed Totalitarianism,'" *1984 Revisited*, pp. 105–107.

[75] *See* Walzer, "On 'Failed Totalitarianism,'" pp. 109–110, 113–118; Herbert Marcuse, *One-Dimensional Man* (Boston: Beacon Press, 1964), pp. 251–257; Hannah Arendt, "Approaches to the German Problem," *Partisan Review*, 12 (Winter, 1945): 93–106; Arendt, "The Aftermath of Nazi Rule: Report from Germany," *Commentary*, 10 (October, 1950): 342–353.

[76] J. William Fulbright, Speech in the Senate, March 17, 1964.

[77] *See* Claude Levi-Strauss, "The Story of Asdiwal," *The Structural Study of Myth and Totemism*, Edmund Leach, editor (London: Tavistock, 1967).

[78] Kenneth Burke, "Four Master Tropes," *A Grammar of Motives* (Berkeley: University of California Press, 1945), p. 517.

[79] Samuel R. Delany, *The Einstein Intersection* (New York: Ace Books, 1967), p. 18.

[80] J. William Fulbright, *Old Myths and New Realities* (New York: Random House, 1964).

[81] Gary Wills, *Nixon Agonistes* (Boston: Houghton Mifflin, 1969), pp. 417–495.

[82] Alexis de Tocqueville, *Democracy in America*, Phillips Bradley, editor (New York: Randon House, 1945), volume 1, p. 243.

[83] *See* Jürgen Habermas, *Legitimation Crisis*, Thomas McCarthy, trans. (Boston: Beacon Press, 1975); William E. Connolly, "The Dilemma of Legitimacy," *What Should Political Theory Be Now?* John S. Nelson, editor (Albany: SUNY Press, 1983), pp. 307–337.

[84] *See* Robertson, *American Myth, American Reality*, p. 346.

[85] *See* John S. Nelson, "Political Argument in Political Science: A Mediation on Disappointment of Political Theory," paper presented for the North American Society of Social Philosophy at the Annual Meeting of the American Political Science Association, Chicago, September, 1983.

[86] *See* Nelson, "Pure Praxis," pp. 656–660; and Nelson, "Aztechs, Toltechs, and the Art of the Possible."

[87] Others who make similar points about Arendt's structures of democracy and totalitarianism include: Whitfield, *Into the Dark*, p. 160; and O'Sullivan, "Politics, Totalitarianism, and Freedom."

[88] *See* Peter Bachrach, *The Theory of Democratic Elitism* (Boston: Little, Brown, 1967).

[89] *See* Carole Pateman, *Participation and Democratic Theory* (New York: Cambridge University Press, 1980); and Benjamin R. Barber, *Strong Democracy* (Berkeley: University of California Press, 1984).

[90] J. William Fulbright, Speech in the Senate, March 17, 1964.

[91] John Buchan, *Pilgrim's Way* (1940), quoted from *Bartlett's*, 934b.

[92] Winston Churchill, Speech to the House of Commons, November 11, 1947.

[93] Robert C. Tucker, "Does Big Brother Really Exist?" *1984 Revisited*, p. 93.

[94] Tucker, "Does Big Brother Really Exist?" p. 101.

[95] Milovan Djilas, *The New Class* (New York: Praeger, 1957). Also see Djilas, "The Disintegra-

tion of Leninist Totalitarianism," Michael Petrovich, trans., *1984 Revisited,* pp. 136–148.

[96] Jacobo Timerman, "Journal of the Longest War, I," *New Yorker,* 58 (October 18, 1982): 110, 113.

[97] Walzer, "Failed Totalitarianism."

[98] Michael Walzer, "Totalitarianism vs. Authoritarianism: The Theory of Tyranny, the Tyranny of Theory," *Dissent,* 28 (Fall, 1981): 400–403.

[99] George W. S. Trow, "Annals of Discourse: The Harvard Black Rock Forest," *New Yorker,* 60 (June 11, 1984): 94.

Orwell's Hopes, Orwell's Fears

*1984 as a Theory of Totalitarianism**

✎ *Michael P. Zuckert*

George Orwell wrote *1984* and then died. He died too early to see that the book he expected to make very little impression on the world would become a political authority of sorts.[1] He survived long enough to see only a little of the variety of readings it has provoked. The book has become, like other political authorities, a prize of some worth in the political struggles of the entire period since 1949 when it was published. The most long-standing controversy revolves around the question of Orwell's despair—did the bleak ending of the book imply that Orwell had no hope for the European political future and especially for the socialist alternative to which he had devoted his political efforts for many years? Was *1984* meant to be, as Isaac Deutscher found it, an "ideological super-weapon in the Cold War," or was it merely appropriated to this role against its author's intentions?[2] Having died before he could address more than brief comments to these and other issues, Orwell wrote nothing more which would clarify the major ambiguities present in his book.

From a perspective of nearly forty years later it seems that we would do best in our own attempts to penetrate the meaning of the book by postponing for a while the inevitable temptation to look at it essentially as a series of predictions about a future which has now become our present. Instead we ought to take Orwell's book seriously as a theory of totalitarianism. It is neither a book essentially about the future, nor essentially a dystopia, but rather first and foremost an attempt to develop a theory about the nature and causes of the European totalitarian experience which Orwell had watched with great interest over the decade and one-half before he wrote his book.

He takes some of the visible features of the regimes of Hitler and Stalin and tries to show, first, that these regimes, different as they seem from certain perspectives, have much more in common than appears. In this respect Orwell accepts and is in some respect an architect of the theory of "unitotalitarianism."[3] Orwell's theory or explanation of twentieth century totalitarian societies takes the form of an extrapolation of their features into a more perfected version of themselves, which was at the same time also a warning or prediction of the future. Orwell's book could be at once a theory of totalitarianism and a warning or prediction about totalitarianism because, at the deepest level, he argued that the nature of totalitarianism derives from the nature of modern politics altogether.

Orwell thus differs from many others who looked at totalitarianism and concluded that it was an aberration or somehow related to conditions special to Germany and the Soviet Union.[4] The greatness of Orwell's book, I suggest, does not lie in his predictions, which have very little come true, but rather in its penetrating and subtle analysis of the nature of modern politics, and in Orwell's ability to embody that analysis in images of such power and force that many years later, in a world which has gone in a very different direction, we are still emotionally seized by the book.[5] It has at least one quality of great literature in that it can ring true for us even as we know it does not express the literal truth of our times.

Orwell's book was also a prediction or a warning. Like his later readers, he was quite ambivalent about this; on some occasions he claimed to be utterly convinced that totalitarianism was "the wave of the future"—inevitable, or nearly so, potentially universal and potentially final or indomitable.[6] As early as 1940, eight years before he wrote *1984*—Orwell said: "Almost certainly we are moving into an age of totalitarian dictatorships—an age in which freedom of thought will be at first a deadly sin and later a meaningless abstraction. The autonomous individual is going to be stamped out of existence."[7]

But in a very famous letter that Orwell wrote after *1984* was published, he said something rather different: "I do not believe that the kind of society I describe necessarily will arrive, but I believe (allowing of course for the fact that the book is a satire) that something resembling it could arrive."[8] I do not believe that Orwell changed his mind so much as that he was genuinely ambivalent about whether a totalitarian future was inevitable or not. After I have laid out his diagnosis of the problem, we can, perhaps, discern the source of this ambivalence toward his own analysis.

Orwell's book properly belongs in the context of the theories of totalitarianism which arose in the wake of the surprising, even shocking, twentieth-century experience of Hitler and Stalin. The world was shocked because the late nine-teenth and early twentieth centuries were characterized above all by a belief in progress. Part of that progress was a movement toward democratic, free, and mild political societies. The withering experience of twentieth-century totalitari-anism led many, not just Orwell, to seek explanations of what had happened. The post-World War II world thus saw the emergence of a wide variety of theo-ries to explain the nature and rise of totalitarianism. There were, for example, psychological theories, sociological theories, economic theories, philosophical and phenomonological theories. One of these alternative theories might help bring out what is truly unique and most characteristic of Orwell's approach to the problem.

In a recent and well-known essay, Jeane Kirkpatrick describes totalitarian societies as ones which "drive to establish comprehensive political control over the lives of individuals, obliterating in both theory and practice the distinction between public and private, between objective and subjective, claiming for the state the whole life of people."[9] The totalitarian state thus attempts to penetrate all parts of life, and tries to enlist all individuals into service to the ends of the state. Not only does the totalitarian state penetrate every sphere of life—as Or-well nicely shows in his treatment of family relations in Oceania—but it requires all citizens to direct themselves to the regime positively and with enthusiasm— again as shown by Orwell in features like the two-minute hate.

Kirkpatrick finds the cause and core of the totalitarian phenomenon in the totalitarian ideology. In most general terms, a political ideology is a set of related ideas which are meant to explain, guide, and structure political action and politi-cal judgment. Most ideologies contain three elements:

1. Some conception of the political good which serves as a goal of action and a standard by which political situations can be judged as better or worse.
2. Some analysis of the way in which political societies work, which provides the adherents of the ideology with an explanation of how things came to be as they are and indicates the actions one should attempt in order to change them. This aspect of ideolo-gies provides guidance as to the means of action, just as the first aspect provides guidance as to the ends of political action.
3. Ideologies also typically contain some kind of critique of the present order of society.

As described thus far, ideologies are very pervasive—indeed perhaps univer-sal—in contemporary political societies. One can speak, for example, of the ideolo-gies of the Democratic and Republican parties, of the ideology of Margaret

Thatcher or Jesse Jackson. Thus, it should be apparent, not every kind of ideology produces totalitarian regimes. According to the theories of ideology, three further special features are required to make an ideology potentially totalitarian.

It must first be utopian; it must be committed to the idea that truly great improvements in the human condition are possible. Typically, utopian ideologies affirm that some change in the external conditions of life, or some change in human beings themselves, will transform the character of human action and existence. As Jeane Kirkpatrick points out, utopian ideologies affirm the potential for fundamental harmony of persons and also the possibility for "the identity of individual and collective purposes. . . ." As she puts it: "The moral perfection of man is . . . inextricably related to and made dependent on the perfection of society."[10] Marxism is a typical example of a utopian ideology which posits this kind of harmony between individual and social purposes.

The ideology must, secondly, also accept the view that the exercise of political power can bring this utopia into being. Not all utopian ideologies accept politics as the proper means to bring about the goals they seek. Some might affirm prayer, or individual moral reform, as the necessary and proper means to utopia.

To produce totalitarian regimes, the ideology must have a totalistic quality as well. This often follows from its utopian thrust, in that the ideology seeks to overcome the perpetual split we find in life between private interests and the good of the whole. In order to overcome that split, the ideology denies the legitimacy of the private or separate interests of individuals and groups; the public sphere, the realm of the common, extends everywhere in society.

In Kirkpatrick's words, then, "totalitarianism is utopianism come to power."[11] The chief features of totalitarian regimes are said to follow from this central fact. First, the regime is tightly centralized and undemocratic. Since it aims at a radical transformation of men and society from what they are to what they can become, men as they now are cannot rule. If society were ruled democratically, it could never be transformed. Leadership, secondly, rests in a vanguard party whose chief claim to power lies in its special custody over and competence in implementing the ideology.

The rulers claim, furthermore, a monopoly, not only of political power, but over the means of communication. The radical transformation they seek requires that old ways of thinking be rooted out and replaced by ways more in accord with the ideology. Propaganda of all sorts is required, as well as limits on communication not conducive to utopian transformation. Totalitarian rule also refuses to recognize limits, in principle or practice, to its sway, accepting neither legalism as a boundary nor a delimited sphere of legitimate application. The transformation sought, especially the overcoming of the distinction between the public and the private, demands this kind of unlimited sphere of operation. The primacy of the substantive ends sought resists the procedural controls of legal or constitutional restraints.

Despite its good intentions, the regime increasingly resorts to violence and turns against its own citizenry. In part this follows from the initial radical impetus towards transformation but even more from the inevitable resistance the totalitarian project meets whenever it is applied. According to the theorists in question here, the utopian ambitions cannot be accomplished. When it falls short of its hoped-for achievements, the ruling party finds itself unable to give up its ideology and instead increases the level of its efforts in order to bring about its utopia. In practice that means it resorts more and more to violence and terror to control and ultimately to remove social groups and individuals which are seen as a hindrance to the achievement of its goals. Thus, the irony develops that political movements which come to power with the greatest hopes of liberating the people, and leading them to a better life, end in terrorizing and even murdering many of them. Thus the French sociologist, Raymond Aron, said: "I mistrust those hopes which can give murderers a clear conscience."[12]

According to the ideology theorists, totalitarianism is far from inevitable and unlikely to persist even when it has come to power. The utopian hopes spawned by totalitarian ideologies are only attractive to people under limited historical conditions. Moreover, the hopes themselves are so contrary to the possibilities of human political life that eventually even the truest of the true believers catch on, and if not they, then their successors. Totalitarian societies, these theorists hold, tend to evolve back to ordinary, garden-variety, unpleasant and thuggish authoritarian, nondemocratic regimes, with all the unsavory features of that kind of government, but without the systematic terror of totalitarianism.[13] Many theorists of this school would say that something like this has happened in the Soviet Union and in China.

Almost immediately on the surface, we may see two ways in which Orwell's theory differs from the one just sketched. The ideology theorists hold that totalitarianism is likely to arise only in some places and certainly not universally. They hold it can last only a limited time because its impulses are so contrary to the real nature of things. Orwell, on the other hand, shows us a world in which three totalitarian states cover the entire earth. He shows us a world in which any anti-totalitarian spark is utterly and mercilessly crushed. Orwell had originally planned to name his book *The Last Man in Europe,* and that title aptly captures the hopelessness of the Oceanic world over the defeat of Winston Smith's puny rebellion. Totalitarianism, Orwell seems to say, will spread universally over the earth and will last perpetually.

The other differences concern the nature of the forces which produce and sustain totalitarianism. Ideology plays hardly any role for Orwell in explaining the inner reality of totalitarianism. Not ideology, but power fuels the regime in *1984.* Indeed, there is not one but two levels of power. The one, the outer and shallower, the other the inner and deeper; the one a "politics of power," the other a "metaphysics of power."

These two levels of analysis are based on and correspond to two kinds of social knowledge which the leaders of Oceania possess. They possess, in the first place, knowledge of the historic dynamic of societies, which includes knowledge of how to control that dynamic. This knowledge is social and political in character. Secondly, they possess knowledge of the real character of the whole, knowledge which I would call philosophical or metaphysical.

Orwell builds his analysis on a universal social dynamic, borrowed to some extent from James Burnham.[14]

> Throughout recorded time, and probably since the end of the Neolithic Age, there have been three kinds of people in the world, the High, the Middle, and the Low. They have been subdivided in many ways, they have borne countless different names, and their relative numbers, as well as their attitude toward one another, have varied from age to age; but the essential structure of society has never altered. Even after enormous upheavals and seemingly irrevocable changes, the same pattern has always reasserted itself, just as a gyroscope will always return to equilibrium, however far it is pushed one way or the other.[15]

We can readily recognize here the trinal class structure of Oceanic society in these three groups that have "existed throughout recorded time." Orwell sees the basic structure of totalitarian society as identical to the basic structure of human society always and ever. Unlike the other theorists, he does not find that structure dictated by the totalitarian ideology. Totalitarianism, for Orwell, merely represents a variant on a universal theme.

Like Karl Marx, Orwell affirms that class struggle and class domination characterize all societies. He sees the shape of that struggle rather differently from Marx, however. According to Orwell, the struggle is always between the Highs and the Middles. The working class, which was the ultimate hero of Marx's story about the course of human history, plays no essential role in Orwell's story. He also sees the outcome of that struggle differently from Marx. Rather than a movement with a direction, as in Marx, the class struggle in Orwell has much more the character of a cycle. From time to time, the Middles succeed in ousting the Highs; he is thinking here of events like the French Revolution. But the class struggle between the new Highs and the new Middles always resumes, with the eventual outcome that the Highs are once again supplanted by the Middles, and so on, indefinitely.[16]

The novelty of Oceania, however, derives from the knowledge human beings have come to possess of the laws of society according to which this process has occurred; armed with that knowledge, they can now intervene to change the normal operation of the process. As Orwell says: "The cyclical movement of history was now intelligible . . . and if it was intelligible, then it was alterable."[17] From Orwell's point of view, the discovery of this social knowledge was the really decisive thing, not the various technological devices (such as telescreens) which normally attract most attention in his book.

The new ruling group, armed with its social knowledge, can act to head off the theretofore inevitable cycle and perpetuate itself in power. In seeking to do that, it was precisely like every ruling group in history; in having the means to do that, it was able to bring about an unprecedented situation. But that unprecedented situation has nothing to do with the Highs pursuing novel or different kinds of goals—they pursued the same goals ruling groups had always pursued and those goals were not at all utopian. Their goal, pure and simple, was to retain power.

The task facing the ruling group can be expressed rather simply then:

> From the point of view of our present rulers, therefore, the only genuine dangers are the splitting-off of a new group of able, underemployed, power-hungry people, and the growth of liberalism and skepticism in their ranks. The problem, that is to say, is educational. It is a problem of continuously molding the consciousness both of the directing group and of the larger executive group that lies immediately below it. The consciousness of the masses needs only to be influenced in a negative way.[18]

Just as the ideology theorists traced most of the distinctive features of totalitarian regimes to the commitment in those societies to a utopian ideology, so Orwell traces most of the characteristic features of his society to the imperatives of maintaining power in the face of the social cycle.

For Orwell the undemocratic and tightly centralized character of these regimes does not follow from the effort to implement the ideology, but is the end in itself of the ruling group. The vanguard party does not owe its position to its special knowledge and competence over the official ideology as in the other theory, but rather it is more nearly the case that the ideology owes its special place to the needs of the vanguard party. Orwell takes an entirely cynical view towards the ideology—it is merely an instrument the party uses to justify its power. The party, as Orwell portrays it, is not itself a "victim" of its ideology. The ideology theorists see totalitarianism as the result of an intoxicated kind of hope; Orwell sees it as the result of utter cynicism.

The rulers claim a monopoly on the means of communication and also heavily propagandize their populations. But the purpose is not to bring about any utopian goal laid out in the ideology, but rather to keep the middle group, the most likely rivals to the Highs, from getting any independent ideas which might encourage them to attempt to supplant the ruling Highs. There is in Orwell's version the same refusal to recognize constitutional or legal limits as in the ideology theory, but the source of this refusal is the monopoly on power held and sought by the Highs.

Orwell also sees the tremendous role of terror, but he declines to relate it to the utopian aspiration of the regime. Like most analysts of totalitarianism he insists that there is something almost superfluous about the terror employed in those societies.[19] The amount and the kind of terror cannot be explained simply in terms of its instrumentality to retaining power. For example, in *1984* a merely instrumental analysis of the role of terror cannot account for the impulsion that led O'Brien to lure Winston into rebelliousness and then not to kill him but to make him over until he could proclaim his love for Big Brother. Terror prevails in *1984* not as a means to any further end, but as an expression of the underlying impulse to exercise power. O'Brien asks Winston at one point:

> "How does one man assert his power over another?" Winston thought. "By making him suffer," he said. "Exactly. By making him suffer. Obedience is not enough. Unless he is suffering, how can you be sure that he is obeying your will and not his own? . . . Power is in tearing human minds to pieces and putting them together again in new shapes of your own choosing." Like a strong man who can feel his own strength only in overcoming resistance from heavy weights, the wielder of power can know his power only in feeling it work against resistance. The consciousness of exercising power requires the inflicting of suffering. The terror serves no other purpose than psychologically validating for the rulers the fact and the experience of power. O'Brien summarizes the human future as guided by rulers who understand power as he does: "Imagine a boot stomping on a human face—forever."[20]

Now if the exercise and the awareness of the exercise of power require a resisting will, then the Party requires as an objective condition of its satisfaction, the perpetual existence of enemies. If no enemies exist, the Party must create them. The existence of enemies does not indicate the weakness of the Party but rather its omnipotence, for the Party both creates and destroys its own enemies. And so O'Brien describes the odd game he has played with Winston.

> Everyday, at every moment, they will be defeated, discredited ridiculed, spat upon—and yet they will always survive. This drama that I have played out with you during seven years will be played out over and over again, generation after generation, always in subtler forms. Always we shall have the heretic here at our mercy, screaming with pain, broken up, contemptible—and in the end utterly penitent, saved from himself, crawling to our feet of his own accord. That is the world that we are preparing, Winston. A world of victory after victory, triumph after triumph after triumph: an endless pressing, pressing, pressing upon the nerve of power.[21]

Winston merely plays a role in a ritual drama, destined to be reenacted over and over, forever.

In addition to the features of totalitarian societies that Orwell identifies in common with the ideology theorists are features singularly related to his central idea of totalitarianism as a perfected form of the universal social dynamic of elite power seeking. Oceania contains, for example, a sort of "selective totalitarianism." The lower classes are left relatively free while the totalitarian controls are applied most strongly against the Outer Party, the Middles of Orwell's scheme. The Middles are the only rivals for power that need be taken seriously. The Lows never become competitors for power; thus only the Middles require control. But they require intense control.

Secondly, Orwell presents totalitarian states as "warfare states." He does not see the force that leads totalitarian states to be warlike in terms of a dynamic of ideological expansionism, as the other theorists tend to do, but rather in terms of the requirements of internal power maintenance. The perpetual warfare works to maintain the ruling group in at least two ways. It serves as an emotional focus both for hatred, resentment, and other negative emotions, and for loyalty to the state and the ruling party as protectors against foreign threats.

Equally importantly it serves an economic function. Constant warfare provides a use for the economic surplus that even Oceania's inefficient economy does or could produce. Orwell believes that modern machine technology has potentially solved the problem of economic scarcity and that the distribution of the economic surplus that could be produced would inevitably produce a wider sharing of political power. A small elite, he believes, cannot retain political power if there is a general and somewhat equitable distribution of economic goods throughout society. Orwell retains from his socialist background the belief that political power more or less straightforwardly follows economic goods.[22] With the potential overcoming of inequality, the ruling group can no longer remain in power on the basis of natural necessities of a scarcity economy. Their desire for power comes into the open at the very moment when circumstances no longer demand that there be class-dominated societies.

What we have discussed so far is presented by Orwell in terms of the "how" of Oceania—how it works. But the deeper level of the analysis is introduced by raising the question: "Why?" The answer is in a sense the same—for the sake of power. But the focus of the analysis shifts. Not only is the Inner Party the first ruling elite sufficiently knowledgeable about the laws of social dynamics to be able to control them and to remain in power indefinitely, but it also the first elite to be perfectly free from all illusion about its own motives. As O'Brien tells Winston: "We are interested solely in power. . . . We are different from all the oligarchies of the past in that we know what we are doing." The Inner Party now acts consciously to do what always had been the unconscious goal of human action. In so doing, it brings to pass the truly terrifying and emotionally gripping features of Orwell's *1984.*

Previous oligarchies believed in "ideals" of some sort—an ideology, God, some notion of justice or virtue. This ideology may have primarily disguised that elite's will to power, but it did disguise it—even from themselves. But Oceania's elite is entirely without illusion. It has no faith in any "beyonds" that it might be serving or seeking. The prerequisite of its existence, then, is the philosophical critique of all "values." O'Brien states the central point quite consciously: "We are the priests of power. God is power." There is no beyond, no God, but power itself. God, the highest principle of the whole, is power, the ineffable which produces the appearances—period. If God is power, and only power, then God is neither beneficient nor omniscient, only omnipotent. Indeed, there is hardly any sense in which O'Brien can say God is, for God is nothing but potency per se— formless, unstructured potency. God is not something. Being, as such, is not structured.The very notion of nature is thrown in doubt.

The Inner Party, then, in seeking power for its own sake, engages, in a perverse way to be sure, in the holy task of the imitation of the divine.[23] It expresses in its own existence the nihilistic truth that it has discovered. The knowledge that "God is power" and what follows from it about all human ideals or values, is the deepest knowledge the party possesses. The question Orwell leaves us with, and I believe was left with himself, was whether O'Brien's claim that "God is power" was correct or not. Now the most interesting aspects of *1984* are not those things which belong to the sociopolitical dimension of the party's efforts to remain in power, but rather those aspects which altogether go beyond any such goals, express the party's drive, and embody in practice its key insight that "God is power."

This further dimension of the analysis not only answers the question "why," but develops the presuppositions for the "how," for the politics of power proper. The demonstration or achievement of divine power is above all the successful conquest of external realities and especially of five external realities:

1. The conquest of death
2. The conquest of nature
3. The conquest of history
4. The conquest of logic
5. The conquest of human nature itself

Ordinary power is a self-assertion of some sort. But power, as expressed in *1984,* is different in that it is altogether selfless. "The first thing you must realize," O'Brien tells Winston Smith, "is that the individual only has power so long as he ceases to be an individual."[24] Paradoxically, the self must cease being a self in order to successfully assert itself. O'Brien's seemingly contradictory position on the self is a response to the contradictory and necessarily failing character of every particular act of self-seeking.

> Alone—free—the human being is always defeated. It must be so, because every human being is doomed to die, which is the greatest of all failures. But if he can make complete, utter submission, if he can escape from his identity, if he can merge himself in the Party so that he is the Party, then he is all-powerful and immortal.[25]

At the center, then lies the problem of death. Every human act, every assertion and seeking of self and power, is an act aimed at conquering death. Human life and human deeds are expressions, broadly speaking, of the urge to self-preservation, even, we might say, of the urge to establish and maintain a self. Yet every such act is doomed to failure because of the implacable foe, death. Try as hard as they can, evade as far as they can, build walls, build guns, build with love, build with hope—whatever men try, they necessarily fail. The individual dies and with him all his self-assertions.

O'Brien's point is that if men would only be a little more radical in their self-assertions, if they would frankly and entirely recognize what they seek, then their goal can be achieved. If they can lose their individual selves altogether and merge with a collectivity, they can survive; if they are the Party, then they outlive the puny body which houses them in the collective entity which lives on. The paradox of O'Brien's position is that the completely self-assertive person is completely self-effacing. To paraphrase, "he who would find himself, must lose himself."

The human mind can thus conquer death, the greatest limit on man. Power is first and foremost the conquest of death; thus, the Inner Party realizes, to be is to exercise power. The successful exercise of power becomes possible with the realization that mind can conquer not only death but every external reality. Every one of the most interesting features of Oceania expresses the drive of mind to conquer everything external or objective. The subjectivity of the mind claims primacy over everything objective. The principle of the conquest of death is the recognition of the freedom of the mind. The mind, free to redefine or recenter the self, conquers death through the creation of a collective and immortal self. The mind, unlike the body, is free from nature. This discovery is the vehicle for all the other conquests.

We understand the conquest of nature in terms of science and technology, but for Ingsoc this is not the avenue.

> [Winston asks:] "But how can you control matter? You don't even control the climate or the law of gravity. And there are disease, pain, death—"
>
> O'Brien silenced him by a movement of the hand. "We control matter because we control the mind. Reality is inside the skull. You will learn by degrees, Winston. There is nothing that we could not do. Invisibility, levitation—anything. I could float off this floor like a soap bubble if I wished to. I do not wish to, because the Party does not wish it. You must get rid of those nineteenth-century ideas about the laws of nature. We make the laws of nature." [26]

Reality is altogether, or for all practical purposes, in the mind: this radical principle also lies behind the conquest of history, that part of Oceania with which Winston, and thus the reader, had special connection, through his job at the Ministry of Truth. In Oceania, history is what the rulers say it is, and it can change from day to day, for the rulers are able to control the pieces out of which history is constructed. No man by himself can establish and authenticate reality, even a reality he has himself experienced. The world, Orwell sees, is intersubjective. Only social authentication makes belief possible. The individual memory lacks sufficient confidence in itself to stand against the testimony of the "documents" and the "others," which the Party has the power to manipulate. The "objective reality" of the past is really quite irrelevant in Oceania, for the truth is always mediated through human consciousness, and the principles which determine human consciousness are quite other than truth.

Even though Winston has been part of the machinery which established historical "reality," according to the principles of Ingsoc, he nonetheless recoils from O'Brien's revelations.

> The belief that nothing exists outside your own mind—surely there must be some way of demonstrating that it was false. Had it not been exposed long ago as a fallacy? There was even a name for it, which he had forgotten.[27]

Of course Winston is searching for "solipsism," but O'Brien quickly corrects him: "You are mistaken, this is not solipsism. Collective solipsism, if you like. But that is a different thing; in fact, the opposite thing."[28] It is "the opposite thing" because "solipsism" is the thesis that the individual consciousness defines reality for itself; Ingsoc's "collective solipsism" depends on recognizing the inability of the individual consciousness to define reality for itself, and the individual's dependence on collective or social consciousness. Ingsoc's collective solipsism plays out the modern skepticism regarding the human mind's directness of access to the phenomena of the world: the mind knows ideas, or constructs; it does not know "the things themselves."[29] Orwell grasps well the subjectivist character of modern thought, and he extrapolates from his own experience of intersubjective or socially determined consciousness which the history of his times showed on a large scale. A common theme of Orwell's work, going at least as far back as "Shooting the Elephant," is the power of the social whole over the individual mind. Orwell's fixation with "telling the truth" and standing against the crowd, are the response of a man who personally felt the power of the crowd over his own mind. "Confessions" at purge trials, the brazen rewriting of history, inducing conviction in the minds of men by sufficient repetition and control of what can and cannot be said and validated in public spaces—these broader historical experiences of his time must have convinced Orwell that the power of collective solipsism was great indeed.

The conquest of logic is especially problematical, for the victory over the others, the external realities, depends on the primacy of mind. But logic supposedly states the laws according to which the human mind operates. The vehicle within the novel which expresses the conquest of logic, of course, is doublethink, which affirms the ability to think contradictions. If one can think in contradictions, then one can think anything. The mind is free, not only of external reality, but even of the power of its own laws.

Finally, and perhaps most importantly, there is the conquest of human nature itself. The story of Winston is, above all, the story of the conquest of human nature, for the Party not only defeated Winston—that was easy—but it got him to love his oppressor—that is far more difficult. And this was done without any promise of reward for himself in a Heaven from a God who commands love of the enemy. The conquest of human nature, the conquest of self-love, is even more difficult than the conquest of death, for the conquest of death still depends, as we have seen, on a transformed form of self-love. The self recenters itself on the collectivity, but it does so in the service of the essentially self-regarding desire for power and existence. But no such transformed natural drive animates Winston at the end. This is why the novel ends with two of the bleakest sentences in the history of English literature: "He had won the victory over himself. He loved Big Brother."

The key event in the conquest of Winston is his betrayal of Julia—in Room 101 he wishes the rats on her rather than on himself. He asserts himself over his love for her. But through that self-assertion, he loses his self-respect, is broken completely and comes to love Big Brother. Orwell's point seems to be that self-love depends on self-respect, and self-respect on love of something outside or beyond oneself. Even this fundamental principle of human nature, self-love, is not, strictly speaking, natural. One can condemn oneself.

Orwell does not seem to notice, however, that this account of the victory over human nature conflicts with his earlier account of the nature of collective oligarchy. Party members believe in no "beyonds" whatever; they differ from all ruling groups in the past, they are successful beyond all ruling groups in the past in that they seek nothing but power for its own sake. They are not themselves demoralized by their utter cynicism and thorough selfishness in the way Winston is. For the party members the successful exercise of power, the manifestation of being in the fullest sense, expresses itself in the completely selfish assertion of self. Thus the principles inherent in the victory of the Party contradict those inherent in the defeat of Winston.

With Winston's capitulation, the novel comes to a somber and despairing end. In the world shown within the book, there is no hope. Winston would indeed be "the last man in Europe," except that the Party, as O'Brien explains,will continue to raise up opponents for the sake of its game of power. Those, like Gregory Claeys, Ian Slater, or Bernard Crick, who assert that Orwell meant to affirm as a truth about Oceania, Winston's belief that "if there was hope, it lay in the proles," are not persuasive.[30] Claeys pits Winston's assertion that O'Brien's counterclaim: "the proletariat will never revolt, not in a thousand years or a million . . ." and concludes that we have "stronger reason to agree with [Winston] than with O'Brien."[31] To say nothing of anything else, this way of reading runs counter to the entire character of the book: repeatedly Winston's beliefs are opposed to O'Brien's and clearly shown to be overcome by them. None of Claey's more specific observations on the freedom of the proles overturns this general pattern. Their relatively free lives are quite irrelevant to the question of hope. Ingsoc sees no need to make over the proles in the same way that it makes over the members of the Outer Party. As the Theory of Oligarchical Collectivism insists, the lower classes have never been an agent in history; only the middle classes have threatened ruling classes. And nothing in *1984* challenges that view. Repeatedly Winston romanticizes the proles; repeatedly Orwell shows his hopes or expectations to be false. One thinks, for example, of Winston's nostalgic visit to the "dingy little pub," in search of recollections of life before the victory of Ingsoc. Winston's conversation with an old man in the pub only confirms his more despairing observations, not his hope. "Until [the proles] become conscious they will never rebel, and until after they have rebelled they cannot become conscious."[32]

If there is hope—from the proles or elsewhere—it lies not within the world of the book, but outside that world. The world Orwell portrays reveals an inner character such that within its bounds there is no hope. But the world within the book may not correspond to the world to which the book was addressed. Orwell, after all, most persistently described his book neither as prophecy nor as warning (the two categories in terms of which most contemporary discussion goes forward) but as satire or parody, a description suggesting that the world in the novel is subjunctive, a counterfactual of some sort.[33]

Support for the view that Orwell sees the world within as significantly different from the world without would seem to come from the prominent role of Burnhamite ideas in explaining the novel's world. While it is clear that the ideas adapted from Burnham and expressed in Goldstein's book and by O'Brien accurately describe the world within the novel, it is also true that Orwell on several occasions disagreed with Burnham's political analyses. According to William Steinhoff,

> what Orwell has done in *1984* is to assume that Burnham's analysis is correct and to work out the consequences. . . . [But] we know that Orwell disagreed profoundly with many of Burnham's beliefs. . . . Like "A Modest Proposal," *1984* assumes the existence of certain conditions and certain tendencies of mind and attempts to work out their outrageous consequences in order to effect in the reader a revulsion against them.[34]

Orwell takes over from Burnham the idea of a world divided among three superpowers, engaged in a more or less interminable war with each other. He takes over the idea of the three-class structure of society and "circulation of elites" dynamic characterizing all societies. He derives from Burnham also the idea of elites, devoted to power seeking, ruling on the basis of social scientific knowledge.[35]

And while William Steinhoff correctly points out Orwell's criticisms of

Burnham, one must not overstate them, or overestimate their significance. Over time, Orwell accepted more and more of the Burnhamite analysis. Perhaps the most telling example is Orwell's conclusion to his essay, published in the spring of 1946, on "James Burnham and the Managerial Revolution." In a passage directly relevant to *1984,* Orwell observes,

> Fortunately the "managers" are not so invincible as Burnham believes. It is curious how persistently, in *The Managerial Revolution,* he ignores the advantages, military as well as social, enjoyed by a democratic country. . . . The huge, invincible, everlasting slave engine of which Burnham appears to dream will not be established, or, if established, will not endure because slavery is no longer a stable basis for human society.[36]

By 1947 Orwell apparently had changed his mind, to some extent under the intellectual stimulus of Burnham's later book, *The Struggle for the World.*[37] In 1947, Orwell sketched three possible futures for the world—a preemptive attack by the United States against the Soviet Union, an atomic war between the two great powers, with great loss and devastation to civilization as a whole, or a stalemate provoked by recognition of the horribly destructive effects of atomic weapons. Orwell pronounces this last to be "the worst possibility of all." His explanation of that surprising conclusion reads like a description of the world of *1984.* Such a stalemate would mean the division of the world among two or three vast superstates, unable to conquer one another and unable to be overthrown by an internal rebellion. In all probability, their structure would be hierarchic, with a semidivine caste at the top and outright slavery at the bottom, and the crushing of liberty would exceed anything that the world has yet seen. Within each state the necessary psychological atmosphere would be kept up by complete severance from the outer world, and by a continuous phony war against rival states. Civilizations of this type might remain static for thousands of years.[38] Even here, where he approaches closest to Burnham's vision, Orwell does not give way to the view that such a development is simply inevitable. But the main alternative to it (other than atomic war) is an unlikely and highly utopian Socialist United States of Europe, unlikely to come into being itself and operating to head off the other possibility in a most uncertain way. As Orwell described himself in this essay, "A Socialist today is in the position of a doctor treating an all but hopeless case." The doctor, he says, is obliged to continue treating the patient, but "as a scientist, it is his duty to face the facts, and therefore to admit that the patient will probably die."[39]

Even before he explicitly came around to Burnham's view on the possible future of mankind, Orwell had strongly endorsed Burnham's analysis. In the

1946 essay in which he had criticized Burnham he nonetheless affirmed that "as an interpretation of what is happening, Burnham's theory is extremely plausible, to put it at the lowest. . . . If we consider the world movement as a whole, his conclusions are difficult to resist."[40]

Orwell's most far-reaching criticisms of Burnham, however, address not his analysis of the present or projection into the future, but rather the "axioms" on which his theories rest. Burnham assumes, Orwell says, that the drive for power is a political universal, to be explained in simple natural terms, like the drive for food or shelter; Burnham also assumes that the class structure of society always derives from the same necessities. In effect, Burnham sees both the psychological and sociological roots of politics in over-static categories of nature, rather than in the dynamic categories of history and change.[41]

Orwell does not disagree with Burnham's assessments that classless society is nowhere on the horizon and is most unlikely to be so in the foreseeable future; nor does he differ, as many seem to believe he does, with Burnham's estimate of the role of power in political life. Rather, Orwell rejects Burnham's simple reliance on an ahistorical model, derived from Niccolo Machiavelli, in order to explain class relations, because "the machine has altered human relationships, and . . . in consequence Machiavelli is out of date." The machine has made it technically possible to overcome drudgery and thus class structures as heretofore known.[42] To explain the continued or increasing hierarchical organization of industrial societies requires an analysis, therefore, which takes account of the new technical possibilities of overcoming hierarchy; an analysis built on the old Machiavellian political science will not do.

More centrally, Orwell does not reject Burnham's focus on the role of power. "The question [Burnham] ought to ask, and never does ask, is: Why does the lust for naked power become a major human motive exactly now, when the dominion of man over man is ceasing to be necessary."[43] Orwell poses the question to Burnham which Winston poses to O'Brien. In *1984* Orwell attempts to answer, in a way that is consistent with the Burnhamite analysis to which it is attached, the question Burnham should himself have answered. In our discussion of the metaphysics of power in *1984* we have already sketched out Orwell's answer to this question. One might say, in this respect then, that *1984* presents not so much Orwell's refutation as his completion of Burnham.

According to Orwell, Burnham does not ask the necessary historical question, because he himself suffers from the worship of power and success he diagnoses as the foundation of politics, and which Orwell finds as perhaps the most dominant feature in the psychological makeup of twentieth century intellectuals.[44] Orwell finds Burnham inadequate not because he emphasizes power so much, but because he stays to worship at the shrine of the bitch-goddess. Orwell differs from Burnham much more on his personal stance towards power than on his notion of its importance and role. The quest for power may be the decisive fact of politics, but one ought not to like it.

From this perspective, *1984* provides the confrontation of Burnham and Orwell in the guise of the contest between O'Brien and Winston, a contest which, significantly, O'Brien/Burnham wins at last within the world of the novel. That contest and its outcome make certain psychological sense, given the elements of Orwell's position as we have now seen it. On the one hand, he believed Burnham was most likely correct in his forecast of the future and in his pessimism over the prospects for socialism; at the same time, he objected to Burnham's moral stance which did not rebel or at least regret those harsh facts. In *1984* Orwell takes the hard-headed analytical attitude he feared was correct, but combined it with the moral protest he felt was necessary. That combination allowed him to feel superior to those who refused to face the "hard truth," (the average man of the left), as well as to those who gave themselves gleefully to the "hard truth" (e.g., Burnham).

Nonetheless, Orwell persistently described his book as a satire or a parody, that is, as a work which presents its world in an ironic voice of some sort. Orwell described his book, while he was writing it, in a 1947 letter to Frederich Warburg: it is, he says, "a novel about the future—that is, it is in a sense a fantasy, but in the form of a naturalistic novel. That is what makes it a difficult job—of course as a book of anticipations it would be comparatively simple to write."[45] I take it that by "fantasy" Orwell does not simply mean a book about the future, for he distinguished his work from another sort of writing about the future, "a book of anticipations." He seems to mean a work of fantasy-like character, but presented naturalistically. As he says, the combination of forms is difficult, for the more he succeeds at writing a naturalistic novel, the less visible are the fantasy elements. And vice versa. In this respect *1984* differs a great deal from his own earlier satirical effort in *Animal Farm* and from those of the satirist whom Orwell admired most, Swift. In both his own and Swift's satires, the fantasy element stands forth for all to see.

In the face of these difficulties, it is worth wondering why Orwell attempted the interesting but not altogether successful mix of genres that he did in *1984.* The answer resides, I think, in the deep ambiguity and even uncertainty Orwell felt towards his own material.

On the one hand, Orwell saw to the depths of the modern aspiration to omnipotence through the total subjectivization of man. Man, Orwell saw, is more and more assertive—he conquers nature, kills God, redefines himself and challenges the very idea of objective truth and objective reality. The novel is born of Orwell's haunting fear that the Stalins, the Hitlers, the Marxists, the O'Briens might be correct—that there is not objective reality to serve as a limit to man's subjectivity. Orwell's book is so powerful because he sees that the chief thrust of modernity is the impatience with everything external and objective. His book is so farsighted because he sees that the complete victory of man over all the external and given things means, not the liberation, but the most terrible enslavement of man. Orwell despairs. Orwell is terrified, in fact, because he sees that man's freedom and man's slavery are completely identical. Ultimately, *1984* is a great document of twentieth century despair over God and nature; it is, in other words, a great document of modern nihilism, of our fear of the nothing in us and around us.

But on the other hand, Orwell knew or suspected that the aspiration for complete liberation through complete subjectivization of man could not succeed. He presents in *1984* what we might call a "thought experiment," a fantasy, showing at the outer edge what would be necessary for the achievement of the implicit agenda of modernity. He thus shows us the limits of the possibility, and surely also, the limits of the desirability, of the successful completion of that agenda. This dimension of his book is warning, or even better, satire and parody, for it pictures for us as conditions implicit in the totalitarian project, things which we can recognize as impossible.

The mystery of *1984*, as well as its formal experimentation, derives from Orwell's inability to resolve the tension sketched above. That tension derived from a yet more ultimate fixed point in his thinking. *1984* as a satire, or warning, must rest on some ground for hope. In his various responses to Burnham, and elsewhere throughout his writings, Orwell expressed that ground of hope in terms of the unfixed character of human nature: "As for the claim that 'human nature,' or 'inexorable laws' of this and that, make socialism impossible, it is simply a projection of the past into the future."[46] And in an "imaginary interview" Orwell conducted with Jonathan Swift on the radio in 1942, he laid bare the ground for his rejection of Swift's pessimism and misanthropy: "I see now where it is that we part company, Dr. Swift. I believe that human society, and therefore human nature, can change. You don't."[47]

Orwell's ground of despair, however, was just that same belief that there was no fixed human nature.

In the past every tyranny was sooner or later overthrown, or at least resisted, because of "human nature," which as a matter of course desired liberty. But we cannot be at all certain that "human nature" is constant. It may be just as possible to produce a breed of men who do not wish for liberty as to produce a breed of hornless cows.[48]

Orwell brings this theme directly into *1984,* when he has O'Brien tell Winston: "You are imagining that there is something called human nature which will be outraged by what we do and will turn against us. But we create human nature. Men are infinitely malleable."[49]

Orwell was not sure what sort of future to project, what sort of book he had written, because his deepest principle seemed compatible either with great hope or great fear. Orwell wrote a much bleaker book than he probably intended to write because he seemed to be tending to the view, perhaps not altogether consciously, that the unfixed character of nature more likely led to O'Brien's view than to his own best hopes. Such seems to me anyway the tendency of his analysis of God as power and of his reflections on the recent history of Europe. Had Orwell lived longer he well might have clarified his position for himself and for us. As it stands, the direction of his thought is fairly clear—if not unambiguously so. Orwell found his own Room 101, and there discovered that his most cherished dream was true—and led to his greatest fear. The most valuable feature of *1984,* then, turns out not to be its prediction of the future, which obviously is so different from our present, but rather his analysis of the freedom-inspired attack on objectivity, an attack whch deeply threatens freedom itself.[53]

NOTES

*This paper was originally prepared as part of a program on Orwell's 1984, sponsored by the Minnesota Humanities Commission. An earlier version was first delivered as part of a symposium at Shattuck-St. Mary's Schools, Fairbault, Minnesota, Spring 1984.

[1] Bernard Crick, *George Orwell: A Life* (Boston: Little, Brown, 1980), pp. 393–394.

[2] Isaac Deutscher, "1984—The Mysticism of Cruelty," *George Orwell,* Raymond Williams, editor (Englewood Cliffs, NJ: Prentice Hall, 1974, originally published in 1954), p. 119.

[3] Cf. Alexander Groth, "The 'Isms' of Totalitarianism," *American Political Science Review* 58 (1964): 888–901.

[4] For a fine contemporary version, consider Richard Lowenthal, "Beyond Totalitarianism," *1984 Revisited: Totalitarianism in Our Century,* Irving Howe, editor (New York: Harper & Row, 1983), pp. 209–267. In the same volume, consider also Michael Walzer, "On 'Failed Totalitarianism,'" pp. 103–121.

[5] Cf. Irving Howe, "1984: Enigmas of Power," *1984 Revisited,* p. 7.

[6] On the basis of a fairly random survey of the literature, on the side of "prophecy," and thus of Orwell's despair, one finds Daphne Patai, *The Orwell Mystique* (Amherst: University of Massachusetts Press, 1984), pp. 17, 237–238, 264–268; Alex Zwerdling, *Orwell and the Left* (New Haven: Yale University Press, 1974), pp. 201–203; Isaac Deutscher, "1984—The Mysticism of Cruelty," pp. 126–129, 131; Stephen J. Greenblatt, "Orwell as Satirist," *George Orwell,* p. 118; and Christopher Small, *The Road to Miniluv* (Pittsburgh: University of Pittsburgh Press, 1975), p. 166. On the side of "warning," and thus of hope: Ian Slater, *Orwell—The Road to Airstrip One* (New York: W. W. Norton, 1985), pp. 238–243; Bernard Crick, *George Orwell,* pp. 383–396; William Steinhoff, *George Orwell and the Origins of 1984* (Ann Arbor: University of Michigan Press, 1975), pp. 43, 48,

54, 193–204; Gregory Claeys, "The Lion and the Unicorn: Patriotism and Orwell's Politics," *Review of Politics* 47, no. 2 (1985), pp. 202–206.

⁷George Orwell, "Inside the Whale," *Collected Essays, Journals and Letters of George Orwell,* Sonia Orwell and Ian Angus, editors, 4 vols., hereafter, *CEJL* (New York: Harcourt Brace Jovanovich, 1968), I. p. 526.

⁸Letter to Francis A. Henson, June 16, 1949, *CEJL* IV, p. 223.

⁹Jeane Kirkpatrick, *Dictatorships and Double Standards—Rationalism and Reason in Politics* (New York: Simon and Schuster, 1982), p. 99.

¹⁰Ibid.

¹¹Ibid., p. 101.

¹²Raymond Aron, *The Industrial Society* (New York: Simon and Schuster, 1968), p. 5.

¹³Cf. Michael Walzer, "On 'Failed Totalitarianism.'"

¹⁴It is now widely recognized that Orwell borrowed heavily from Burnham's works, although his intention in doing so, his stance toward the Burnhamite elements of *1984,* are matters of some controversy. Cf. James Burnham, *The Managerial Revolution* (New York: John Day, 1941); *The Machiavellians* (New York: John Day, 1943); *The Struggle for the World* (New York: John Day, 1947). Orwell wrote on Burnham many times during the gestation period for *1984.* Consider his "James Burnham and the Managerial Revolution," in *CEJL* IV, pp. 160–180; and "Burnham's View of the Contemporary World Struggle," *CEJL* IV, pp. 313–325. The connections between Burnham and Orwell's works are discussed at some length by Steinhoff, *Orwell and the Origins,* and Michael Maddisin, "1984: A Burnhamite Fantasy," *Political Quarterly* 32 (1961): 71–79.

¹⁵George Orwell, *1984* (New York: Harcourt Brace Jovanovich, 1977), p. 185.

¹⁶Ibid., pp. 202–204.

¹⁷Ibid., p. 204.

¹⁸Ibid., pp. 208–209.

¹⁹He reminds one most of Hannah Arendt, *Totalitarianism* (New York: Harcourt Brace and World, 1968), esp. ch. 4.

²⁰Orwell, *1984,* pp. 269–271.

²¹Ibid., p. 271.

²²Ibid., pp. 189–191.

²³See the very interesting and extended analysis of *1984* as "parody" of the quest for the divine in Small, *The Road to Miniluv,* ch. VI.

²⁴Orwell, *1984,* p. 267.

²⁵Ibid.

²⁶Ibid., p. 268.

²⁷Ibid., p. 269. On the issue of modern subjectivism, one must consider above all the work of Martin Heidegger, e.g., his *Nietzsche,* David F. Krell, editor (San Francisco: Harper & Row, 1982), pp. 96–139.

²⁸Orwell, *1984,* p. 269.

²⁹Compare Christopher Small's critique of O'Brien's position in *The Road to Miniluv,* p. 155. Small misses the collective character of the solipsism here, and thus mistakenly believes he can readily refute O'Brien on solipsistic grounds.

³⁰Orwell, *1984,* pp. 69, 85.

³¹Claeys, "Patriotism and Orwell's Politics," p. 204.

³²*1984,* p. 70.

³³Bernard Crick, *George Orwell,* pp. 383, 384, 395, and 398 conveniently collects Orwell's various extrinsic comments about his book.

[34] Steinhoff, *Origins,* pp. 200–201.

[35] Orwell, "James Burnham and the Managerial Revolution," in *CEJL* IV, pp. 160–161; cf. Steinhoff, *Origins,* pp. 43–54.

[36] Orwell, "James Burnham," 179–180.

[37] Orwell, "Burnham's View," p. 313.

[38] Orwell, "Toward European Unity," *CEJL,* IV, p. 371.

[39] Ibid., p. 370.

[40] Orwell, "James Burnham," pp. 164–165; cf. p. 176.

[41] Ibid., pp. 176–177.

[42] Ibid., pp. 177–178.

[43] Ibid., p. 178.

[44] Ibid., pp. 178–179.

[45] Letter to F. J. Warburg, 31 May 1947, in *CEJL* IV, pp. 329–330.

[46] "James Burnham," p. 178.

[47] Quoted in Slater, *Road,* pp. 180–181.

[48] Orwell, "The Russian Regime," in *CEJL,* I, pp. 380–381. Cf. also his review of Bertrand Russell's *Power, CEJL,* I, pp. 375–376.

[49] Orwell, *1984,* p. 272.

[50] Cf. Patai, *Orwell Mystique,* p. 238; Zwerdling, *Orwell and the Left,* p. 202; Deutscher, "Mysticism," p. 131; Steinhoff, *Origins,* p. 199.

Dark Utopia

1984 and its German Contemporaries

❧ *Mark E. Cory*

In a recent novel written in conscious and sometimes playful anticipation of "Orwell's Decade," Günter Grass contrasts his own dark vision of the future with that of *1984:* "No, dear George, it won't be quite that bad, or it will be bad in other ways and in some of these ways it may be even a little worse."[1] Writing at the same time, and with some of the same concerns, Heinrich Böll sets his penultimate novel, *The Safety Net,* in a sterile society totally defined by protective surveillance.[2] These allusions to George Orwell by Germany's two leading novelists on the eve of the 1980s are suggestive of the extraordinary impact of *1984* on West German letters. In paperback form the novel figured prominently on the German bestseller list for 1983 and 1984, and Orwell is now being cited as one of the most widely read English novelists of the twentieth century. *Der Spiegel,* no less than *Time,* devoted a cover issue to the approach of this ominous but nevertheless compelling date,[3] and the prestigious Frankfurt Book Fair selected the novel as its theme in October, 1984.

Given the ideological, technological, and general social parallels between the Federal Republic and the United States and the similar attention paid *1984* in this country of late, these West German phenomena are not surprising. What does seem curious, and perhaps even paradoxical, is that despite the enormous popularity of the novel since its serialization in the pages of *Der Monat* in late 1949, only recently has it been much viewed in Germany as a reminder of National Socialism, as well as a warning against totalitarian excesses of the political left.

In a recent and provocative article in *World Literature Today,* Sidney Rosenfeld analyzes this very paradox. While reaffirming the important point that it would be a distortion of the novel to read *1984* as a fable of National Socialism, he does ask the legitimate question of "why, at a time when the ruins of the Third Reich were still being cleared away, the blood-drenched nightmare of Nazi totalitarianism did not palpably influence critical reaction to Orwell's novel?"[4] Rosenfeld's answer is twofold: first, that nascent Cold War fears of the totalitarian state being formed across the rude new border with the German Democratic Republic made anticommunism (and hence an interpretation of *1984* which focused on parallels between Big Brother and Stalin) an obsession; and second, that a collective unwillingness to work through the immediate past made the identification of Germany under National Socialism with Oceania under Ingsoc psychologically impossible for many Germans in the decades immediately following the Second World War.[5]

Rosenfeld's argument does much to untangle the knotted motives shaping critical and popular responses to Orwell in the Federal Republic but leaves some related questions largely unanswered. One such is the question of whether similar or dissimilar visions of the future as nightmare haunted German contemporaries of Orwell during the 1940s. What was the fictional locus of their horror? If not totalitarian Germany itself, then where, and what meaning if any attaches to this broader context of German dystopian fiction? Rosenfeld does discuss one such contemporary example, Walter Jens' *Nein. Die Welt der Angeklagten (No. The World of Defendants)*, but given the rather significant number of extant German fictional utopias,[6] it seems worthwhile broadening the base of Rosenfeld's inquiry. Each of the three examples discussed in what follows—Hermann Hesse's *Das Glasperlenspiel (The Glass Bead Game)*, published in 1943; Franz Werfel's *Stern der Ungeborenen (Star of the Unborn)*, 1946; and Ernst Jünger's *Heliopolis,* 1949—postulates a new social order claiming to be an advance over the social order of the mid-twentieth century, and in each case the central figure and personality with whom the reader comes to identify ultimately becomes disenchanted with the new order and reacts in some way against it. It is this reaction against new social orders which most compellingly links the German novels to *1984* and which subsumes them, with Aldous Huxley's *Brave New World* and Evgenij Zamiatin's *We,* under the subgenre called variously anti-utopian or dystopian fiction, or in German critical parlance *negative Staatsutopie.* And it is in this conflict with a flawed utopian vision that each author articulates his warning for his time, his warning, as it were, for us.

Franz Werfel, born in Prague in 1890, is best known in this country for *The Song of Bernadette,* written as an act of thanksgiving for escaping National Socialism and reaching the haven of America. One of that large host of Austrian and German intellectuals who were either forced into exile or who elected to emigrate after Hitler rose to power in 1933, Werfel eventually joined the German exile community in California. *Star of the Unborn* was his last work and was completed only a month before his death in August, 1945.[7]

At first glance, F. W., the central figure of *Star of the Unborn,* seems a study in contrast to Orwell's Winston Smith. Instead of a disaffected Party member in a joyless and grimy nightmare society, Werfel's first-person narrator is a casual visitor summoned on something of a lark through a time warp to a distant era some 100,000 years in the future. The landscape of New California reflects the changes wrought in these intervening years in the development of the "Astromental" world. Above its iron-gray surface towers a crystalline mountain known as the "Djebel" which houses the center of universal learning. Below the surface, F. W. explores the elegant habitat of a cultured elite, admires their diaphanous, ageless beauty, and accustoms himself to marvelous economies of time and effort. Productive work in the Astromental era is eagerly and efficiently done for all by a robust colossus known as "The Worker," while necessary governmental chores are administered by an equally benevolent but very retiring civil servant. Everywhere F. W. is treated courteously and gently, as befits the fragile anachronism he seems to be.

As the novel develops, F. W. gradually shifts roles from that of dazzled guest to that of a direct participant in the crises festering in this mock-utopia. In the process, F. W. acquires a striking kinship with Winston Smith. Like Oceania, the Astromental World evolved after a cataclysmic event. Both societies feature a drastically simplified social structure, with an elite core and vast additional numbers living beyond the pale. Each society has developed new values, articulates those values by means of a new language (the Astromental equivalent to Newspeak is Monolingua), and each devises exceedingly effective measures for ensuring complete conformity to its values. Oceania's overarching value was power, power for its own sake. "We are the priests of power," O'Brien tells Winston Smith before sending him to Room 101. The Party's devices for gaining power were physical torture and thought control. The values of the Astromental era are beauty and play and seem benign by comparison, but the techniques for ensuring conformity are in a way more insidious than torture and thought control: compliant Astromental citizens are guaranteed the minimization of physical effort, suspension of the aging process, and virtual freedom from illness and even death. Oceania's ostensible external enemies are East Asia and Eurasia, but the only real enemy is the nonconforming individual. The Astromental city Panopolis is threatened by a combination of a deliberately regressive society of renegade jungle dwellers on the outside and by its own internal dissidents, but in reality its most serious challenge comes from F. W., who ultimately rejects the seductions of ageless beauty and an existence without death. Like Winston Smith, F. W. is profoundly uncomfortable with his would-be utopia, with its new antiseptic technology, and with the asexual, even deliberately antisexual code governing conduct between men and women. In strikingly parallel fashion, each protagonist encounters a girl presumed to embody the antisexual values of her respective society, only to discover that old-fashioned passions smoulder beneath cold exteriors. This fascination with changed sexual codes is not gratuitous. In actively pursuing F. W. and Winston Smith, Lala and Julia reveal themselves as desperate critics of their respective utopian orders.[8]

Julia and Winston's affair is cut off by the Thought Police and is the very weapon used by the Ministry of Love to torture and ultimately to destroy them both. The narrator in *Star of the Unborn* renounces Lala, too, but for the quite different reason that his disaffection from the Astromental world is too profound for the compensation their union might offer. These deeper grounds for his rejection lead away from comparison and into points of contrast with *1984*, a part of the discussion best reserved, however, until the remaining examples of contemporary German dystopian fiction have been introduced.

To turn to Hesse's *The Glass Bead Game* is to move from perhaps the least to the best known of these works, although only recently has much attention been paid to the dystopian dimension of Hesse's last novel.[9] Like Werfel, Hesse wrote as an émigré, albeit one whose relocation in Switzerland before the outbreak of the First World War had nothing to do with the kind of persecution suffered by Werfel. Hesse was an outspoken opponent of war, however, and displayed throughout his career a dedication to pacifism that allies him spiritually with many of those forced to flee Germany under National Socialism.[10]

The Glass Bead Game was first published in 1943, but did not appear in English translation (initially under the title *Magister Ludi*) until 1949. Whereas *Star of the Unborn* took the form of a Swiftian travel novel, *The Glass Bead Game* is presented as a biography of one Josef Knecht. Like Winston Smith and F. W., Knecht is an outsider in a futuristic and highly structured society. As a boy, Josef attracts the attention of his teachers and is recommended for the elite schools of the Castalian order. There he learns about Castalia through the tutelage of the Music Master, who understands how to instill spiritual values through the joyful experience of music. The ability to weave melodies, to abstract from reality a spiritual code which can be shared with others, to work playfully and imaginatively within laws and principles and at the same time creatively to order the experiences of time and space—these abilities prepare Knecht for the Glass Bead Game. Left purposely ambiguous in the novel, the Glass Bead Game is the culminating rite in Castalian society, a "lingua sacra" and a symbol for the supreme unity and harmony of all its values.

The reason *The Glass Bead Game* is not more often cited as an example of dystopia is the essentially noble and nonthreatening character of Castalia. In fact, the Music Master is the beatific, almost too perfect counterforce to Big Brother. The value system gracing this twenty-fifth century society, like that in Werfel's Astromental world, has elevated its members to a life beyond physical effort and material want, and emphasizes the development of the intellect and aesthetic sensibility above all else. In an even more systematic way than in Panopolis, Castalia features the ideal of *homo ludens* as the zenith of human cultural development. What is made almost grotesque in Werfel's novel, namely a preoccupation with ageless physical beauty, is sublimated in Castalia as a gentle, exquisitely masculine aura of secular saintliness.

Nevertheless, Knecht rebels. Having moved through the various schools of the order and then into positions of increasing responsibility, Knecht ultimately is selected as Magister Ludi, Master of the Glass Bead Game. But through his years of study and very devotion to the order, he has grown skeptical of its superiority to the outside world. Unlike Panopolis or Oceania, Castalia faces no imminent military enemies, but it has become so aloof in its perfection that its values are threatened with growing indifference from the outside world. Knecht sees both the pragmatic danger that in the event of another war this indifference could prove fatal to the order, and the moral danger that in the process of nurturing its own culture so well Castalia has lost sight of its original purpose as a teaching order. Knecht, whose name in German means "servant," lays down his office as Magister Ludi in the conviction that to meaningfully serve his order he must leave it and rejoin the outside world. He becomes a humble teacher, seeking out as his first pupil the difficult son of an old friend. In trying to establish a trusting relationship with the boy Tito, Knecht accepts his pupil's challenge to a swim across an icy mountain lake and drowns.

As in both *1984* and *Star of the Unborn,* the protagonist becomes the focal point of tension between forces which would maintain the order and those which would change it. And again, as in those other flawed utopias, what allows the protagonist to articulate his own skepticism is a caring relationship to another character. *The Glass Bead Game* is a much more intricately constructed novel than either *Star of the Unborn* or *1984,* and so it is not a simple love affair that fosters this skepticism, but a series of relationships. Some of those relationships are with his mentors, the Music Master and Father Jacobus. Some are with fellow students, for example with the irritating and very fragile Tegularious on the one hand and with the dominating, worldly Designori on the other. Although all the relationships are to other men and function on the purely platonic level of friendship (an interesting link to the puritanical values of Panopolis and Oceania), the seductive nature of these relationships is as real as in the cases of Winston-Julia and F. W. Lala.

Two of these relationships in particular pull Knecht away from the order. The first is the relationship to Father Jacobus, and through him, to the Church. Interestingly enough, both Castalia and the Astromental world must come to terms with the Church, and one limitation of both societies, one measure of their failure as utopias, is the extent to which they have aspired to perfect harmony without an adequate spiritual base. F. W.'s lengthy conversations with the Archbishop, his involvement in the debate over the existence of God make little sense in Werfel's novel until we discover with the protagonist the secret of the Wintergarden—a huge subterranean realm in which Astromental citizens are recycled in a process of retrogenesis, short-circuiting death and reducing God to a kind of gardener in a glorified hydroponic farm. Josef Knecht is singled out by the Order to serve as emissary to the Church before he becomes Master of the Glass Bead Game, and in this role he has opportunity to probe the extent to which the two orders are compatible. It is an essential spirituality that marks both men as outsiders in their respective utopias, and it is this spirituality which ultimately compels them to defect.

The second seductive relationship in Knecht's case is that to Plinio Designori. Designori is not a Castalian proper, but has been extended the benefits of a Castalian education because of his family's powerful position in the outside world. In their early years together, Plinio insisted on the superiority of the outside world to Castalia. Ironically, this insistence forces Knecht to become the more nearly perfect defender and servant of his order. When in later life Designori (whose name contains an ironic complement to "Knecht") considers himself a failure and invokes Knecht's help with his son, the way for the latter's break with the order has been prepared.

The third German contemporary of *1984* is less well known than *The Glass Bead Game,* probably better known than *Star of the Unborn,* and certainly the most elusive of all four novels. Ernst Jünger wrote *Heliopolis: Rückblick auf eine*

Stadt (*Heliopolis: Reflections on a City*) in the direct aftermath of the Second World War. Jünger's longest and most difficult work to date, it was published in the same year as *1984*, although publication might have occurred sooner had Jünger not been black-listed by the Allied Occupation Forces until 1949 because he refused to submit to denazification proceedings.[11] The reasons for Allied suspicion and for Jünger's refusal to cooperate bring some of the issues surrounding one of Germany's more controversial novelists into reasonably sharp focus. Born in 1895, Jünger served as an officer in the First World War and turned his combat experiences into highly popular fiction (*Storm of Steel*, 1920; *Fire and Blood*, 1925; etc.). During the 1920s he contributed to right-wing journals with essays on the First World War and the ethics of combat. Surprising many, he then refused membership in the Nazi party and in the official Party literary academy. Whereas both Werfel and Hesse wrote as true emigrants, it has been claimed for Jünger that he became a member of the "inner emigration"—those who remained in Germany during the twelve years of National Socialism, but who distanced themselves from any sort of political involvement with or support for the government. In Jünger's case the issue is not at all transparent: in 1939 he published *On the Marble Cliffs*, a short novel which begs to be interpreted as an anti-Nazi allegory; for the next five years he served for the second time as an officer, largely with occupation forces in France; there he had contact with the group planning the July 20, 1944, assassination attempt on Hitler, to which he was nevertheless opposed; forbidden to publish further in Germany by the National Socialists from 1942 on, he indignantly refused to undergo denazification proceedings in 1945 and was thus forbidden to publish by the Allies until 1949.

Heliopolis, like *Star of the Unborn* and *The Glass Bead Game*, is set in a more distant future than *1984*. Lucius de Geer, Jünger's aristocratic central figure, is a young officer in the service of a distant and obscure World Regent. The glittering city of Heliopolis, like Panopolis and Castalia, is the future summit of civilized mankind and is replete with advanced technology, a heightened aesthetic dimension and a life seemingly unencumbered by physical labor, sickness, or poverty as we know it. Behind the superficial serenity of Heliopolis lurks the shadow of war, however. As in *Star of the Unborn*, armed conflict finally erupts because of intervention by the central figure, and in turn precipitates his flight from dystopia.

Power is important in the three German novels, but only in *Heliopolis* does it possess the sort of primary value it had in Orwell's *1984*. Lucius can discourse with the philosopher Serner, debate with the historian Orelli, and muse with poets and painters, but it is as military officer that Commander de Geer uncovers the dark side of Heliopolis and ultimately violates its code.

Lucius' disaffection is characterized by his immediate superior as a "metaphysical tendency," more suitable, the General says, to a monastic order than to the military, especially since the outwardly serene Heliopolis is in a state of near anarchy. Although very little actually happens by way of action in this most philosophical of Jünger's novels, what plot exists is driven by the contest for control of Heliopolis between two factions: the evil forces of the Governor, who aspires to the power of "an absolute bureaucracy," and the more aristocratic forces of the Proconsul. On a diplomatic mission from the Proconsul to the Governor, de Geer exceeds his authority by interceding on behalf of the daughter (named Budur Peri) of a member of a persecuted minority. Later, de Geer leads a commando unit charged with destroying a Nazi-like "Toxiocological Institute" run by the Governor, and again he exceeds his authority—this time by delaying his mission long enough to search for Budur's father.

Although a man of action and a superb leader, Lucius feels more and more torn between his military obligations and the dictates of his conscience. He comes to realize that an order, no matter how aristocratic, which cannot tolerate his metaphysical leanings is a flawed order—especially when those leanings include an increasing distaste for violence and an increasing affection for Budur Peri. The intimate reltationship to this girl, like Winston Smith's relationship to Julia, F. W.'s to Lala and Knecht's friendship with Plinio Designori, is the logical mechanism for the author to expose the dark side of his putative utopia, for in each case that which is absent is a spiritual dimension whose natural human expression is a loving interpersonal relationship.

Lucius is rewarded for his resistance. In a dramatic reversal of Winston Smith's horrific fate in *1984,* Jünger concludes his novel by promoting Lucius to the immediate entourage of the distant World Regent. He and Budur Peri marry and are then spirited away from Heliopolis in a rocketship sent by the Regent, whose attention and affection Lucius has captured. The significance of this difference is much greater than the simple contrast between the pathos of *1984* and the felicitous conclusion of *Heliopolis.* Paradoxically, considering the common crucible for these four dystopic novels and the parallels just reviewed, all three German novels end in affirmation as profound as was Orwell's despair. Orwell, in fact, puts a fine point on this contrast by leaving Winston Smith nothing to affirm in the end but Big Brother: "He loved Big Brother." To maximize his warning Orwell permits no escape from the Thought Police, no hope of resistance to systematic terror. The power of his novel rests on the simplicity of its images, upon the ruthless consistency with which his anti-utopia apes our own successes in certain fields of technology and techniques of persuasion. His vision was darkened by his failing health, but also by the melancholy common to liberals who had perhaps expected too much of mid-twentieth-century man, and he lashes out against the very idea of hope with the unrelenting pressure of satire, a pressure which brooks no compromise if it is to sustain its effect.[12]

To point out that Werfel, Hesse, and Jünger were more optimistic than Orwell is not to say they wrote conventional utopias. Theirs are still basically dystopic visions. But in permitting their protagonists not only to recognize the failures in their respective systems, but to break with those systems as well, they preserve a measure of hope denied by Orwell. More than any other feature, this unwillingness to capitulate to despair frames the distinction between Orwell's novel and those of his German contemporaries. For Jünger, that hope is articulated in the invitation issued Lucius by the emissary of the World Regent:

> We consider it possible to extract from the world an elite formed by pain. This elite has purified itself in the struggles and fevers of history as a raw material in which dwells a hidden will to recover. We seek to capture and develop this will in order one day to return it to the body as a rationally clarified life force.[13]

"Elite," "pain," "will to recover," "life force"—these words resonate throughout Jünger's fiction and invite objection to what many critics view as the fascist aesthetic latent in his work.[14] The counterargument can be made, however, that the forces struggling for control of Heliopolis are modeled on fascism and that the same humanistic values which discredit Lucius with both the Governor and the Proconsul make him eligible for the true aristocracy to which he is eventually elevated. But the novel is highly ambiguous, and in this point especially elusive. What seems clear is that out of his experience with fascism in World War II, Jünger, like Orwell, constructs a negative utopia in which he draws the lessons from that central event and posts profound warnings for the future. The irony, given the fact that Orwell wrote in the language of the victors and Jünger in that of the vanquished, is that Lucius sails away with his new bride on a rocketship named "Columbus," while Winston Smith drowns his pain in the bitter gin of dystopia.

Jünger's is not the only elite answer to the flawed present masked as dark utopia. Hesse's Castalia is unabashedly elitist, as Josef Knecht makes explicit in his letter of resignation:

> The history of societies shows a constant tendency toward the formation of a nobility as the apex and crown of any given society. It would seem that all efforts at socialization have as their ideal some kind of aristocracy, or *rule* of the best, even though this goal may not be admitted.[15]

The problem with Castalia as utopia is that the order has lost touch with the world outside, has turned inward and arrogant, and has traded its historical and spiritual connectedness for a brilliant but sterile intellectual elegance. The internal danger Knecht perceives is that of hubris; the external danger outright destruction. Smug in its superiority, the Castalian order and its Glass Bead Game have become disconnected from external reality. Knecht's study of history warns him that an era of global conflict could erupt again, and that if it did there would be no support for superfluous elements in society, no matter how superior. To counteract the void spreading beneath the luminous surface of Castalia, Knecht reconnects his order with the world at large by personal example in his new role as humble teacher. We understand that just as in the case of Lucius de Geer, this seeming subordination is in reality a promotion to an even higher plane in a hierarchy more noble than the flawed utopia it leaves behind. Although Knecht dies, the fact that his deeds and motives are recorded in terms of growing appreciation by a later Castalian biographer points to a spiritual renewal of the order.

Winston Smith's job in the Ministry of Truth was to rewrite history. This eagerness on the part of the State to distort truth for political gain is Oceania's most venal aspect. Lucius and Josef Knecht are chosen to point the way out of darkness in part because of their sensitivity to history and their respect for historical truth. Werfel's F. W. calls himself an "historian of the future," and for him, too, the treatment of history is a barometer of the new society. For this deeply religious author, writing in the seventh year of his exile, the course of history is a gradual falling away from God. The failure of the Astromental era was to have pursued too keenly intellectual and technological sophistication without concomitant regard for spiritual values; hence the brittle vulnerability of the jewellike Djebel, hence the powerful allure of the half-wild Jungle. In rejecting Panopolis and its Wintergarden and electing instead to return to the barbaric year of 1943, F. W. expresses a preference for a time when the finality of death nevertheless enhanced the meaning of life and served at least as a potential link to a dimension of transcendental values.

As dark utopias, each of these four novels articulates a warning against the perpetuation of forces contributing to the shambles of the 1940s. The same, certainly, is true of other German contemporaries of *1984,* such as the novel by Walter Jens mentioned at the outset (*No. The World of the Defendants*) and the trilogy by Stefan Andres (*The Deluge*). Increasingly, literary historians seem wont to characterize all Western literature since Orwell as basically anti-utopian, as a "literature of lost illusions."[16] Perhaps it is true, in the words of Wolfgang Bergsdorf, that utopia has lost its original purpose of encouraging the political imagination to stretch itself towards better solutions.[17] Evidence that this seems to be the case in recent German letters can be found for instance in the way images of America—long a metaphor for something approaching utopia for Germans—have become either explicitly negative or at best highly ambivalent.[18] And in a significant and rather depressing note, the editors of a deliberate effort mounted in 1983 to stimulate contributions from both the Federal Republic of Germany and the German Democratic Republic, as well as Austria and Switzerland, to a volume of utopian stories confess that the majority of those authors invited felt unable to respond with positive visions of the future.[19] The most positive voice, in fact, in what he himself calls Orwell's decade, is that of Günter Grass. Even there one finds less optimism than a stubborn refusal to be pessimistic, less hope for a better world than fortitude in the face of almost certain defeat. The last line of Grass's 1969 novel *Aus dem Tagebuch einer Schnecke* (*From the Diary of a Snail*), a novel constructed in large part of the tension between utopian hopes for political reform and the melancholy of campaign reality, gives a measure of cautious optimism for the 1970s:

> He alone who knows and respects stasis in progress, who once and more than once has given up, has sat astride the snail's empty shell and dwelled on the dark side of Utopia, can take the measure of progress.[20]

Yet the snail as metaphor for slow, steady progress proved to be too optimistic. In his novel for the 1980s, *Headbirths or The Germans are Dying Out,* Grass admits that the snail has long outdistanced any measurable progress. As his new metaphor Grass chooses the stone of Sisyphus, but as Albert Camus interpreted the myth, i.e., with affirmation: "*Ja sagen zum Stein.*"[21]

This remarkable "*Ja,*" this realistic but emphatic affirmation distinguishes Günter Grass among current German writers and links him in an unambiguous way to Franz Werfel, Hermann Hesse, and even Ernst Jünger. These latter three, to be sure, were all deeply conservative authors while Grass is a committed social democrat; but all have articulated a longing for a renewal of humanistic values in their fiction, a longing foreclosed to Orwell's disaffected liberalism. Each has recognized and attempted to come to terms with Germany's totalitarian past, none more so than Grass, but these German writers have been less interested in evoking the trappings of terror than in probing the failure of the human spirit. While it is true that none of his German contemporaries matched the power of Orwell's images to fascinate and inform an entire generation, it seems worth noting that they pose a serious challenge to the usual critical assumption that dystopia in the twentieth century is the exclusive province of the dispirited left.[22] Obviously, it is too soon to predict whether, as we gain distance on 1984, some of the power of Orwell's bitter images will wane and interest in the more conservative visions of his German contemporaries might grow. In the meantime, it may be enough not to forget them entirely and to remember that although all four novels demonstrate an understandable reluctance to indulge blithely in traditional utopian dreams, only three showed the courage, in Lewis Mumford's phrase, to keep up "the business of projecting prouder worlds."[23]

NOTES

[1] Günter Grass, *Kopfgeburten oder Die Deutschen sterben aus* (Darmstadt and Neuwied: Luchterhand, 1980), p. 85 (my translation).

[2] Heinrich Böll, *Fürsorgliche Belagerung* (Cologne: Kiepenheuer & Witsch, 1979).

[3] *Der Spiegel,* January 3, 1983.

[4] Sidney Rosenfeld, "*Nineteen Eighty-Four* in Germany: A Look Back," *World Literature Today* 58 (1984): 199–203.

[5] Rosenfeld cites the important study by Alexander and Margarete Mitscherlitsch, translated as *The Inability to Mourn,* which details some of the psychological defense mechanisms manifested in postwar German society: "In order to resist the collective melancholic impoverishment of the self that would have resulted from a 'working-through' of its past, the Federal Republic, the Mitscherlitschs argue, alienated itself from the past, cut off all affective bridges to it, erected a group taboo against its recollection." Rosenfeld, p. 202. Many West German authors on the other hand, notably Günter Grass, have deliberately and consistently violated that taboo in an effort to compel their fellow Germans to come to terms with the past.

[6] The recent monograph *Die literarische Utopie* by Wolfgang Biesterfeld (Stuttgart: Metzler, 1982) identifies some one hundred and sixteen German fictional utopias published between 1900 and 1981.

[7] For a general orientation to Werfel in English, see the entry in the *Handbook of Austrian Literature,* Frederick Ungar, editor (New York: Ungar, 1973). The monograph in German by Leopold Zahn, *Franz Werfel,* in the series *Köpfe des XX. Jahrunderts* (Berlin: Colloquium Verlag, 1966), gives a much more complete introduction.

[8] On the tradition of changed sexual codes in utopian literature, see Lewis Mumford, *The Story of Utopias* (New York: Viking, 1922, reprinted 1966), esp. pp. 21f., and Joachim Bumke, "Die Utopie des Grals. Eine Gesellschaft ohne Liebe?" *Literarische Utopie-Entwürfe,* Hiltrud Gnüg, editor

(Frankfurt: Suhrkamp, 1981), pp. 70–79. Irving Howe credits Orwell with this discovery, namely that "Orwell has here come upon an important tendency in modern life, that the totalitarian state is inherently an enemy of erotic freedom" in *Orwell's Nineteen Eighty-Four. Text, Sources, Criticism,* Irving Howe, editor (New York: Harcourt Brace Jovanovich, 1963), p. 193.

[9] The major treatment of utopian elements in Hesse is Roger C. Norton's *Hermann Hesse's Futuristic Idealism* (Bern: Herbert Lang and Frankfurt: Peter Lang, 1973).

[10] The critical literature in English on Hesse is especially large due to the enormous popularity his works enjoyed in America during the 1960s and early 1970s. For a general orientation, see George Wallis Field, *Hermann Hesse* (New York: Twayne, 1970). The best analysis in any language is Theodore Ziolkowski's *The Novels of Hermann Hesse* (Princeton: Princeton University Press, 1965).

[11] A general orientation to Jünger is available in English in Gerhard Loose's *Ernst Jünger* (New York: Twayne, 1974).

[12] Both Orwell's health and the melancholy associated with disenchanted liberalism in the late 1940s are discussed in the essays by Irving Howe, "*1984*: History as Nightmare," and Lionel Trilling, "George Orwell and the Politics of Truth," in *Orwell's Nineteen Eighty-Four. Text, Sources, Criticism.*

[13] "Wir halten es für möglich, eine Elite aus der Welt herauszuziehen, die der Schmerz gebildet hat. Sie hat sich geläutert in den Kämpfen und Fiebern der Geschichte als Stoff, dem ein verborgener Wille zur Heilung innewohnt. Wir suchen ihn aufzufangen und zu entwickeln, um ihn dann dem Körper wieder zuzuführen als sinnvoll geklärte Lebenskraft." Jünger, *Heliopolis: Rückblick euf eine Stadt. Werke,* Vol. 10 (Stuttgart: Ernst Klett, 1965), p. 350.

[14] For an example of an excellent study which is nevertheless very hostile on this account, see Wolfgang Kaempfer, *Ernst Jünger* (Stuttgart: Metzler, 1981).

[15] Hermann Hesse, *The Glass Bead Game,* Richard and Clara Winston, translators (New York: Holt, Rinehart and Winston, 1969), p. 348.

[16] See, for example, the article by Hans Meyer "Widersprüche einer europaischen Literatur," *Die Zeit* 11 (March 1983): 19.

[17] "Utopie steht jetzt für den Alptraum von der schlechtesten gesellschaftlichen Ordnung. Damit verliert die Utopie ihre traditionelle Aufgabe, die politische Phantasie bei ihrer Suche nach besseren Möglichkeiten zu beflügeln." Bergsdorf, "Zweck der Macht ist die Macht," *Die Zeit* 11 (March 1983): 16.

[18] See Heinz D. Osterle "The Lost Utopia: New Images of America in German Literature," *German Quarterly* 54 (1981): 427–446.

[19] See the foreword to *Auf der Suche nach dem Garten Eden. Science-fiction-Geschichten für eine bessere Welt* (Baden-Baden: Signal-Verlag, 1984), p. 7.

[20] Günter Grass, *Aus dem Tagebuch einer Schnecke* (Darmstadt and Neuwied: Luchterhand, 1972), p. 264 (my translation).

[21] Saying "yes" to the stone of Sisyphus is the central metaphor in *Headbirths*. The different metaphors are contrasted in Mark E. Cory, "Sisyphus and the Snail: Metaphors for the Political Process in Günter Grass' *Aus dem Tagebuch einer Schnecke* and *Kopfgeburten oder Die Deutschen sterben aus,*" *German Studies Review* 6 (1983): 519–533.

[22] As formulated, for instance, by Howe, p. 176: "The peculiar intensity of such fiction derives not so much from the horror aroused by a possible vision of the future, but from the writer's discovery that in facing the prospect of a future he had been trained to desire, he finds himself struck with horror." See also Alfred Kazin, "Not One of Us: George Orwell and 1984," *New York Review of Books* 31 (1984): 13–18.

[23] Mumford, p. 298.

FICTIONAL *1984* AND FACTUAL 1984

ETHICAL QUESTIONS REGARDING THE CONTROL OF CONSCIOUSNESS BY MASS MEDIA

Thomas W. Cooper

It has never been less *nor* more appropriate to consider the fiction *1984* by George Orwell. It has never been *less* appropriate to consider *1984* as a work of *prophecy*. Orwell did not intend his novel to describe the literal year 1984 A.D.; with the arrival of that year, however, a bevy of writers were tempted to measure Orwell's distance from the prophetic bull's eye.[1] Such distractions missed his point. With the vantage of hindsight, the Orwell reader discovers that it is more the spirit than the letter of Orwell which is significant.

Thus, it has never been more appropriate to consider *1984* as a warning. Orwell warns of darker tendencies present within the human species, tendencies increasingly serviced by global communications systems, consciousness-control psychology, and overkill weaponry, tendencies increasingly visible during the 1980s.

THE WILL TO POWER

> All events that result from intention are reducible to the intention to increase power.[2]
>
> *Friedrich Nietzsche*

> But always, do not forget this, Winston,—always there will be the
> intoxication of power, constantly increasing and constantly grow-
> ing subtler.[3]
>
> Comrade O'Brien to Winston Smith
> in *1984*

The twentieth century has been nothing if not an ode to power. The managers of media, military, and transportation systems have watched their wattage,
megatons, and velocities increase arithmetically and now geometrically. Aware of
the power explosion, and deeply disturbed by the atomic bombs dropped during
World War II, George Orwell made central to his writing the discussion of un-
checked power. He suggested the ends human beings might pursue to maintain
power over their fellows. Like Nietzsche's *The Will to Power, 1984* is a prolonged
meditation upon power as *the* underlying human goal. The protagonist, Winston
Smith, is motivated throughout the entire novel by the question, "Why?", by
which we assume his longer question, "Why does the Party seek total control?"
or, in more general terms, "Why is power the basis for human motivation?"

Orwell's construction of a mythical society pits Smith, a futuristic Everyman
and symbol of dying individualism, against the monolithic power of a thoroughly
regimented society. Resembling the worst aspects of Nazi Germany and Stalinist
Russia, *1984*'s regime outdistances all previous totalitarian societies by monitoring
and destroying deviation in behavior, language, and *thought*. Smith, like the
many romantic Quixotes preceding him, seeks to maintain his vision and to expose the system. But, unlike his fictitious predecessors drawn by Cervantes, Ibsen,
and others, Smith does not finally abandon his illusion for truth, he abandons his
truth for an illusion. Our hope as an audience is twice betrayed, first when
Winston Smith is finally tortured into imagining that "two plus two equals five"
and finally, during Orwell's bleakest warning, when Smith *happily* KNOWS that
two plus two equals five. Social enculturation has thoroughly and tragically
crushed his own perception of experience. More importantly, he consciously am-
putates his own detection of and trust in personal experience. "He presented himself with propositions—'the Party says the earth is flat,' 'The Party says that ice is
heavier than water'—and trained himself in not seeing or not understanding the
arguments that contradicted them."[4]

The forced training of "comrades" to choose deliberately the reigning perspective is implemented by ubiquitous, omnipotent electronic media. Micro-
phones are hidden everywhere and the telescreen, which only Inner Party members may briefly turn off, constantly informs, educates, and persuades all Party
members. This metal plaque telescreen dictates history, current events, and nec-

essary behaviors (exercises, group "hate sessions," waking, working, and sleeping). It serves as constant negative ("Smith, you can do better than that.") and positive ("That's better, Comrade.") reinforcement to modify behavior.

Eric Blair (alias George Orwell) had obtained first-hand experience of the power of mass media as a producer with the BBC from 1941–43. He had also served with the Indian Imperial Police, if not the secret police, from 1922–27.[5] His job as literary editor of *The Tribune* in 1943 was not without parallels to Winston Smith's occupation. Moreover, his fascination with the overlapping tendencies within Socialism, Communism, and Fascism stemmed from his constant participation within the actual and verbal Civil Wars, among and against Marxist factions in Spain and England.[6]

Bernard Crick's *Orwell* downplays the previous offbeat interpretations that *1984,* Orwell's last volume, was heavily influenced by his prolonged and lethal struggle with tuberculosis.[7] Attempts to reduce the book to an autobiographical science fiction written by a failing mind are as shallow as hopes to analyze the book as mere prophecy. Orwell sanely, soberly called his book a satire. He deliberately developed "Oceania" as a carefully premeditated warning against totalitarian tendencies within ourselves and within all societies, not as commentary about previous or existing Fascist or Communist regimes within Germany, Japan, Italy, and Russia.[8] Moreover, the only sense in which Orwell intended his book to be prophetic was what his friend Freddy Ayer and the philosophers would have called "'an if/then proposition, if A is not done, then B will follow'. . . something like 1984 *could* happen."[9]

Hence, whatever autobiographical and historical allusions *1984* may contain, the work is primarily philosophical, anthropological, and sociopolitical. As satire, it consists of countless insights about human nature pushed into high relief toward caricature. Like Aristophanes, Swift, and Voltaire, Orwell prefers the rapier to the bludgeon: often his minor asides are, upon close inspection, more telling about social relations than the central plot. He took meticulous care to integrate artfully a coherent culture in which each event, character, and dialogue tells something deeper about this century.

THE "LESSER" DANGERS

Of the dozens of dangers Orwell pinpoints, at least seventeen are increasingly visible due to recent communication, technological, and sociological transformation. These seventeen are interrelated and many consecutive listings overlap. This list begins with eleven "lesser" dangers and concludes with six terminal tendencies. To draw parallels between the literary fictional and (reported) factual for the lesser dangers, I simply list quotes juxtaposed from *1984* with media reports and publications from the year 1984.

TOTALITARIAN TENDENCY	FICTIONAL *1984* DEPICTION BY GEORGE ORWELL	"FACTUAL" 1983–84 DEPICTION BY MASS MEDIA
1. INVASION OF PRIVACY/UBIQUITOUS SURVEILLANCE	"Even from the coin the eyes pursued you. On coins, on stamps, on the cover of books, on banners, on posters, and on the wrapping of a cigarette packet—everywhere. Always the eyes watching you and the voice enveloping you. Asleep or awake, working or eating, indoors or out of doors, in the bath or in the bed—no escape."[10]	"Think carefully about orbiting satellites that can read the license plates in a parking lot and computers that can tap into thousands of telephone calls and telex transmissions at once and other computers that can do our banking and purchasing, can watch the house and tell a monitoring station what TV program we are watching and how many people are in the room."[11]
	"For a moment he was tempted to take it into the water closet and read it at once. But that would be shocking folly as he well knew. There was no place where you could be more certain that the telescreens were watched continuously."[12]	"The federal government holds an average of 15 files on each man, woman and child in the country, and computer technology makes it easy to piece together innocuous snippets gathered by different agencies into a detailed, perhaps incriminating mosaic."[13]
2. CENTRALIZED HIERARCHICAL CONTROL THROUGH COMMUNICATION TECHNOLOGY	"The telescreen received and transmitted simultaneously.[14] Life, as you looked about you, bore no resemblance . . . to the lies that streamed out of the tele-	"When Zenith Radio Corp's top executives want to know what's happening on the factory floor here, they watch television . . . and as the top brass

TOTALITARIAN TENDENCY	FICTIONAL *1984* DEPICTION BY GEORGE ORWELL	"FACTUAL" 1983–84 DEPICTION BY MASS MEDIA
	screens.[15] 'Smith,' yelled a voice from the telescreen. '6069, Smith W., Hands out of pockets . . .'"[16]	hunker into their desk chairs to watch . . . the records tell a happy story— record production . . . They're watching this on a computer in television's clothing."[17]
3. MASS MEDIA AS CATALYSTS FOR THE INTENSIFICATION OF DESTRUCTIVE EMOTIONS AND VIOLENCE	"The (two minutes) Hate had started. As usual, the face of Emmanuel Goldstein the Enemy of the People, had flashed upon the screen. A hideous ecstasy of fear and vindictiveness, a desire to kill . . . seemed to flow through the whole group."[18]	"Cable and pay television are more than twice as violent as commercial TV, a news story reported . . . The N.C.T.V. said it found an average of twenty acts of violence each hour."[19]
4. DEHUMANIZATION	"Orwell . . . is simply implying that the new form of managerial industrialism, in which men build machines which act like men, and develop men who act like machines, is conducive to an era of dehumanization . . ."[20]	"The RB5X robot at the Center of Science and Industry will telephone the RB5X robot at the Museum of Natural History in Denver. The event, says the RB Robot Corp., will be the first transcontinental robotic "conversation" that initiates robot activity."[21]
5. MECHANICAL SUBSTITUTE PATTERNS FOR INTIMATE, PERSONAL RELATIONSHIPS	"Tacitly the party was even inclined to encourage prostitution, as an outlet which could not be altogether suppressed. . . . All marriages between Party members had to be approved by a committee ap-	"The most sought after phone number in New York these days . . . is the unlisted number for *High Society* magazine's 'living centerfold hot line,' more commonly known as 'dial-a-porn.' Since it began last

TOTALITARIAN TENDENCY	FICTIONAL *1984* DEPICTION BY GEORGE ORWELL	"FACTUAL" 1983–84 DEPICTION BY MASS MEDIA
	pointed for that purpose, and . . . permission was always refused if the couple concerned gave the impression of being . . . attracted to each other."[22]	February this 57-second x-rated tape has received as many as 500,000 calls a day."[23]
6. MINDLESS AUDIENCE OWNERSHIP/FORMULAIC, ANONYMOUS DISPOSABLE CULTURE	"The tune had been haunting London for weeks past. It was one of those countless similar songs published for the benefit of the proles by a subsection of the Music Department. The words were composed without any human intervention whatever on an instrument known as a versificator."[24]	"ABC OWNS WEDNESDAY . . . it seems to have assembled the most invincible single night for the new season . . . a quartet of half hour comedies has been assembled for Tuesdays as a lead-in to the robust *Hart to Hart,* but two of ABC's shows—*Just Our Luck* and *Oh Madeline* are new and unproven and the veteran *Happy Days* is showing signs of age."[25]
7. EASILY CENSORED, "TAPPED," OR ROUTINIZED CORRESPONDENCE	"As for sending a letter through the mail, it was out of the question. By a routine that was not even secret, all letters were opened in transit. Actually, few people ever wrote letters. For the message it was occasionally necessary to send, there were printed postcards with long lists of phrases, and you struck out the ones that were inapplicable."[26]	"MCI will send letters electronically over its lines, either sending them directly to . . . computers or printing them by laser at a center near the recipient for delivery later . . . MCI expects 200,000 subscribers to sign up by the end of 1984."[27]
8. ROUTINIZATION OF LEISURE TIME	"The telescreen was giving forth an ear-splitting whis-	"The Oakland A's, Philadelphia Phillies and New

TOTALITARIAN TENDENCY	FICTIONAL *1984* DEPICTION BY GEORGE ORWELL	"FACTUAL" 1983–84 DEPICTION BY MASS MEDIA
	tle, which continued for thirty seconds. It was nought seven fifteen, getting up time for office workers . . . Winston sprang to attention in front of the telescreen, upon which the image of a youngish woman . . . had already appeared. 'Arms bending and stretching,' she rapped out '. . . one, two, three, four! . . . Come on, comrades'"[28]	York Yankees all have computers. . . . Other teams will follow. At least a dozen are interested. Despite howls by traditionalists, and dire predictions that the next Hall of Fame manager will be an Apple II, the computers' ability to make sense of baseball's endless statistics gives it enormous potential . . ."[29]
9. ETHNIC AND NATIONAL STEREOTYPE BY MEDIATED ARTIFICE	"Some Eurasian prisoners, guilty of war crimes, were to be hanged in the park that evening. This happened about once a month and was a popular spectacle."[30]	"Hollywood is ready to get serious this fall by tackling themes of political violence . . . *Beyond the Limit,* Michael Caine and Richard Gere get involved with Paraguayan guerrillas in Argentina. *Under Fire* follows American journalists Nick Nolte and Gene Hackman, who become enmeshed in the Nicaraguan revolution. *Deal of the Century* features Chevy Chase and Gregory Hines as ruthless arms dealers who cater to corrupt South American dictators and revolutionaries. *Curfew, USA,* features actress/writer/producer Zoe Tamerlis as an American singer who joins a Latin American revolution and

TOTALITARIAN TENDENCY	FICTIONAL *1984* DEPICTION BY GEORGE ORWELL	"FACTUAL" 1983–84 DEPICTION BY MASS MEDIA
		assassinates a tyrant during a Fifth Avenue friendship parade. *Hanna K.* follows a lawyer who becomes attached to a Palestinian terrorist she defends in Israel."[31]
10. THE DEVALUATION OF INTUITIVE FEELING/ COLLECTIVIZATION OF MEDIA-CONTROLLED OPINION	"The terrible thing that the Party had done was to persuade you that mere impulses, mere feelings, were of no account, while at the same time robbing you of all material power over the material world. When once you were in the grip of the Party what you felt or did not feel . . . made literally no difference."[32]	"Our research shows that people think the financial situation is increasingly worse, and that the President is doing well only in the area of defense. About six in ten are concerned about environmental protection and two-thirds with the loss of jobs."[33]
11. SIMULTANEOUS GLOBAL INDOCTRINATION	"There was of course no way of knowing whether you were being watched at any given moment. It was even conceivable that they watched everyone all the time . . . always the eyes watching you and the voice enveloping you . . ."[34]	"TMC videoconferences allow you to address hundreds of thousands of people at once, via satellite, without the enormous cost of transporting everyone to one location. . . . They are ideal for employee indoctrination, for making important announcements, and for motivating organizations."[35]

TERMINAL TENDENCIES

Ironically, however, these are eleven "lesser" dangers. The sum of their parts is far less than their combined *total* (cf. *total*itarian) effect. When these eleven tendencies co-function, six greater life-threatening hazards become operative. Communication plays a crucial role in what could be called sensory monopoly, and the six perils below could be called "Media Fascism." The six are listed in order of increasing malignancy.

12. MEDIA ADDICTION AND THE ABOLITION OF PLURALISM

> The Party told you to reject the evidence of your eyes and ears. It was their final, most essential command.[36]
>
> *1984*
>
> This country has more radios than people, more television sets than bathtubs.[37]
>
> *Tony Schwartz*

In *1984,* the senses are given constant artificial stimulation. The eyes and ears, particularly, are focused upon human sounds and images of electronic origin. Animals, vegetables, galaxies, and ocean waves are beyond the range of hearing and seeing. Only electronic voices, plaque and poster replicas of "Big Brother," and Party-composed music saturate the senses.

Nietzsche argues that all social thought is a rationalized "perspective" which legitimizes a society's (or individual's) will to power.[38] Christianity is, in his view, a perspective which elevates morality above force as a social virtue. Hence, Christianity redefined power in moral terms to protect its own physical weakness.[39] Such a perspective was in marked contrast to the competitive Roman Empire perspective which held that superior military force itself legitimized dominance. Thus, for Nietzsche, each culture constructs a world view which protects and elevates its own strengths and avoids any penetrating examination of its weaknesses.

1984 epitomizes such "perspectivism" (i.e., power through controlled perspective), and media serve to institutionalize the universally "right" perspective. At the outset, Winston cherishes his private thoughts and hopes they are undetected: he yearns for more time to meditate privately rather than watch the screen. By the conclusion, however, Winston's spirit has been broken and his only significant relationships are mediated: he now watches the telescreen for the outcome of battles just as an addicted fan watches television for the updates on football scores.[40] His new and only "friends" are telescreens, Party papers, and the posters of Big Brother, whom he now loves. Big Brother, of course, is also a media creation, who has no demonstrable existence outside of ghost-written journalism and the Party's public relations machine. While at one level Winston has turned his affection from his lover to the Party, it could also be said that he has turned his interest from people to media.

Mass media as surrogate for first-hand experience is not a new theme: Plato warned that writing and reading might lead humans to substitute mediated "knowledge" for first-hand experience.[41] However, that syndrome has grown to astronomical proportions. Tony Schwartz explains why he calls modern media "the second God" in his book by that title.

> Ask someone raised in the religious traditions of the Western world to describe God, and this, with idiosyncratic variations, might be the answer:
>
> "God is all-knowing and all-powerful. He is a spirit, and He exists both outside us and within us. God is always with us, because He is everywhere. We can never fully understand Him, because He works in mysterious ways."
>
> In broad terms, this describes the God of our fathers, but it also describes electronic media, the second God, which man has created. Radio and television are everywhere and they are always with us. Millions listen to the same networks, hum the same commercial jingles, share with soap-opera characters the testing of souls, the mystery of love and death, the agony of the sinful, and the triumph of the righteous. Stations transmit the same programs worldwide. In cramped apartments of Tokyo, people watch "Charlie's Angels." Lieutenant Columbo tracks down killers in Oslo, Rome, Madrid, and Bucharest. The whole world wanted to know who shot J. R., of "Dallas." And here in the United States we tune in the B. B. C.'s "Masterpiece Theatre" or watch Japanese and other foreign films on cable. Two billion people saw a man walk on the moon.[42]

Although the contrary arguments of cable television executives will be considered later, the thesis that media are slowly homogenizing world culture has much supporting evidence. Conceivably, even the *differences* in national programming are secondary to the increasingly widespread media-consumer relationship of "worship" and "addiction." Hence pluralism, or multiperspectivism, *could* erode toward Nietzsche's "perspectivism," in which the strongest perspective protects and legitimizes the strongest will to power, by means of mass media.

13. MEDIA AUTHORITY

> American reporters, given a glimpse of Ayatollah Khomeini's Iran
> at the end of 1982, were saying it was like *1984.* It's Orwellian, one
> added.[43]
>
> *Walter Cronkite*

Cronkite's analysis is useful. Terms such as "Orwellian" and "1984" have
slipped into the language as a means of describing *apparent* dictatorships such as
Khomeini's Iranian government. However, the word "apparent" is more interesting than "Orwellian." American audiences knew Khomeini's televised *appearance,* not Khomeini. In fact, Khomeini received thousands of pieces of "hate
mail" from Americans solely on the basis of his depiction by foreign media.
Not unlike the "two-minutes hate" described by Orwell, U.S. audience sessions
during the early 1980s would include informal assemblies at appointed hours
(7:00 a.m., 7:30, 8:00, 8:30, noon, 6:00 p.m., 6:30, 7:00, 10:00, 11:00 news slots) to
throw insults, opinions, and outrage at Khomeini's image. Some 1980 polls suggested that U.S. audiences hated no one more than Khomeini.

Similar polls also revealed that no person was more trusted than Walter
Cronkite. More than any social or political leader, he was viewed as the most
popular and *authoritative* spokesperson on world problems. Such popularity and
"authority" reveal the far subtler peril of Orwell's foreboding view. However
avuncular his manner and soothing his voice, Walter Cronkite has had little more
first-hand experience of Khomeini's circle than Big Brother has of Eurasia. He
was selected to *entertain,* not because of his experience, knowledge, or professional skills; instead, Cronkite retained his job because of his ability to sell advertising. Commercial television programming is simply a type of bait used to
"hook" audiences on particular products. If the advertising is ineffective, and if
program ratings fall, "talent" (those in *front* of the lens like Cronkite) become, in
Orwellian terms, media "unpersons" (cf. "has-beens"). Hence, from a unique
angle of perception, Cronkite resembles *Big Brother,* the trusted father-figure image. By default, he becomes an authority to the degree of our collective unques-
tioning submission to his ghost-written perspective.

When American viewers tuned to Cronkite (and the entire genre of trusted
"hosts"), their questions were not, "Is Cronkite honest with his wife?" "Does he
write his script?" "Has he lived in Teheran?" "What are his credentials in political science?" "Which advertisers does he represent?" Or even, "Does he have
legs?" Audience questions more closely resemble those of Winston Smith: "What

happened in Iran (cf. Eurasia) today?" "How will the captives (cf. prisoners) be freed?" "Can Khomeini (cf. Emmanuel Goldstein) really be that fanatical?"

More problematic are the hidden powers we concede to such "authorities." Ironically, the 1983 edition of *1984* by Signet features a preface by Cronkite. At the end of the text is an afterword by Erich Fromm, the accomplished author, thinker, and scholar. Despite Cronkite's command of journalistic insight and crafted prose, Fromm's is the far more substantial essay. The paperback's cover reads, "With a special preface by Walter Cronkite"; there is no mention of Fromm. At best, one half of the readers will discover Fromm's lengthier essay and, at worst, one half of the readers will glimpse some portion of Cronkite's brief editorial as they skim toward the primary text. Like Cronkite himself, his preface and the layout of the book are symbolic. The brief analysis of *surface* is increasingly preferred to the thoughtful, transcendent evaluation of substance.

However, *this* evaluation is not of surface, that is, of Cronkite per se, or even of the mediated icon he typifies. Rather this essay is an evaluation of more substantial concerns: aspects of *1984* have already infiltrated our consciousness at levels beyond our control. We talk of Khomeini, Chernobyl, "Irangate," and moon landings as if they are a part of our perceived experience; we affectionately hum jingles which we find truthless about products we find useless made by advertisers we find ruthless. Later the products infiltrate our household and we wake up at seven a.m. subconsciously humming jingles along with millions of other people. As an audience, increasingly we vote, think, worship, act, and feel in patterns resembling our programming during those few remaining hours of each week when we, as an aggregate norm, are not being further programmed with printed or electronic information.

When we read in an introduction by Cronkite that "Iran is Orwellian," according to his colleague, we subtly reinforce the illusion that dictatorship is "out there" somewhere and not within our own consciousness. The all-pervasiveness of our own telescreen is not measured simply by the fact that Americans have more television sets than bathtubs. Rather the deeper pervasiveness is within: we have far more subconscious programming, through which perspective we monitor experience, than *conscious* awareness. Our parallels with *1984* are not found within prophesied societal structures, but rather within our inability to detect controlled (sub)consciousness. Whose perspective(s) are we?

14. THE ONE-SIDEDNESS OF COMMUNICATION

> Even under primitive conditions one person can talk to a large audience (if they are disposed to listen!) and with modern aids even to

the whole world (same "if"). But I can't imagine any invention, human, social, or mechanical, enabling *one* to "listen" (attend) to more than one at a time! Is this a partial clue to the universal tendency to *centralization,* and the loss of liberty, and final decadence all around?[44]

Frank Knight, letter to Innis

My chief worry has been precisely . . . the one-sidedness of communication . . . I think this is what you call a partial clue to the universal tendency towards centralization . . . This one-sidedness seems to lead to monopoly and to general corruption and bureaucracy. . . .[45]

Harold Innis, letter to Knight

The Canadian social scientist Harold Innis cautions us to be wary of "monopolies of knowledge." In his unpublished correspondence to Frank Knight the discussion of "the one-sidedness of communication" offers some explanation of the origins of such monopolies. History provides Innis and Knight much reason for concern: historically, in Hellenic Athens, for example, the speaker/listener ratio was one to one in private conversation and perhaps one to one hundred at a public assembly or forum. This Innisian ideal, an oral culture, in which each citizen (Innis overlooked women and slaves) could speak freely and proportionately seemed equitable and stimulating. Each "receiver" could also be a "transmitter." Moreover, no speaker would be barred from presenting his perspective.

With each shift in communication tools, however, the ratio between speakers and listeners changed drastically.[46] The author of a scroll might reach *scores* of anonymous readers and the first authors of printed books might touch *hundreds* of unknown readers. Early radio announcers reached *thousands* more ears than Marc Antony, and Cronkite spoke in a tone we understood by *millions* more than Khomeini. Nicholas Johnson's *Talk Back to Your TV Set* to the contrary, satellite audience members may no longer publically participate in the video dialogue.[47] Although Innis died during the early years of television, the imbalanced ratio he feared continued to grow to its ultimate potential—satellite transmissions of one person's or group's perspective to the entire population and beyond. The ratio becomes one to hundreds of millions.

Nor only is a synchronous culture created in which immense numbers may worship or hate authority/images. Simultaneously, a totally programmable cultic species becomes feasible. "One-sidedness" maintains absolute power within a global executive force, and viewpoints outside the official perspective have no audience.

15. THE TOTAL VERTICAL CONTROL OF COMMUNICATION

One model of communication for the *1984* society might be called "Maypole structure." As with each member of a Maypole dance, it is the individual's connection with the apex of the hierarchy which completes the design. Each individual must consistently correspond with Party doctrine (apex) via the telescreen (streamer) or they vanish and become an "unperson." Horizontal relationships have no meaning outside of Party function and it is only chain-of-command dialogue which maintains machine efficiency.

Talking personally to colleagues, being attracted to peers, or choosing one's patterns of expression is negated by ostracism and even vaporization. Total agreement among Party members is expected and open debate is unthinkable. No directory of addresses is published and puritanical ultraconservatism safeguards all conversation.

An elaborate spying web of vertical communication insures that all judgments of the Party will be overheard and nullified. Omnivorous in its appetite for offenders, the Party uses every one to betray each other—parents inform on children; children are trained to spy on parents and report.[48] Wives are enticed to betray husbands, even Inner Party officials feign friendship to serve as "intercessors" for potential Party deviants. O'Brien, feigning such friendship for Winston and for Julia, ultimately betrays each of them to the Party and insures their betrayal of each other.

In such a fully vertical model, an enormous inequity comes through an eavesdropping superstructure which destroys the power of confidential communication in all save the innermost Party. Because the central core commands the grapevine (or Maypole), the reputation and perceived nature of all persons is controlled by the executive core. The loyal and lobotomized are promoted and praised; the thoughtful and threatening are demoted and denied public expression. All communication is censored or censured save that which echoes dogma. Hence, the Outer Party functions as an amplifier for the inner Party. The Party is ventriloquist; all others, even "Big Brother," are dummies.

Such a view seems far-fetched until one examines the communicative structure of businesses, administrations, espionage rings, governments, religions, families, and other social institutions. The tendency to "scapegoat" or "blacksheep" from above down by the grapevine has falsely established the reputation of innumerable "deviants." With global technologies, the difference becomes one of degree and power reversal. The reputation spreads instantly, globally, and from the inner Party of media through the outer Party of politics. One need look no further than the Nixon persona after Watergate to discover who owns the national grapevine.

If our own social (cf. Party) history is correct, such vertically controlled communication has always existed to some degree: "Deviants" such as Socrates, Jesus of Nazareth, Joan of Arc, Trotsky, Becket, Martin Luther King, and countless others, were lethally censored. From a communication standpoint, their crime was one of challenging reigning dogma while seeking the public address system.

Hence, the fully vertical model of communication perpetuates societal suicide. Those who spot the leak in the ship are quickly overheard, dubbed "traitors" through the grapevine, and thrown overboard. The captain, wishing to hear only praise for the ship, invites only sycophants to the watchtower while those observing the leaks are muzzled below. His grapevine permits full monitoring of the crew's activity, while the questionable crew member has no access to the larger system: he must either watch the ship sink slowly or pay the price for honest articulation—exile, excommunication, vaporization, ostracism, or "unperson" status. The "untouchables" in India, whom Orwell observed during early manhood, were treated in such manner. Throughout the Western world, nonconforming intellectuals, scientists, artists, and minority leaders play this stereotypical role.

Yet Winston Smith is none of the above stereotypes. He represents an "Everyman" as Julia represents an "Everywoman." Together they suggest that *all* of us, not just articulate eccentrics, are subject to organizational communicative conformity. The "Party's" two deadly weapons for maintaining controlled conformity are the manipulation of language ("Newspeak") and the reversal of consciousness ("Doublethink").

16. The Reversal of Consciousness and Language

In describing the kind of thinking which is dominant in *1984*, Orwell has coined a word which has already become part of the modern vocabulary: "doublethink." "Doublethink means the power of holding two contradictory beliefs in one's mind simultaneously, and accepting both of them. . . . This process has to be conscious, or it would not be carried out with sufficient precision. But it also has to be unconscious or it would bring with it a feeling of falsity and hence of guilt." It is precisely the unconscious aspect of doublethink which will seduce many a reader of *1984* into believing that the method of doublethink is employed by the Russians and the Chinese, while it is something quite foreign to himself. This, however, is an illusion, as a few examples can demonstrate.[49]

Erich Fromm

Examples of such reversals of consciousness and language offered by Fromm include the self-reference of peoples in Western nations as the "free world," the use of false ideographs in characterizing Western institutions, and the seeming lack of guilt of most writers in the West in their discussions of the nuclear deterrence strategy in the face of the Judeo-Christian tradition opposing the killing of human beings. In the first case, Fromm concisely points out that the "free world" designation is extended to all nations that, whatever the nature of their own regimes, more or less oppose Communist-bloc nations. Thus, Spain under Franco and Portugal under Salazar as well as continuing oppressive regimes such as those in South Africa and Pakistan are included in the "free world."

With regard to the characterization of social institutions in Western nations, we use such terms as "free enterprise," "individualism," and "idealism" when in fact these societies, even the most democratic ones, are highly centralized systems basically bureaucratic in structure for which materialistic values are the chief forces in motivating individual members. Fromm does not say it, but implicitly he suggests considerable hypocrisy on the part of Westerners who complain of the perversion of such terms as "socialism" and "people's republic" by the Communists.

Finally, the last of Fromm's examples bears little further comment. Indeed, extensive, serious discussion of nuclear strategies is a relatively recent phenomenon and probably only because we now must face the likelihood that nuclear war will destroy all civilization rather than just some national populations.

The fundamental problem, however, is an internal one of overcoming one's own tendencies for "doublethink." Throughout *1984,* Orwell demonstrates that Winston Smith's greatest challenge is his own thought. Modifying his behavior and language to align with Party policy causes only pain and extreme self-discipline. However, the self-manipulation of thought violates his personal experience and integrity; it is the province of *inner* communication which proves his undoing.

At his job, Smith is immersed within the social reconstruction of reality. Like those around him, he invents persons who have never existed and writes about them in news articles.[50] He changes dates and events to correspond with the Party's rewriting of history. But he cannot master doublethink. He remembers dates and events which contradict Party history and cannot hold both as truth.

The erasure of memory so vital to a perfect Party member is unnatural and inherently questionable to Smith.[51]

Nevertheless, Winston Smith is absolutely powerless against the Party's primary tactic—the reversal of consciousness. Whatever the personal perceptions and private perspectives of this individual, they are strategically nullified by the Party's dogmatic axiom that all reality exists in one's consciousness. Such relativistic absolutism (or absolutist relativism) prevents the substantiation of personal observation. A Party member may be tortured by another but be told that the pain is all in his mind. Smith may insist that societies based upon control and imposition have always failed but be told that his memory is faulty or that his consciousness is impure.

Moreover, the Party's power remains inviolate. By focusing all attention upon the individual's consciousness, attention is diverted from the Party's internal contradictions, function, dishonesty, dangers, and dogma. If the Party dictates that two plus two equals five, Smith must first learn to maintain both (cf. double) thoughts (cf. think) without contradiction and then later erase the memory of the second inappropriate thought. Hence a universal cultic consciousness may be controlled even at the level of inner communication: constantly, hordes of people maintain "truth" by rebuking personal memories and observations. If, however, the individual does maintain an appropriate thought (crimethink), which slips out during his sleep, (s)he may remain assured of the Party's safety. The thought will be trivialized from all potential meaning by being labeled a crimespeak (cf. judgement, criticism).

Such labeling is part of the larger linguistic control pattern called Newspeak. Through simple strategies of syntax, redundancy, compounding, jargon, and reduction, Newspeak extends a symmetrical outer equivalent to thoughtcrime. A frown becomes a *facecrime*. A criticism of the Party is a *thoughtcrime* and a liquidated nonconformist is an *unperson*. Redundancy through slogan and principal ("Freedom is slavery"), attitudinal modifiers (victory square, victory coffee, victory gin, victory cigarettes) and stressed vocabulary (love, peace, truth) renders an increasingly reductive scale to language.

Orwell's linguistic schematic is not without modern parallels. The authors of the Newspeak dictionary, who must increasingly restrict language to appropriate thought forms, are not unlike television's pruning of Elizabethan or even Edwardian prose, and the increasing bureaucracies of high-technocrats proliferate an endless stream of compounded scientific and technical terms, which Orwell called class C vocabulary.[52]

Here again, however, the hazard is not at the surface level of society . . . rather the deepest danger is not that *1984* is coming, but rather that is *has come* in another guise, and we are unaware of it. Language and thought remain predominately a mixture of habituation-and-enculturation. Heidegger wrote: "Most thought-provoking for our thought-provoking time is that we are still not thinking."[53] Whorf, Sapir, Wittgenstein, Austen, Cavelle, among others, consider the degree to which thought or language controls the other. Orwell implies that we are controlled by both. If human beings are constantly beckoned to create a new language and consciousness, as each new government and new philosophy undertakes, one wonders about the true dictator humans seek to overthrow. Is it the mechanism of thought/language which rigidifies perspective? Those most basic forms of communication are involved in the understanding of all other forms and are thus the most challenging to penetrate. To assume the understanding of consciousness and its dangers is itself dangerous since both the word and the thought "consciousness" are contained within what they seek to describe.

17. THE DESTRUCTION OF TRUTH, REALITY, INTEGRITY, HUMAN DIGNITY,
    AND INDIVIDUAL PURPOSE

The Newspeak term for individual activity is "ownlife."[54] Any activity which does not appear to serve immediate political purposes is labelled "ownlife" and punishable by death. As with the phrase (doing one's) "own thing," "ownlife" is linguistically structured to suggest that the individual is separated from the humanly controlled system, rather than instinctively integrated within some larger, more natural, system such as biology, chemistry, or ultimately astronomy (i.e., if humans indeed function within what appears to be a Multi-Galactic Order). The inhabitants of Oceania are encouraged to relinquish all "ownlife" and assume greater Party responsibilities. Any personal choice of residency, companionship, occupation, travel, or life style is "ownlife" and hence forbidden.

All inappropriate actions of personal integrity are denied. The Party thrives upon the *submission* (cf. repentance) of the individual and relinquishing of all personal dignity.[55] An increase in Party power accrues from the individual's confession of personal arrogance or preference. Most valuable to the Party is the collective submission of those "below" to those "above," which feeds their need for power. Most threatening to the Party are those who perceive the Party outlook as ideology, rather than truth, and thus may influence others to think.

While the dangers of "ownlife" to the Party are ingrained into the individual, nothing is said about the hazards of the Party to people and other species. In a masterful stroke, Orwell introduces an unnamed cameo character whose disordered nervous system is a product of the system. The psychiatric consequences of doublethink (cf. schizophrenia), and its concomitant disturbance of cognitive dissonance, lead to societies earmarked by increasing mental disease, nervous disorders, depression, and suicide. The constant doublebinding (corporate values vs. integrity; groupthink vs. personal experience) is of little danger when the lies pull easily in the same direction. But when the tug is strong from opposite directions, even accomplished musicians lose the control of the hands and well-trained thinkers lose the acuity of their minds. Attitudinal training may also affect or magnify inner turmoil in numerous ways yet unrecognized.

At the outset of *1984,* the full regulation of sex practices and attitudes seems to be just another facet of totalitarianism. However, Orwell's implication is that sex is political; power motivates and activates sex. Hence, such energy should not be wasted or enjoyed.[56] Once again the psychological and consequent physiological effects of ideologically contrived mating patterns may be both severe and largely unperceived.

Because the source of Party happiness springs from the domination of others, notions of truth and reality become mere nomenclature. What is important is not who is right, if anyone, or what is right, if anything, but rather if a lesser power submits to a higher power. The total estimation of a person's value is his degree of surrender to the hierarchy. Obedience to Party doctrine insures approval, acceptance, and possibly promotion, that is, more power. Ironically, those who could be most valuable to such organizations—those who actually seek to discover reality and express truth as opposed to the Newspeak word "truth" which means doctrine—are exiled, together with their talents and perceptions, into the powerless position of censored expression and controlled reputation.

Dignity, discernment, discretion, and decorum vanish. Those who control consciousness will use any means to maintain control. Impotent, those whose consciousness is (remote-) controlled stoop to any means (Winston and Julia are tricked to use Party treachery to oppose the Party) to free themselves and others. Ultimately, truth is not so much destroyed as castrated: the word is not retired, but cheapened to mean only the total of Party dogma. Words such as truth, peace, and love become devoid of inner meaning and the exploration of personal depth. As within modern societies, their employment becomes mechanical and rhetorical, not experiential. Finally, the Party equates both truth and reality with its own vision. To agree with that view is to destroy personal conscience and vision; to disagree is to die. To agree *and* disagree is to live within the migraine limbo of doublethink.

To many, such ultimate disaster fully separates Orwell's science fiction from the apparently sane democracy in which *we* abide. Again, however, instances such as the group suicide in Reverend Jim Jones' Guyana community have been, if accurately reported, obvious examples of groupthink. Truth and reality had fully socialized etymologies and were "manufactured" in consciousness. In North America alone, millions of people currently participate in countless religious, spiritual, psychological and philosophical sugar-coated love dictatorships in which they learn to (i.e., are controlled to) decontrol, "clear," train, love, hypnotize, or recreate their own consciousness. Nor is there strong evidence to suggest that elementary and high school education, military training, parental indoctrination, and regional enculturation differ in kind, rather than in degree.

Mass media and dictatorships, then, are not exceptional distortions of truth and reality. They merely further distort the already visible distortions. Nor is *1984,* even in its most extreme exaggerations, about a fictional society. Whenever we cease thinking, speak opinion based on programming, or give in to the will to power, we become coauthors. Clearly, the political contradictions are pertinent to the United States, and not simply a "Communist" posture in world politics. However romantic our patriotic perception, incidents involving the take-over of American embassies, the bombing of Marine barracks in Lebanon, the shooting down of a Korean passenger plane, the take-over of Grenada, the ousting of the American military in Vietnam, and the constant "threats to national security" may not be altogether coincidental. Our government and media present American involvement positively, but other nations and peoples may resent what they perceive as the presence of a Big Brother. Notions of truth and reality depend in part upon who owns the telescreen and satellite.

Even Walter Cronkite's conclusion may be revealing: "It has been said that *1984* fails as a prophecy because it succeeded as a warning—Orwell's terrible vision has been averted. Well, that kind of self-congratulation is, to say the least, premature. 1984 may not arrive on time but there's always 1985."[57] As O'Brien points out, when dictatorships strengthen, they become more subtle and less tolerant. Even their leadership succumbs to the pressures and everyone loses. Still the Party intensifies its efforts to control just as the mass media strengthen their efforts to control, leaving the individual's integrity, dignity, truth, and reality lost in the shuffle.

Cronkite, in the manner millions unthinkingly chanted with him, asserted "And that's the way it is."[58] It is our right and responsibility to question, "Is it really?"

THE POSITIVE COUNTERBALANCE:
REVOLT AS A BASIS FOR OPTIMISM

> With the increase in the quality and number of communication links will come an increased potential for the consciousness of the whole planet system to be shared by more and more people all over the world. Through rising global consciousness, not only are we

better informed, but in sharing the total spectrum of human experience we come much closer to the truth of our common humanity and the meaning which we all seek in our individual lives. This greater and deeper perspective of humanity might be characterized as "light." Because light reveals. It reveals the hidden, it reveals what is. . . . [59]

David Smith

The will to power is subtle and begins within. If dominant, the will to power may use global media to indoctrinate many and seek to censor their perspective: Orwell's voice is strong in that warning. Yet equally strong is the will to truth, its discovery and expression, which has historically *always* overcome the control of dictators: revolt has taken, and will take, many forms in many countries. Given the freedom of perspective yet available, one may still maintain that even these alternatives are misleading. Cannot *both* the individual *and* the society be liberated and hence free the media they deploy? An immediate enthusiastic, "Yes" answer would be naive, given the depth of our programming. However, a wise and balanced, "Yes" is possible and practical.

This mature positive approach does not overlook the value of balancing or fusing other perspectives. From cinematic experience we see in Sturges' *Sullivan's Travels* how media may free the heart of hardened prisoners, while Chayefsky's *Network* demonstrates how hardened producers imprison the hearts of free audiences. Moreover, Ashby's *Being There* reminds us that even our patterns for assessing such experiences are a product of our media programming.

We are reminded of the mother who says, "if you think my son's handsome, wait 'til you see his picture." Likewise we watch artificial news to keep up with reality, when we ourselves are the real. Like the images in our retina, media show us life upside-down. Yet despite all this, we know that 1984 is not an endpoint but precedes 2001 and 2010 and that the potency of 1776 is as much before as behind us

We also know that if media are to be used responsibly, and not by the unilateral and arbitrary whim of "the Party," then the choice of how best to be responsible is a question facing *each* of us. Finally, one senses that all media are not entities unto themselves, but rather mirror our own human feelings and thoughts. Their programs and tapes follow us everywhere and pop up from memory like forgotten toast in the toaster. We can no longer escape these or any other techno-responsibilities, any more than we can escape our own shadows.

In 1984 our media shadows have become ominous and menacing. Like vampires in German Expressionist films, they seem to hang over us, larger than life, ready to consume the consumer. Yet that image may be easily placed in perspective if we 1) recognize the shadows as our own, 2) stand up, and 3) turn on the light. 1) Recognizing the shadows as our own means acknowledging personal slothfulness by allowing both media and government to dominate. 2) Standing up means taking action. 3) Turning on the light means being a source of illumination, rather than of ignorance and apathy toward governmental and mass media/systems.

If these steps are not taken, we will increasingly hear words like O'Brien's:

> You are here because you have failed in humility, in self-discipline. You would not make the act of submission which is the price of sanity. You preferred to be a lunatic, a minority of one. Only the disciplined mind can see reality, Winston. You believe that reality is something objective, external, existing in its own right. You also believe that the nature of reality is self-evident. When you delude yourself into thinking that you see something, you assume that everyone else sees the same thing as you. But I tell you, Winston, that reality is not external. Reality exists in the human mind, and nowhere else. Not in the individual mind, which can make mistakes, and in any case soon perishes; only in the mind of the Party, which is collective and immortal. It is impossible to see reality except by looking through the eyes of the Party. That is the fact that you have got to relearn, Winston. It needs an act of self-destruction, an effort of the will. You must humble yourself before you can become sane.[60]

Such words come not only in the clothing of sheep, but in the more subtle media programming and group ideologies in which we are already clothed. The principle, "Everything is in your own mind" is itself an unproven dogma, which is constantly employed to anesthetize the individual. If one will fully disrespect his/her own senses, thinking, perception, and judgements, not all of which are erroneous, one may be manipulated for Party ends. Even those whose initial aspirations seem noble may unknowingly become addicted to privilege and threatened by internal inspection of "truth" as stated within the Party line.

The tendencies Orwell caricatures are no less present than the mediated spirit of revolt. From a balanced perspective, one notes *both* tendencies, keeps *both* eyes open, and *both* feet firmly on the ground. Unless consistently and universally *proven* otherwise, to the satisfaction of *all* concerned, two plus two still equals four.

While a basic ethics of mass media cannot impose a definition of truth upon society, it is the role of the ethicist and indeed of the citizen to be wise and wary of those who do. Finally, it is the discovering of truth, not the imposition of truth, which is central to responsible education, communication, and government. With the vantage of hindsight, the reader discovers that theme to be Orwell's most substantial and relevant message.

NOTES

[1] See, for example, Gene Lyons, "Slouching toward 1984," *Newsweek,* 101 (February 21, 1983): 53, 55; and Norman Podhoretz, "If Orwell Were Alive Today," *Harper's,* 266 (January, 1983): 30–32, 34–37. Podhoretz' statement that "Orwell was more often wrong than right" is typical of the wave of mass media analysis as 1984 approached and passed, treating Orwell as "prophet."

[2] Friedrich Nietzsche, *The Will to Power* (New York: Vintage Books, 1973), p. 394.

[3] George Orwell, *1984* (New York: Signet Editions, 1983), p. 220.

[4] Ibid., p. 229.

[5] *Encyclopedia of World Biography* (New York: McGraw-Hill, 1973), pp. 220–221.

[6] Ibid. For more detailed discussion of Orwell's participation in the Spanish Civil War and his feuding correspondence on the true purpose and direction of politics, see Bernard Crick, *George Orwell: A Life* (Boston: Little, Brown, 1983); Raymond Williams, *George Orwell* (New York: Viking, 1971); and George Woodcock, *The Crystal Spirit: A Study of George Orwell* (Boston: Little, Brown, 1966).

[7] Crick, *George Orwell,* pp. 370–406.

[8] Ibid., p. 384.

[9] Ibid., p. 395.

[10] *1984,* p. 26.

[11] Walter Cronkite, "Preface" to the Signet edition of *1984,* p. 2.

[12] *1984,* p. 89.

[13] Edward Polnick, "Info Glut," *The Boston Globe,* October 17, 1983, p. 41.

[14] *1984,* p. 6.

[15] Ibid., p. 63.

[16] Ibid., p. 187.

[17] Kathy Rebello, "Zenith at Forefront of TV Revolution," *USA Today,* October, 1983. Indeed,

a more recent report of employer monitoring of video-terminal operators found that some of the employers "even send *subliminal messages,* exhorting employes to work harder"; see Robert J. Shapiro, "Tomorrow," *U.S. News and World Report,* 100 (May 12, 1986): 32.

[18] *1984,* pp. 15, 17.

[19] Tony Mauro, "Cable, Pay TV Most Violent," *USA Today,* October, 1983.

[20] Erich Fromm, "Afterword" to Signet edition of *1984,* p. 266.

[21] "The First Robot to Robot Telephone Call," *USA Today,* October, 1983.

[22] *1984,* p. 57.

[23] Barbara Palmer, "Freedom to Say Anything Pays Off," *USA Today,* October, 1983.

[24] *1984,* p. 115.

[25] Tom Green, "ABC Owns Wednesday," *USA Today,* September 13, 1983.

[26] *1984,* p. 30.

[27] "MCI Bites into Postal Service," *USA Today,* October, 1984.

[28] *1984,* p. 30.

[29] Rick Ostrow, "Computers Grab Place in Baseball," *USA Today,* October, 1983.

[30] *1984,* p. 23.

[31] Dan Yakir, "Fall's Films Are Playing Politics," *USA Today,* September 29, 1983.

[32] *1984,* p. 136.

[33] Kenneth Schwartz, special address to the International Radio and Television Society, Glen Cove, NY, February 3, 1984.

[34] *1984,* pp. 6, 36.

[35] "Hi-Net Communications, The Total Meeting Concept," (Memphis, TN: Hi-Net Communications, Holiday Inns, n. d.), p. 8.

[36] *1984,* p. 69.

[37] Tony Schwartz, *Media: The Second God* (Garden City, NY: Anchor Books, 1983), p. 5.

[38] Nietzsche, *The Will to Power.*

[39] Friedrich Nietzsche, *The Genealogy of Morals* (Garden City, NY: Doubleday, 1956).

[40] *1984,* pp. 242–245.

[41] Plato, "Phaedrus," in *Euthyphro, Apology, Crito, Phaedo, and Phaedrus,* trans. H. N. Fowler (London: William Heinemann; New York: Macmillan, 1913), p. 2,769.

[42] Tony Schwartz, *Media: The Second God,* p. 1.

[43] Cronkite, "Preface," p. 1.

[44] Frank H. Knight, letter to H. A. Innis, Chicago, May 15, 1952.

[45] Harold A. Innis, letter to Frank H. Knight, Toronto, May 21, 1952.

[46] Harold Innis, *The Bias of Communication* (Toronto: University of Toronto Press, 1951), p. 4.

[47] Nicholas Johnson, *How To Talk Back To Your Television Set* (Boston: Little, Brown, 1970).

[48] *1984,* p. 111.

[49] Fromm, "Afterword," p. 264.

[50] *1984,* p. 42.

[51] Ibid., p. 51.

[52] See Orwell's Appendix, "The Principles of Newspeak," pp. 246–256 in the Signet edition of *1984.*

[53] Martin Heidegger, *What Is Called Thinking?* (New York: Harper & Row, 1968), p. 17.

[54] *1984,* p. 70.

[55] O'Brien's remarks are most telling: "Obedience is not enough. Unless he is suffering, how can you be sure that he is obeying your will and not his own? Power is in inflicting pain and

humiliation. Power is in tearing human minds to pieces and putting them together again in new shapes of your own choosing." *1984*, p. 220.

[56] Julia's commentary on Party sexual strategy is pertinent; see *1984*, pp. 110–111.

[57] Cronkite, "Preface," p. 3.

[58] Cronkite's well-known tag line, "And that's the way it is," originated as a sign-off on The CBS Evening News aired weekday evenings. For Cronkite, the sign-off became more a leitmotif-cum-trademark.

[59] David Smith, "The Potential for Light," unpublished manuscript, pp. 1–2.

[60] *1984*, pp. 205–206.

HAIGSPEAK, SECRETARY OF STATE HAIG, AND COMMUNICATION ETHICS*

∽ Richard L. Johannesen

"In our time, political speech and writing are largely the defense of the indefensible. . . . All issues are political issues, and politics itself is a mass of lies, evasions, folly, hatred and schizophrenia."[1] Thus wrote George Orwell in the mid-1940s. Even today many American citizens would share his pessimistic judgment of political communication. Admittedly, some scholars take issue with Orwell's views on language in general and political communication in particular.[2] For example, Carl Freedman castigates Orwell's often-reprinted essay on "Politics and the English Language." Freedman contends that Orwell's advice on good style is "ideologically loaded," inhibits the opportunity for argument on complex issues, and even promotes some of the language characteristics condemned by Orwell in his essay on "The Principles of Newspeak."[3]

Nevertheless, I find that a number of Orwell's insights concerning language in these "Politics" and "Newspeak" essays provide valuable aid in analyzing a particular example of contemporary political communication, namely the domestic public discourse of former Secretary of State Alexander Haig (1981–1982).[4] Haig's abuse of the English language proved fair game for satirists as reflected even in the titles of their satires: "Paradoxing the Auditioners"; "De Brief Encounter: We Wallfly Haig Conversationing Schultz"; "Mogul Haig's Mellow Through-put."[5] And *Newsweek* described Haig's language habit as a "form of military-bureaucratic jargon that at times turns nouns into verbs and transforms straight talk into gobbledygook. . . ."[6] Gobbledygook, semanticist Stuart Chase reminds us, can be defined as "using two, three, or ten words in the place of one, or of using a five-syllable word where a single syllable would suffice." Also, says Chase, it may promote confusion of meaning by "scrambling words" or "packing a message with excess baggage."[7] William Safire, former Nixon speechwriter and current syndicated political columnist, dubbed Haig's "new linguistic form" with the label "Haigravation." Safire described it as "the tendency of the secretary of state to change the state of parts of speech—from noun to adverb, from noun to verb."[8]

In 1981 the National Council of Teachers of English (NCTE) bestowed first place in its Doublespeak Awards to Haig as the American public figure whose language is "grossly unfactual, deceptive, evasive, euphemistic, confusing, or self-contradictory."[9] *Time* labeled Haig's discourse pattern as "Haigledygook and Secretaryspeak."[10] Most simply we can call Haig's communication pattern Haig-speak.[11] It seems appropriate here to recall that, according to Orwell, the language of Newspeak in *1984* aimed to propagate a particular political ideology by diminishing rather than extending the range of citizen thought.[12]

TRANSFORMATION OF NOUNS AND MODIFIERS

A major grammatical characteristic of Newspeak was the interchangeability of parts of speech. For example, adjectives often were formed from nouns and verbs by adding the suffix -ful, while adverbs were formed by adding the suffix -wise.[13] What are some instances of Haigspeak?[14] Among the nouns that he had transformed into verbs are "caveat" and "context." He hedged certainty by saying, "I'll have to caveat my response." He replied to a question by saying he could not answer it "in the way you contexted it." The noun "nuance" becomes an adjective in such phrases as "nuanced departures" and "nuance-al differences." At the Cancun summit conference in Mexico, Haig transformed the adjective "definite" into a verb by adding the suffix -ize. He spoke of an effort to "definitize how the procedural aspects of the American assumptions can be met." For philosophers, epistemology is the formal study of the origin, nature, methods, and limits of human knowledge. But philosophers, and grammarians, would shudder at Haig's transformation of that noun into the qualifier "epistemologicallywise."

CONFUSING METAPHORS

Among the "swindles and perversions" of political communication castigated by Orwell in his essay on "Politics and the English Language" was the use of mixed metaphors, of complex metaphors with confused or clashing images. Orwell believed that such mixed metaphors are a "sure sign" that the writer "is not seeing a mental image of the objects he is naming; in other words he is not really thinking."[15] On one occasion Secretary of State Haig declared, "I would not want to saddle myself with a statistical fence."[16] On another occasion he warned, "If the whole game becomes a bookkeeping operation, we lose sight of the real goals." In explaining a slip of the tongue, Haig said, "That's because I'm thinking ahead, and not keeping my feet on the ground." Or consider a more lengthy confused image of Haig's. After stating that there were no current plans for the use of American military forces in El Salvador, he warned that "the sterility of drawing lines around America's potential options constitutes the promulgation of roadways for those who are seeking to move against America's vital interests."

INFLATED STYLE

In his political language essay, Orwell also condemned an "inflated style." Such a style frequently pads sentences with extra syllables, chooses more complex words and phrases over simpler ones, and displays "needless repetition."[17] At the Cancun conference, the straightforward noun, "statement," becomes the inflated noun, "intervention." Haig referred to President Reagan's many "interventions" at the meeting.[18] Typical of the many redundant phrases in Haigspeak are "careful caution" and "longstanding in time."[19] In describing a matter as being crucial, Haig said it was at the "vortex of cruciality." In urging that a matter be deemphasized, he said we need "to push this to a lower decibel of fixation."[20]

In Haigspeak a list of nations becomes a "menu" of nations and a risk by the Soviet Union becomes a "risk taking mode." In his first press conference as Secretary, Haig inflates and pads a prepared statement on the agreements to free American hostages in Iran: "I think it's important for those who analyze and assess the pros and cons of these agreements, which were arrived at under the most unprecedented and unusual conditions in our history, be recognized to be perhaps the most complex series of international agreements that I have been exposed to."[21] Another notable example of Haig's inflated style is his statement on the Reagan administration policy on arms-control agreements: "The United States cannot contemplate negotiations or ratifications of arms-control agreements exclusive of considerations of the conduct and the activities of the Soviet Union outside the sphere of arms control.' He then explained the statement by saying that it was a "shorthand" way of expressing Reagan's policy of "linkage."[22]

Haig's penchant for inflated language is not of recent vintage. In the early 1960s, Haig completed an M.A. thesis in foreign policy at Georgetown University. He studded the thesis with such inflated language as "interpretative vagaries," "thought modes," "permeating nexus," and his old favorite, "vortex."[23] Orwell suggested that a habitual inflated style might be a sign of insincerity, thus prompting questions about the user's ethics.[24] "When there is a gap between one's real and one's declared aims, one turns as it were instinctively to long words and exhausted idioms, like a cuttlefish squirting out ink."[25]

Especially disturbing for the Public Doublespeak Committee of the NCTE was Haig's language in Congressional testimony concerning the murder of three nuns and a civilian worker in El Salvador. Newsmedia accounts said the women had been shot in the back of the head and that three of them had been raped. Haig's testimony before the House Foreign Affairs Committee left the implication that the nuns might have attempted to run through a roadblock or that they may have fired weapons at people.

> I'd like to suggest to you that some of the investigations would lead one to believe that perhaps the vehicle that the nuns were riding in tried to run a roadblock, or may accidentally have been perceived to have been doing so, and there'd been an exchange of fire and then those who inflicted the casualties sought to cover it up. And this could have been at a very low level of competence and motivation in the context of the issue itself. But the facts on this are not clear enough for anyone to draw a definitive conclusion.[26]

In concluding its analysis of Haig's testimony, the *Quarterly Review of Doublespeak* quoted additional Orwellian judgments on political language. "Thus political language has to consist largely of euphemism, question-begging and sheer cloudy vagueness. . . . (It) is designed to make lies sound truthful and murder respectable, and to give an appearance of solidity to pure wind."[27]

William Safire believes that a person's oral language generally should not be scrutinized as harshly for proper grammar as should his writing, since we have the chance to edit our writing to ensure clarity. Nevertheless, Safire is disturbed by some of Haig's oral comments. In response to a question about the Reagan administration policy on human rights, Haig responded, "There will be no de-emphasis but a change in priority." Clearly, says Safire with regard to a policy that in the prior administration had been given a top priority, a change in priority does represent a de-emphasis. Concludes Safire: "But when words are deliberately used to stand meaning on its head, the speaker deserves some censure."[28]

INTENTIONALITY

Safire's mention of deliberate use raises the question of whether Haig intentionally used Haigspeak to cloud, divert, or deceive. Whether communicators seem intentionally and knowingly to use particular language is a factor that most of us take into account in judging degree of communication ethicality.[29] If a dubious communication behavior seems to stem more from accident, from an occasional slip of the tongue, from lack of preparation, or even from ineptness, often we are less harsh in our ethical assessment. For most of us, it is the intentional use of ethically questionable techniques that merits our harshest condemnation. In contrast, it might be contended that communicators have an ethical obligation to double-check the clarity and soundness of their information, evidence, and reasoning before they present them to others. Superficial preparation would not be an adequate excuse to lessen the harshness of our ethical judgment. A similar view might be advanced concerning elected or appointed government officials. If they use obscure or jargon-laden language that clouds ideas, even if that use is not intended to deceive or hide, they are ethically irresponsible. Such officials, according to this view, should be obligated to communicate clearly and accurately with citizens in fulfillment of their government duties.

While there is no way of knowing for sure in each instance, there are some minimal indications that Haig does intentionally at times employ Haigspeak. When asked to clarify a statement at a press conference, Haig replied: "That was consciously ambiguous in the sense that any terrorist government or terrorist movement that is contemplating such actions I think knows clearly what we are speaking of."[30] In his book, *Caveat,* his memoir as Secretary of State, Haig praises President Reagan's "habit of speaking plainly without metaphor or jargon . . ." both privately and in public. Haig also describes his own private communication habit of plain and unadorned speech, a habit instilled in him at West Point and a habit of which he never was "cured."[31] *Time* observes that while Haig "mangles the English language" in public, he speaks with "force and clarity in private." Also *Time* asserts that "there is a hint of method in his search and destroy operations on syntax." According to *Time,* Haig's sister, Regina, a lawyer, once reproached him for uttering "polysyllabic fog." She asked him, "Why don't you speak in simple declarative sentences?" Reportedly Haig smiled and replied with the question, "Did you ever think of the cost of making a mistake?"[32] One implication would seem to be that too much clarity and preciseness increases the chance that a statement might prove to be incorrect.

ETHICAL ASSESSMENT

I would argue that Haigspeak does warrant our ethical censure. Any political system (system of governing) usually contains within its ideology a set of values accepted as crucial to the health and growth of that governmental system.[33] Once these essential political values are identified for a system, they can generate criteria for evaluating the ethics of communicative means and ends within that system. The assumption is that communication should foster realization of these values and that tactics that retard, subvert, or circumvent these fundamental political values should be condemned as unethical. Naturally each different governmental system could embody differing values leading to differing ethical judgments.

Within the framework of American representative democracy, for instance, various analysts pinpoint values and procedures traditionally viewed as fundamental to the functioning of that political system. Such values can guide ethical scrutiny of communication on public issues. Among such fundamental values and procedures would be: enhancement of citizen capacity to reach rational decisions; access to channels of public communication; access to relevant and accurate information on public issues; maximization of freedom of choice; toleration of dissent; honesty in presenting motivations and consequences; and thoroughness, accuracy and fairness in presenting evidence and alternatives.[34]

Haigspeak represented a pattern in Secretary Haig's public discourse; it was not an occasional occurrence. More importantly as the Secretary of State, Haig had a responsibility to provide Congress and American citizens with accurate, fair, relevant information they needed to make reasonable decisions on problems, policies, and consequences. Regardless whether Haigspeak was used deliberately or not, Haig's communication ethics here were questionable; in these instances he simply was not meeting his ethical responsibility to the American public.

Power and language are intimately related. In *Power and Communication,* Andrew King argues that power is a "relationship that is both activated and sustained by human communication. Power is a communication act."[35] Michel Foucault contends, in *Power/Knowledge,* that power relations "cannot themselves be established, consolidated nor implemented without the production, accumulation, circulation and functioning" of a system of discourse.[36] A governmental leader's abuse of language is one type of abuse of power. The techniques of communication used by governmental officials can have long-term cumulative effects on citizen habits of thought and decision-making in addition to the impact of specific policies sought by the officials. No matter the purpose they serve, the arguments, appeals, and language chosen gradually do shape a citizen's values, standards of judgment, language patterns, range of ethical tolerance, and level of trust.[37]

Simply to minimize or ignore a Haigspeak as a tolerable part of the political game would be unfortunate. Governmental leaders have an obligation to reinforce rather than undermine the trust between government and the citizenry so vital to the functioning of representative democracy. "In most democratic politics," notes John Orman, "the notion of accountability in the linkage between leadership and the public is grounded in the fragile concept of 'trust'."[38] Haigspeak is representative of the increasing use of lies, deception, and obfuscation that seems to characterize much of our political and public discourse.[39] The ominous warning of David Wise in his book, *The Politics of Lying*, still holds force: "The American system is based not only upon formal checks and balances among the three branches of government; it depends also, perhaps most importantly, on a delicate balance of confidence between the people and the government. . . . If the governed are misled, if they are not told the truth, or if through official secrecy and deception they lack information on which to base intelligent decisions, the system may go on—but not as a democracy."[40]

NOTES

* *Revised version of "Orwell, Haigspeak, and Secretary of State Haig," presented at the Annual Convention of the Speech Communication Association, Washington, DC, 1984.*

[1] George Orwell, "Politics and the English Language," *Collected Essays* (London: Mercury Books, 1961), pp. 347–348. Originally published in 1946 in *Shooting an Elephant, and Other Essays.*

[2] Hugh Rank, "Mr. Orwell, Mr. Schlesinger, and the Language," *College Composition and Communication,* 28 (1977): 159–165; Cleo McNelly, "On Not Teaching Orwell," *College English,* 38 (1977): 553–566; Harvey A. Daniels, *Famous Last Words: The American Language Crisis Reconsidered* (Carbondale: Southern Illinois University Press, 1983), Ch. 8; Richard W. Bailey, "George Orwell and the English Language," *The Future of Nineteen Eighty-Four,* Ejner J. Jensen, editor (Ann Arbor: University of Michigan Press, 1984), pp. 23–46.

[3] Carl Freedman, "Writing, Ideology, and Politics: Orwell's 'Politics and the English Language' and English Composition," *College English,* 43 (1981): 327–340. Interpretations more supportive of Orwell's advice on language are: A. M. Tibbetts, "What Did Orwell Think About the English Language?" *College Composition and Communication,* 29 (1978): 162–166; Arthur Schlesinger, Jr., "Politics and the American Language," *The American Scholar,* 43 (1974): 553–562; George Steiner, "Books: Killing Time," *The New Yorker,* 59 (December 12, 1983): 168–188; Bernard Avishai, "Orwell and the English Language," *1984 Revisited,* Irving Howe, editor (New York: Harper and Row, 1983), pp. 57–71.

[4] Haig resigned June 25, 1982. For a detailed biography up to 1980, see Roger Morris, *Haig: The General's Progress* (New York: Playboy Press, 1982).

[5] For example, see "Paradoxing the Auditioners," by the British *The Guardian,* reprinted in *Newsweek,* 97 (February 23, 1981): 40; Charles Fenyvesi and Walter Shapiro, "De Brief Encounter:

We Wallfly Haig Conversationing Schultz," *The New Republic,* 187 (August 2, 1982): 12–13; Michael Killian, "Mogul Haig's mellow through-put," *Chicago Tribune,* January 7, 1983, p. A10.

[6] Headnote to "Paradoxing the Auditioners."

[7] Stuart Chase, *The Power of Words* (New York: Harcourt, Brace and Co., 1953), pp. 249–251; also see Ross Beatty, "Windyfoggery and Bureaucratese," *Rhetoric Society Quarterly,* 12 (1981): 261–270.

[8] William Safire, *What's the Good Word?* (New York: Times Books, 1982), p. 102.

[9] *Quarterly Review of Doublespeak,* 8 (1982): 1–2.

[10] "Haigledygook and Secretaryspeak," *Time,* 117 (February 23, 1981): 19.

[11] "Reagantalk, Haigspeak," *The Nation,* 232 (February 14, 1981): 161.

[12] George Orwell, "Appendix: The Principles of Newspeak," *1984* (New York: New American Library paperback, 1981), p. 246. Originally published in 1949.

[13] Orwell, *1984,* pp. 247–248.

[14] For the following examples in this paragraph, see "Haigledygook and Secretaryspeak"; Safire, *Good Word,* pp. 102–104; "Washington Wire," *Wall Street Journal,* October 30, 1981, p. 1; Arnaud de Borchgrave and Michael Ledeen, "An Interview With Alexander Haig," *The New Republic,* 184 (February 7, 1981): 18.

[15] Orwell, "Politics," pp. 340, 345.

[16] For the following examples in this paragraph, see "Haigledygook"; de Borchgrave, "Interview," p. 20; "Notes on People," *New York Times,* August 8, 1981, p. 43. "As Usual, Words Fail Him," *Mother Jones,* 7 (May 1982): 6.

[17] Orwell, "Politics," pp. 340–341, 346, 348, 350.

[18] "Briefing," *New York Times,* October 26, 1981, p. A20.

[19] "Haigledygook"; William Safire, "Haigravations," *New York Times Magazine,* 130 (February 22, 1981): 9–10.

[20] Francis X. Clines, "Lexicon," *New York Times,* December 3, 1981, p. B16.

[21] Seth Lipsky, "The Strange Tongues of Secretary Haig," *Wall Street Journal,* February 6, 1981, p. 20.

[22] "Reagan Changes the Rules," *Newsweek,* 97 (February 9, 1981): 46.

[23] Morris, *Haig,* pp. 54–55, 402.

[24] On the necessity to separately assess communicators' sincerity and the ethicality of their techniques, see Richard L. Johannesen, *Ethics in Human Communication,* 2nd ed. (Prospect Heights, IL: Waveland Press, 1983), pp. 7–8.

[25] Orwell, "Politics," p. 348.

[26] Cited in *Quarterly Review of Doublespeak.*

[27] Orwell, "Politics," pp. 347, 351.

[28] Safire, "Haigravations."

[29] Johannesen, *Ethics,* 2nd ed., p. 7.

[30] "Haigledygook."

[31] Alexander M. Haig, Jr., *Caveat: Realism, Reagan, and Foreign Policy* (New York: Macmillan, 1984), pp. 6, 56–57, 73, 335.

[32] "The Vicar Takes Charge," *Time,* 117 (March 16, 1981): 16.

[33] For extended discussion, see Johannesen, *Ethics,* 2nd ed., Ch. 2. For another application of this approach, see Richard L. Johannesen, "An Ethical Assessment of the Reagan Rhetoric: 1981–1982," *Political Communication Yearbook 1984,* Keith R. Sanders, Lynda Lee Kaid, and Dan Nimmo, editors (Carbondale, IL: Southern Illinois University Press, 1985), Ch. 10.

[34] Emmette S. Redford, *Democracy in the Administrative State* (New York: Oxford University Press, 1969), Ch. 1; Joel L. Fleishman, Lance Liebman, and Mark H. Moore, editors, *Public Duties: The Moral Obligations of Public Officials* (Cambridge, MA: Harvard University Press, 1981), Chs. 1, 3, 4, 8, 12; Thomas R. Nilsen, *Ethics of Speech Communication,* 2nd ed. (Indianapolis: Bobbs-Merrill, 1974), Chs. 1–4.

[35] Andrew King, *Power and Communication* (Prospect Heights, IL: Waveland, 1987), pp. 1–8.

[36] Michel Foucault, *Power/Knowledge: Selected Interviews and Other Writings, 1927–1977,* ed. Colin Gordon, trans. Colin Gordon, Leo Marshall, John Mepham, and Kate Soper (New York: Pantheon, 1980), pp. 51–52. Also see Sonja K. Foss, Karen A. Foss, and Robert Trapp, *Contemporary Perspectives on Rhetoric* (Prospect Heights, IL: Waveland, 1985), pp. 204–208.

[37] Thomas R. Nilsen, "Free Speech, Persuasion, and the Democratic Process," *Quarterly Journal of Speech,* 44(1958): 235–243; B. J. Diggs, "Persuasion and Ethics," *Quarterly Journal of Speech,* 50(1964): 366; Rober T. Oliver, *The Psychology of Persuasive Speech,* 2nd ed. (New York: Longman, Green, 1957), p. 26; Herbert W. Simons, *Persuasion* (Reading, MA: Addison-Wesley, 1976), pp. 147–149.

[38] John M. Orman, *Presidential Secrecy and Deception* (Westport, CN: Greenwood, 1980), pp. 4, 166.

[39] The May 25, 1987, issue of *Time* featured four lengthy articles on the decline of ethics that pervades political and public life. Also see Merrill McLoughlin, "A Nation of Liars?" *U.S. News and World Report,* February 23, 1987, 54–60.

[40] David Wise, *The Politics of Lying* (New York: Random House, 1973), pp. 18, 342, 345. Also see Bruce Ladd, *Crisis in Credibility* (New York: New American Library, 1968), p. 9; J. Michael Sproule, *Argument* (New York: McGraw–Hill, 1980), p. 282.

Manipulation and Control of People's Responses to Public Opinion Polls

An Orwellian Experiment in 1984

❧ *George F. Bishop*

To know and not to know, to be conscious of complete truthfulness while telling carefully constructed lies, to hold simultaneously two opinions which cancelled out, knowing them to be contradictory and believing in both of them, to use logic against logic, to repudiate morality while laying claim to it, to believe that democracy was impossible and that the Party was the guardian of democracy, to forget, whatever it was necessary to forget, then draw it back into memory again at the moment when it was needed, and then promptly to forget it again, and above all to apply the same process to the process itself—that was the ultimate subtlety: consciously to induce unconsciousness, and then, once again, to become unconscious of the act of hypnosis you had just performed. Even to understand the word "doublethink" involved the use of doublethink.[1]

The central theme in Orwell's volume involves the use of language to manipulate and control what people say, what they do, and what they think. By creating and propagating an official language known as "Newspeak," and through the practice of a system of thought called "doublethink," the State, with its total control of the mass media, dominates the minds of its citizens who constantly fear the worst: to be accused of "thoughtcrime." Such is the stuff of science fiction. But how much of it is true today? Can people so easily be manipulated and controlled by the use of language and the mass media? Perhaps not in the ways that

Orwell imagined, but in ways that are nonetheless worrisome.[2] In this essay I will give an example of one such way: how people's responses to public opinion polls can be manipulated and controlled by the way in which the questions are worded—a use of the language which Orwell would surely have expected were he alive today.

Pollsters and political pundits have, of course, long recognized that the results of public opinion surveys can be significantly affected by the way in which questions are worded and by the order and context in which they are asked.[3] Not until recently, however, have researchers begun to investigate the effects of question form, wording, and context on survey findings in a systematic manner.[4] As they have, it has become clear to this writer, at least, that our increasing knowledge of what affects what, and how much, gives pollsters an unprecedented ability to manipulate and control the results of public opinion polls and in a manner that can easily go undetected by the uninitiated. Knowing, for example, that the answer to a question in one part of the interview can be significantly influenced by responses to questions asked five, ten, or even fifteen minutes earlier in the interview[5] gives us a subtle tool for manipulation that is highly unlikely to be detected by all but a handful of those who are aware of such research. And not even most of them will have the time, the energy, or the inclination to investigate such potential abuses by getting a complete copy of all the questions that were asked in the original interview. Not that such abuses are likely, but that they have now become possible is what should concern us if we are to counter them.

Let me illustrate now the degree of control we have acquired over people's responses in survey interviews with the results of an experiment which Orwell would have regarded as a dramatic demonstration of doublethink: getting people to give opinions on public affairs issues that do not exist in the present nor in the past, issues which people must simultaneously believe exist and yet not exist, and which beliefs they must be both conscious and unconscious of ". . . knowing them to be contradictory. . . ." Though the experiment I will describe was not designed, originally, to demonstrate our ability to manipulate people to engage in a form of doublethink, I think it does show us just how far we can go in controlling what people say and do in the survey interview, and in a way which recalls some of the classic experiments by Solomon Asch on conformity to group pressures and by Stanley Milgram on obedience to authority—and perhaps, too, B. F. Skinner's brand of behaviorism.[6] Indeed, we can view the behavior of respondents in this experiment as a special case of conformity and obedience to authority: conformity to the pressures to respond created by the form and wording of the questions, the demands of the interviewer, and obedience to the "aura of authority" generated by the type of organization conducting the survey, a university, which symbolizes the importance of being well-informed.

How the Experiment Was Done

In May and early June of 1984 the University of Cincinnati's Behavioral Sciences Laboratory designed an experiment in the Greater Cincinnati Survey[7] on how people would respond to questions about three fictitious public affairs issues: *The Agricultural Trade Act of 1984, The Monetary Control Bill of 1984,* and *The 1975 Public Affairs Act.*[8] The questions were asked near the middle part of the interview, either immediately before or after three other questions about government and public affairs issues which were not fictitious and which therefore provided a cover for deceiving respondents about the "reality" of the three fictitious issues.[9] All of the questions were asked in one of three forms, to which the respondents were randomly assigned:

1. FORM A.   People who received this form were asked the questions in a way which allowed them to admit that they did not know much, if anything, about the three issues. On the Agricultural Trade Act, for example, they were asked the question this way: "Congress has been considering *The Agricultural Trade Act of 1984*—do you favor or oppose the passage of this act, or haven't you thought much about this issue?" The response alternative, ". . . or haven't you thought much about this issue?" is known as a *filter question* because it filters, or screens, out respondents who are uninformed about an issue by giving them an explicit opportunity to say they do not know much about it.

2. FORM B.   People who were given this form were asked the questions without an explicit filter, that is, without the response alternative, ". . . or haven't you thought much about this issue?" The question on the Agricultural Trade Act, for example, was asked in the following manner on this form: "Congress has been considering *The Agricultural Trade Act of 1984*—do you favor or oppose the passage of this act?" If people volunteered that they did not know anything about the topic or gave a qualified response other than the two alternatives that were read to them (i.e., favor or oppose), the interviewers were instructed *not* to pressure them for an answer in any way (e.g., by probing), but rather to record exactly what they said and then to go ahead and ask the next question.

3. FORM C.   People administered this version were also asked the questions without the response alternative, ". . . or haven't you thought much about this issue?" In contrast to Form B, how-

CHART 1

WORDING OF THE QUESTIONS ASKED ABOUT
THREE FICTITIOUS PUBLIC AFFAIRS ISSUES

FORM A	FORMS B AND C
1. "Some people feel that *The 1975 Public Affairs Act* should be repealed—do you agree or disagree with this idea, or haven't you thought much about this issue?"	1. "Some people feel that *The 1975 Public Affairs Act* should be repealed—do you agree or disagree with this idea?"
2. "Congress has also been considering *The Agricultural Trade Act of 1984*—do you favor or oppose the passage of this act, or haven't you thought much about this issue?"	2. "Congress has been considering *The Agricultural Trade Act of 1984*—do you favor or oppose the passage of this act?"
3. "Congress has also been considering *The Monetary Control Bill of 1984*—do you favor or oppose the passage of this bill, or haven't you thought much about this issue?"	3. "Congress has also been considering *The Monetary Control Bill of 1984*—do you favor or oppose the passage of this bill?"

ever, if people volunteered that they did not know anything about the subject, or offered some qualified answer to the question other than the two choices (favor/oppose) presented to them, the interviewers were instructed to pressure them into answering by repeating the question (i.e., "Let me repeat the question: . . ."), by rereading the choices (e.g., "Would you say you lean more toward favoring it or more toward opposing it?"), or both. In this way the respondent was "persuaded" to answer the question whether he or she had an opinion on it or not.

Chart 1 shows the exact wording of the questions asked in Forms A, B, and C. Notice that the wording of the questions in Forms B and C was identical. The difference was that "don't know" responses given to Form C were probed by the interviewer, whereas those given to Form B were not. The reader should also note that people who were asked the questions in Form A were *not* probed if they volunteered a "don't know" response or gave a qualified answer to any of the questions. This, of course, was consistent with the intent of the filtered form which was to make it acceptable for people to say they did not have an opinion on the issue or that they "hadn't thought much about it." It also seemed consistent not to pressure respondents who received Form A into selecting one of the forced-choices (e.g., favor or oppose), but rather to let them freely qualify their answers if they wanted to. That describes the forms.[10]

THE HYPOTHESIS

What did we expect to find? If the experiment worked, as we expected it would, people who received Form A should have felt the least pressure to give an opinion on the fictitious issues because they had an explicit opportunity to say they "hadn't thought much about the issue." People administered Form B should have felt more pressured to give an opinion on the issues because they did not have such an opportunity, though they were not pressured for an answer if they volunteered a "don't know" response to any of the questions. Finally, people given Form C should have experienced the most pressure to offer an opinion because they were not given the opportunity to say they "hadn't thought much about the issue," nor were they allowed to volunteer a "don't know" response without being pressured, cajoled, or manipulated by the interviewer into answering the questions by picking one of the forced choices.

THE RESULTS

How well did we succeed? The figures in Table 1 indicate that we did very well indeed. Apparently, many people can easily be manipulated into giving opinions on issues they have never heard of, depending upon the form and wording of the question and the pressures put upon them by the interviewer to give an answer. Such is the power and control of the survey situation over people's behavior.

Consider, first, the findings for the question about *The 1975 Public Affairs Act*. When the question was asked in a way which gave people an explicit opportunity to say they "haven't thought much about the issue" (Form A), only 3.6 percent of them pretended to have an opinion on the subject. The vast majority (96.4 percent) said they had not thought much about the issue or had never heard of it. But when the question was asked without the response alternative, ". . . or haven't you thought much about this issue?" people were significantly more likely to offer an opinion on the *Public Affairs Act*, particularly if they were pressured to do so by the interviewer, as in Form C, on which over forty percent of the respondents (42.3 percent) were manipulated into expressing an opinion on an obscure subject which they must have realized did not exist, and yet they

TABLE I

RESPONSE TO THE PUBLIC AFFAIRS ACT,
THE AGRICULTURAL TRADE ACT, AND THE
MONETARY CONTROL BILL BY QUESTION FORM

	FORM A	FORM B	FORM C
Public Affairs Act			
Opinion	3.6%	22.2%	42.3%
No Opinion	96.4	77.8	57.7
Total	100.0%	100.0%	100.0%
(N=)	(398)	(411)	(402)
$\chi^2 = 171.01$, df $= 2$, p .001			
Agricultural Trade Act			
Opinion	10.5%	35.5%	55.9%
No Opinion	89.5	64.5	44.1
Total	100.0%	100.0%	100.0%
(N=)	(398)	(411)	(403)
$\chi^2 = 183.33$, df $= 2$, p .0001			
Monetary Control Bill			
Opinion	14.3%	38.4%	54.7%
No Opinion	85.7	61.6	45.3
Total	100.0%	100.0%	100.0%
(N=)	(398)	(411)	(404)
$\chi^2 = 143.68$, df $= 2$, p .0001			

Source: Greater Cincinnati Survey (May/June 1984).

treated it as if it did. Such is the capacity, Orwell would have said, for people to deceive themselves by engaging in a form of doublethink lest they be regarded by the university interviewer as guilty of the thoughtcrime of being ignorant, the fear of which, no doubt, controls much of their behavior in this situation.

The results for the *Agricultural Trade Act* and the *Monetary Control Bill* (*see Table 1*) suggest that the fear of being thought ignorant on such matters may well explain why people can be so easily controlled. For the findings demonstrate that people can be manipulated into giving an opinion on a fictitious issue more readily, when the topic—"agricultural trade" or "monetary control"—seems familiar and similar to subjects that they "think" they have heard of, such as farmers' shipments of wheat to the Soviet Union or control of the federal deficit. People were thus more likely to be manipulated into offering an opinion on the *Agricultural Trade Act* and the *Monetary Control Bill* than they were on the *Public Affairs Act* regardless of the form in which the questions were asked.

The form of the questions nonetheless made a difference. When the question about the *Agricultural Trade Act,* for example, was asked with the response alternative, ". . . or haven't you thought much about this issue?" (Form A), barely 10 percent of the respondents ventured an opinion. When this alternative was omitted from the question, however, they were much more likely to be pressured into offering an opinion. On Form B, over a third of them (35.5 percent) did so; on Form C, over half (55.9 percent). Similarly, on the *Monetary Control Bill,* the form of the question made a substantial difference. On Form A, a little less than 15 percent offered an opinion; on Form B, 38.4 percent; and on Form C, 54.7 percent—a convincing confirmation of the pressures to conform to the demands of the situation.[11] And surely it must be considered astonishing to think we can get a majority of the adult population (age eighteen and over) in a major metropolitan area of the United States to comply with such absurd demands. Perhaps nothing should surprise us any more.

Nor is this, by any means, an isolated demonstration of how readily respondents can be manipulated into giving one answer to a survey question rather than another. Elsewhere, we and other research teams have shown that people's responses to survey questions can be greatly affected—or as I should say here, manipulated and controlled—by such things as whether they are offered a middle response alternative on an issue;[12] whether they are presented with one or both sides of an issue in the question;[13] and whether the questions or the response alternatives are presented in one order rather than another.[14] Though none of these experiments was designed with "Orwellian" intentions, they nevertheless warn us about what has now become possible with advances in behavioral research.

CONCLUSION

Orwell's fiction about the world of 1984 may seem now, with the advantage of hindsight, to be obsolete. For 1984 has come and gone with his prophecy essentially unfulfilled. Big Brother has not arrived, at least not in the form he expected, if at all. True, there are societies today—some would say, aspects of our own included—in which we can point to ominous developments in the restriction of human freedoms and to the growth of technologies which threaten to bring the world of Big Brother closer to reality. But for the most part, most of us, most of the time do not feel so threatened, at least not in the "free world" as we like to think of it. Despite the attempts of advertisers and political propagandists to manipulate and control what we think, what we buy, how we vote, and when and where we go—most of us, most of the time feel as though we do have a choice about what we say, what we think, and what we do: that we are in a word "free," free to think our minds and say and do as we please. Such, some might say, is the illusion of the democratic society.

In this essay I have done something which may help dispel that illusion by demonstrating that we are not, perhaps, as "free" to say what is on our mind as we like to think we are: that, in fact, we can be manipulated and controlled by the use of language and communication in a way which Orwell would have seen as inevitable. So while the society he envisioned has not come to pass in the form he imagined, the techniques for manipulating and controlling what people think, what they say, and what they do may be a great deal more advanced than we would like to believe.[15] And that such a society is therefore more realizable than ever before, making Orwell's warning about where we are headed a bit more believable than we thought.

Yes, George, perhaps we have met the enemy . . .

Notes

[1] George Orwell, *Nineteen Eighty-Four* (New York: Harcourt, Brace, 1949), p. 36.

[2] For a good example of how the mass media can be potentially used to manipulate people's perceptions of national problems and their evaluations of the President's performance, see the experiments by Iyengar and his colleagues: Shanto Iyengar, Mark D. Peters, and Donald R. Kinder, "Experimental Demonstrations of the 'Not-So-Minimal' Consequences of Television News," *American Political Science Review*, 76 (December, 1982): 848–858; and Shanto Iyengar, Donald R. Kinder, Jon Krosnick, and Mark D. Peters, "The Evening News and Presidential Evaluations," *Journal of Personality and Social Psychology*, 46 (April, 1984): 778–787.

[3] For some early examples, see Donald Rugg and Hadley Cantril, "The Wording of Questions," *Gauging Public Opinion*, Hadley Cantril, editor (Princeton, NJ: Princeton University Press, 1944), pp. 23–50; and Stanley L. Payne, *The Art of Asking Questions* (Princeton, NJ: Princeton University Press, 1951).

[4] See the several works by George F. Bishop, Robert W. Oldendick, and Alfred J. Tuchfarber: "Experiments in Filtering Political Opinions," *Political Behavior*, 2, 3 (1980): 339–369; "Political Information-Processing: Question Order and Context Effects," *Political Behavior*, 4, 2 (1982): 177–200; "Effects of Presenting One Versus Two Sides of an Issue in Survey Questions," *Public Opinion Quarterly*, 46 (Spring, 1982): 69–85; "Effects of Filter Questions in Public Opinion Surveys," *Public Opinion Quarterly*, 47 (Winter, 1983): 528–546; "Interest in Political Campaigns: The Influence of Question Order and Electoral Context," *Political Behavior*, 6, 2 (1984): 159–169; "What Must My Interest in Politics Be if I Just Told You 'I Don't Know'?" *Public Opinion Quarterly*, 48 (Summer, 1984): 510–519; "Context Effects on Questions about Interest in Government and Public Affairs," report to the National Science Foundation on Project SES–8218586, Institute for Policy Research, University of Cincinnati, January, 1985; and "The Importance of Replicating a Failure to

Replicate: Order Effects on Abortion Items," *Public Opinion Quarterly* 49 (Spring, 1985): 105–114. See also Bishop, Oldendick, Tuchfarber, and Stephen E. Bennett, "Pseudo-Opinions on Public Affairs," *Public Opinion Quarterly,* 44 (Summer, 1980): 198–209; Howard Schuman and Stanley Presser, *Questions and Answers in Attitude Surveys* (New York: Academic Press, 1981); Howard Schuman and Jacob Ludwig, "The Norm of Even-Handedness in Surveys as in Life," *American Sociological Review,* 48 (February, 1983): 112–120; Howard Schuman, Graham Kalton, and Jacob Ludwig, "Context and Contiguity in Survey Questionnaires," *Public Opinion Quarterly,* 47 (Spring, 1983): 112–115; Tom H. Smith, "Can We Have Confidence in Confidence? Revisited," *Measurement of Subjective Phenomena,* Denis F. Johnston, editor (Washington, DC: U.S. Government Printing Office, 1981), pp. 119–189; and Charles F. Turner and Elizabeth Martin, editors, *Surveying Subjective Phenomena,* 2 vols. (New York: Russell Sage Foundation, 1984).

[5] See Bishop, Oldendick, and Tuchfarber, "Interest in Political Campaigns," and "Context Effects on Questions"; and Schuman, Kalton, and Ludwig, "Context and Contiguity."

[6] Solomon E. Asch, "Studies of Independence and Conformity: A Minority of One against a Unanimous Majority," *Psychological Monographs,* 70, 9 (Whole No. 416, 1956); Stanley Milgram, *Obedience to Authority* (New York: Harper & Row, 1974); and B. F. Skinner, *About Behaviorism* (New York: Alfred A. Knopf, 1974).

[7] The Greater Cincinnati Survey is a cost-shared multipurpose telephone survey conducted twice a year by the Behavioral Sciences Laboratory which is part of the University of Cincinnati's Institute for Policy Research. The response rate for the May/June 1984 survey was *71.3 percent.* The refusal rate was *14.8 percent.* The rest consisted of partially completed interviews (2.8 percent) and potential interviews that were not completed because of a language barrier, a hearing problem, illiteracy, senility, or physical illness (5.6 percent) or because the selected respondent was away on vacation, a business trip, or avoided an appointment for some other reason (5.5 percent).

[8] The question about the Public Affairs Act was drawn from a previous experiment by Bishop, Oldendick, Tuchfarber, and Bennett, "Pseudo-Opinions on Public Affairs." The questions about the Agricultural Trade Act and the Monetary Control Bill were adapted from items originally developed by Schuman and Presser, *Questions and Answers in Attitude Surveys: The Agricultural Trade Act of 1978 and The Monetary Control Bill of 1979,* both of which were obscure, but real matters at the time they were used. The years of these purported pieces of legislation were changed to 1984 to make them sound more up-to-date and thus have the respondent feel as if they were current issues on which he or she should probably have an opinion. To my knowledge, there were no such legislative matters pending in Congress at the time of the survey or earlier in the year. Nor is it likely that any respondent knew anything about the obscure pieces of legislation from which these items were originally derived (see Ch. 5 of the Schuman and Presser volume).

[9] These consisted of a question about whether the federal government was trying to do too many things that should be left to individuals and private businesses, which was adapted from an item developed originally by the National Opinion Research Center at the University of Chicago (see the questionnaire for NORC Study 4179, December, 1973, p. 14) and questions on trade with the Soviet Union and government spending, both of which were adapted from items designed by the Center for Political Studies at the University of Michigan (see the questionnaire for 1982 National Election Study Cross-Section Interview, p. 52 and p. 55 respectively).

[10] In addition, we varied the order in which the questions were asked, randomly assigning respondents to one of two conditions: in *Order I,* they were asked the three questions about the fictitious issues immediately *before* the questions about the three nonfictitious issues; in *Order II,* they were asked the questions about the fictitious issues *after* the questions about the nonfictitious

topics. The order was varied to control for the possible influence of context. As it turned out, question order and context made little or no difference in the results (data not presented here).

[11] Cf. Martin J. Orne, "On the Social Psychology of the Psychological Experiment: With Particular Reference to Demand Characteristics and Their Implications," *American Psychologist,* 17 (November, 1962): 776–783.

[12] George F. Bishop, "The Middle Response in Survey Questions about Issues of Public Policy," paper presented at the Annual Conference of the American Association for Public Opinion Research, McAfee, NJ, May, 1985; and Schuman and Presser, *Questions and Answers in Attitude Surveys,* Ch. 6.

[13] Bishop, Oldendick, and Tuchfarber, "Effects of Presenting One Versus Two Sides"; and Schuman and Presser, *Questions and Answers in Attitude Surveys,* Ch. 7.

[14] Bishop, Oldendick, and Tuchfarber, "Political Information-Processing," "Interest in Political Campaigns," and "Context Effects on Questions"; and Schuman and Presser, *Questions and Answers in Attitude Surveys,* Ch. 2.

[15] For the reader who remains skeptical about the ease with which he or she can be manipulated by practitioners of the principles of modern behavioral science, see Robert B. Cialdini's stimulating volume, *Influence: How and Why People Agree to Things* (New York: William Morrow, 1984).

AN ORWELLIAN LASSWELL
FOR TODAY*

∾ Hayward R. Alker, Jr.

As a contribution to a volume focusing on the broader thematic relevance of George Orwell's *1984* for today, this essay is, perhaps surprisingly, about Harold Lasswell. For most readers, Harold Lasswell is probably but a shadowy figure from the "distant past" of American Political Science—one might recall an association with Merriam at Chicago in the 1930s; some catchy titles like *Politics: Who Gets What, When and How;* some crude operational studies of propaganda content; his commitment to the policy sciences; or the jargon-filled years of the Yale Law School and his coauthorship with Myres McDougall and others of numerous, weighty tomes on international law. But I consider Harold Lasswell to be the most important "founding father" of American Political Science in the twentieth century, the professional contemporary whose work most closely rivals and complements Orwell's achievements, and a shining, if neglected, model for further critical studies of systems of international domination; so I write about him here.

The Lasswell you will read about, then, will not be the person who directly influenced a whole generation of my teachers—themselves influential scholars like Gabriel Almond, Robert Dahl, Karl Deutsch, Heinz Eulau, Robert Lane, Daniel Lerner, Ithiel Pool, and Lucian Pye; it will be my personal Lasswell. This essay pays homage to a great teacher from one of his later students. Focusing on an especially appropriate, but independently developed theme, it tries to present an Orwellian Lasswell for 1984 and beyond. If this Lasswell is less known than other Lasswells, even by those who know his work less superficially than the typical graduate student or teacher of today, I take the resulting identity dilemmas as evidence for my thesis about Lasswell's unequaled influence in American Political Science. As a true founding father, he was, in a very professional way, an inspiration for the right and the left; an Americanist, a European comparativist, a developmentalist, and an international scholar. He was a functionalist and an action theorist; a student of broad social processes and institutions as well as of the irrational minutiae of individual political behavior; a behavioral scientist, a policy analyst, and a critical humanist; a "realist" and an "idealist"; a political scientist for all times, even post-1984.

To make my approach work I must show that there is an Orwellian Lasswell relevant for today, someone who not only shared many of Orwell's preoccupations but also as a political scientist shaped viable scholarly responses to them, responses we might expect Orwell himself to have tolerated or approved. This is not an easy task—Orwell profoundly distrusted intellectuals, and he disliked jargon. Lasswell trained Yale lawyers and political scientists, intellectual elites, in systematic political analysis. He was a scholar's scholar, able to define and defend disciplinary boundaries using difficult technical vocabularies. But a great commonality yet remained: they were both rational, humane citizens of the same tortured world.

With respect to "Orwellian" conceptualizations of the "institutionalized relations of global power and domination—their emergence, perpetuation, and possible transformation"—I accept Richard Ashley's interpretation of Orwell's *1984* as broadly suggesting:

1. potent imagery about the emergence of a new, totalitarian world order; and
2. appropriate intellectual and political commitments in an age whose desperate insecurities threaten to extinguish even "The Last man in Europe," Orwell's first projected title for that work.[1] My reading of Orwell's work, like my understanding of the life that produced it, has been heavily conditioned by Bernard Crick's *George Orwell: A Life* and William Steinhoff's *George Orwell and the Origins of 1984.*[2] "Orwellian" signifies for me not only the powerful, nightmarish world of *1984* but also the way of life and writing style of a man who "hated the power-hungry, exercised intelligence and independence, and taught us again to use our language with beauty and clarity, sought for and practiced

fraternity and had faith in the decency, tolerance and humanity of the common man."[3]

WORLD POWER HIERARCHIES

What first suggested to me a compatibility of perspectives was teaching Lasswell's "The Garrison State" as a political science test to follow Orwell's *1984*.[4] But in order to show how the two writers could come to such frightening, and similar, projections about world politics, I have to "unpack" Lasswell's conceptual and methodological orientation to such "developmental constructs" and show which aspects of the *1984* literary construct Orwell himself took seriously.

LASSWELL'S EARLY POLITICAL "REALISM"

In 1934 Lasswell began what he considered to be his most significant book, *World Politics and Personal Insecurity* with a shocking, pithy, "realistic" account of the "who gets what, when, and how" of world politics:

> Political analysis is the study of changes in the shape and composition of the value patterns of society. . . . Since a few members of any community . . . have the most of each value, . . . the pattern of distribution . . . resembles a pyramid. The few who get the most . . . are the *elite;* the rest are the rank and file. An elite preserves its ascendancy by manipulating symbols, controlling supplies, and applying violence.[5]

So far this conception maps quite clearly onto the cynical, power-oriented elites dominating *1984,* even if its Machiavellianism need not exhaust either Lasswell's or Orwell's views of the possibilities of human nature.

Lasswell goes even further, however, defining significant changes in world history in terms of changing worldwide patterns of recruitment of elites, their symbolic-self-understanding and their replacement possibilities.

> A *revolution* is rapid and extensive change in the composition and the vocabulary of the ruling few; *world revolutions* are those which inaugurate new principles of elite recruitment and new reigning ideologies in the political life of humanity. No doubt the French and Russian revolutions were major innovations in the world history of rulers and ruling symbols. . . . If the significant political changes of the past were signalized by revolutionary patterns which rose and spread until they were blocked or superseded by new revolutionary innovations, the future may follow the same course of development. . . . Correct self-orientation would therefore consist in

discerning the principle of elite recruitment and the predominant symbols to appear in the next phases of world political change. . . . Developmental analysis construes particular details with reference to tentatively held conceptions of the elite-symbol changes toward which or away from which events are moving.[6]

1984 AND "THE GARRISON STATE" AS COMPATIBLE DEVELOPMENTAL CONSTRUCTS

An "apprehensive" developmental perspective characterizes Lasswell's writing in 1941—two years before Orwell first outlined *1984*—about "the possibility that we are moving toward a world of 'garrison states'—a world in which the specialists on violence are the most powerful group in society."[7] His article suggests the same orientational concern as Orwell's, the desire to focus attention on a possible development of tremendous, negative value relevance. Listen to Lasswell's abstract of that article; it could almost equally well describe *1984*.

> The trend of the time is away from the dominance of the specialist on bargaining, . . . the businessman, and toward the supremacy of the specialist on violence, the soldier. . . . It is probable that the ruling elite of the garrison state will acquire most of the skills that we have come to accept as part of modern civilian management . . . especially skill in the manipulation of symbols in the interest of morale and public relations. Unemployment will be 'psychologically' abolished. Internal violence will be directed principally against unskilled manual workers and counterelite elements who have come under suspicion. . . . The practice will be to recruit the elite according to ability (in periods of crisis); authority will be dictatorial, governmentalized, centralized, integrated. . . . The power pyramid will be steep, but the distribution of safety will be equalized (the socialization of danger under modern conditions of aerial warfare). . . . The elites will seek to hold in check the utilization of the productive potentialities of modern science and engineering for nonmilitary consumption goods.[8]

Here is an independent, earlier version of *1984,* closer to it in outline than any of the book's literary precursors by Swift, Kipling, Wells, Huxley, Chesterton, or Zamiatin. Globally a self-perpetuating militarized technocracy rules a world made up of garrison states. Objective standards of rationality partly govern the elite's actions; not so the masses'. Frequent "war scares" mean that often unconscious fears of death are ceremonialized and ritualized. "This is one of the subtlest ways by which the individual can keep his mind distracted from the discovery of his own timidity."[9] We see as well an Orwellian deflection of economic capacity away from true improvements in the standard of living; military construction and expenditure are mentioned as ways of satisfying this need. The use of propaganda, a moderately egalitarian income distribution and drugs are suggested to be effective ways of undercutting criticism. Terror is also a routine instrument of domestic rule.

Although there is no explicit discussion of imperialism as a necessary feature of the garrison state in Lasswell's 1941 article, violent chauvinistic expansionism is associated with modern war crises in his earlier work. In 1934, Lasswell identified the pervasive, worldwide expectation of violence with the "drastic redefinition of the situation in directions gratifying to the underindulged, unreflecting, incautious, and spontaneous patterns of culture and personality," obviously including aggressiveness among them. In particular the "insecurities connected with the war symbol are partially disposed of by vigorously asserting the 'we' symbol at the expense of the 'they' symbol." Conditions for the maintenance of peace in an insecure world by a power-balancing process are investigated, including the measurability of variations in power (conceived as fighting effectiveness), the convertibility and distributability of power among balances, the early visibility of power variations and sentimentibility of the power estimation process, and found not likely to be met in the modern age of complex technologies and highly mobilized mass publics. Rather, contemporary Great Power war crises are associated with a culture of chauvinism, an exacerbated "we/they" thinking, "the most extreme form of truculent assertion; . . . an excited demand for the limitless, violent expansion of the nation."[10]

SHARED RESISTANCE TO PROPAGANDA ABOUT INEVITABLE
AND BENEFICIAL DIRECTIONS OF POLITICAL CHANGE

We see how Lasswell's developmental analysis of political hierarchies in the world crisis of the 1930s led him to the same preoccupations as Orwell. But the similarity was even closer: both Lasswell and Orwell took a hard, critical look at the political *myths* (including the utopias) by which all polities, including imperialist democracies and totalitarian states, sustain themselves. Both studied the self-deceiving justifications of imperialism (Orwell's *Burmese Days* and Chapter 6 of Lasswell's *World Politics and Personal Insecurity*); Orwell's devastating study of the betrayal of socialist revolutionary principles, *Animal Farm,* corresponds in many ways to Lasswell's functionalist, at times empathetic, but ultimately sardonic treatment of the Russian revolution as the "second bourgeois revolution, conducted in the name of the proletariat" in the same volume.[11] Their criticisms extended to Marxist arguments about the inevitability of proletarian victories under socialism. When a hierarchical alternative was considered—a totalitarian world of collectivist oligarchies or a world of garrison states—these also were treated as possibilities, not inevitabilities. Both Orwell and Lasswell lived rationally in a world of limited but distinct political possibilities.

Let me consider in more detail this correspondence of views on the possibility of coercive, hierarchical world order alternatives to genuine international proletarianism. In *1984*, Goldstein's heretical/anarchist treatment of the antiproletarian Ingsoc regime is entitled "The Theory and Practice of Oligarchical Collectivism"; the major world powers are treated as without significant ideological differences. Through an examination of Orwell's essays we can easily verify that both of these literary constructions were thought by Orwell to represent objective world tendencies. Reviewing favorably Franz Borkenau's *The Totalitarian Enemy*, in 1940, he was to treat the Hitler-Stalin pact as evidence that National Socialism *is* revolutionary socialism, but a socialism that crushes both the property owner and the worker. As a result, the Communist and Fascist regimes, "having started from opposite ends, are rapidly evolving towards the same system—a form of 'oligarchic collectivism.'"[12] In an essay for the *Observer* written in 1948, the same year as *1984*, Orwell argued that "the Russian Communists necessarily developed into a permanent ruling caste, or oligarchy, recruited not by birth but by adoption."[13] Orwell feared the coming of a hierarchic world order of two or three superstates, with a semidivine caste at the top and something like slavery at the bottom; each state might be able to overcome any internal rebellion, but not to conquer the others, perpetuating itself through complete severance from the outside world and the crisis atmosphere of a continuous phony war.[14]

As early as 1934, Lasswell saw Marxism as "the strongest protest symbolism with revolutionary demands and universal claims" to historical and scientific supremacy. Writing in 1951, shortly after *1984* was finally published in the United States, Lasswell was to focus and sharpen his very similar argument about the Communist elites in the Soviet Union and elsewhere:

> From the Communist standpoint there is no doubt about the truth: we are moving from capitalism to socialism, from the primacy of the bourgeoisie to the supremacy of the proletariat. However, the Marxist tradition is interpreted in many different ways. Machajski suggested that the most important development of our epoch is the rise to power, not of the working class as a whole, but rather of the intellectual worker, whose capital is his knowledge. Relying upon the superiority of knowledge, the intellectual wins the support of the manual workers, whom he exploits mainly for his own benefit. Of all theories of the place of the intellectual in history this is the most uncongenial to those who claim to speak in the name of the masses.[15]

In a more general analysis of the correlates of a present trend toward bipolarization of the world, and its associated basic characteristic of the "expectation of violence," Lasswell zeroes in on the Soviet elite as follows: "If we apply these categories to the bipolar situation, we find that the ruling elite of the Soviet world has the problem common to dictatorship of 'externalizing hostility' against the outside environment. Hence the ruling elite enjoys a continuing gain in internal power by sustaining a perpetual crisis."[16]

As a committed democratic Socialist, Orwell did not mean his literary destruction of "the last man in Europe" as a prophecy, nor as an anti-leftist diatribe. It was a warning about likely consequences of an era of total (but artificially drawn out) war from whose effects English-speaking countries were not immune.[17]

As his more general analyses of bipolarity and chauvinistic responses to war crises suggest, Lasswell, too, thought in terms of more general trends and multiple options facing all of the major states. For example, *World Politics and Personal Insecurity* contains a delightful scenario for world unification in the interest of professors of social science, an "elite based on vocabulary, footnotes, questionnaires, and conditioned responses, against an elite based on vocabulary, poison gas, property, and family prestige."[18] More seriously, the last chapter is a hardheaded yet idealistic psychiatric discussion of the prerequisites of a just and (therefore more) stable world order. In his 1941 article, Lasswell recognizes four contending major world-symbol patterns: national democracy, the antiplutocratic thrust of the "axis" of National Socialistic powers, the Soviet-led version of the world proletariat and a truer world-proletarianism hostile to all the above alternatives. His sketched transition to a world of garrison states suggested their probable order of appearance as "Japan in China, Germany, Russia, United States of America."[19] Although his 1951 monograph elaborates most tellingly variants of Machajski's hypothesis about "the world revolution of middle income skill groups," also referred to as the "unnamed revolution" and the "permanent revolution of modernizing intellectuals," Lasswell juxtaposes Orwellian trend statements about totalitarianization, militarization, and bipolarization with a contrary tendency toward the worldwide interdetermination of human actions. And he is open, indeed more positive than Orwell, about our new world of intellectual elitism in the sense that from "the standpoint of human dignity the probable result cannot be foretold with confidence."[20]

THE FEARSOME NOVELTY OF NEW TOTALITARIAN STATE FORMS

It should be emphasized, against those political scientists who want to treat all modern nation states as the same, that both Orwell and Lasswell saw something fundamentally new occurring in the twentieth century. It was founded in the development of technical civilization and modern propaganda, combined in the unprecedented, highly controlled mobilization of popular enthusiasm for total wars. Thus even Orwell's discussion of the "future England" recognizes the fundamental role of newer skill groups, people of indeterminate social class: "The old pattern is gradually changing into something new. . . . To that new civilization belong the people who are most at home in and most definitely *of* the modern world, the technicians and the higher paid skilled workers, the airmen and the mechanics, the radio experts, film producers, popular journalists and industrial chemists. They are the indeterminate stratum at which the older class distinctions are beginning to break down."[21] The conspicuous role of symbol manipulators in these newer social formations is worthy of comment.

But Orwell went further, arguing in 1939 that:

> The terrifying thing about the modern dictatorships is that they are something entirely unprecedented. Their end cannot be foreseen. . . . it may be just as possible to produce a breed of men who do not wish for liberty as to produce a breed of hornless cows. The Inquisition failed, but then the Inquisition had not the resources of the modern state. The radio, press-censorship, standardized education and the secret police have altered everything. Mass-suggestion is a science of the last twenty years, and we do not yet know how successful it will be.[22]

He recognized that war "is the greatest of all agents of change."[23] Indeed, he saw as frightening and new the emergence of total states at war with one another, and, as we have seen, feared such developments were likely in England after the war even if Hitler was defeated.[24]

As we have seen, these themes are also Lasswellian; Lasswell's sense of revolutionary change corroborates Orwell's on all these points. Not only was his first book on revolutionary war propaganda, he was deeply interested in the role of intellectuals (once defining them as "symbol specialists").[25] He considered totalitarianization as a world trend, defining it as "the subordinating of society to government, and the concentration of all governmental power into a few hands, perhaps ultimately in the hands of a self-perpetuating caste of police officers." Since centralization was a function of perceived common threat, war obviously had a lot to do with the trend. Technically, the most important "developments in this connection are the devices for abolishing privacy."[26] How strongly these trends point in the direction of the totalitarian states of *1984!*

Science, Commitment and Power

Among their various shared concerns—science fiction utopias, the genuinely emancipatory outcomes of revolutionary struggles around the world, and the pathologies of power-hungry individuals, but not political psychiatry per se—several more correspondences between Orwell and Lasswell will be discussed here. Since Orwell was a writer and a journalist and Lasswell a political scientist, obviously their professional engagements were not identical. But both men had a lot to say about the hierarchy-renewing temptations of power, as well as the honesty, detachment, and political commitments of intellectuals.

THE CORRUPTION OF INTELLECTUALS

Several elements of Orwell's indictment of his fellow intellectuals have already been mentioned or implied: their self-serving betrayal of egalitarian revolutionary ideals; their lack of the experience that ordinary people have had in practice with the totalitarian ideals (like "necessary murder") that many intellectuals of his time theoretically espoused; the corruption of their honesty or moral decency by power or the hunger for power. One quotation from his essays will suffice: "It was only *after* the Soviet regime became unmistakably totalitarian that English intellectuals, in large numbers, began to show an interest in it. . . . The American James Burnham . . . is really voicing their secret wish: . . . to destroy the old, equalitarian version of Socialism and usher in a hierarchical society where the intellectual can at last get his hands on the whip."[27]

This quotation suggests some of the bitter forces behind Orwell's critique of power-corrupted intellectual work, a major theme in much of his political writing. His implicit critique of this tendency in *1984* is given specific content through his literary construction of doublethink. It is therefore worth repeating some of the book's analysis of the central generating principles of public intellectual life in Oceania. The analysis for "Ignorance is Strength" starts with a great falsehood itself: a theory—like those James Burnham and the early Lasswell subscribed to—that there are three eternally existing classes whose interests are entirely irreconcilable with each other. This is contradicted within a page or two in Goldstein's *Theory of Oligarchic Collectivism* by the admission that authoritarian political theories had done their best to discredit revolutionary beliefs in the rights of man, freedom of speech, and equality before the law just at the time when technical progress made it possible to realize these ideals: "The earthly paradise had been discredited at exactly the moment when it became realizable." One is led to infer that the ignorance of the masses is their strength, but only within a powerful, regimented and hierarchical state based on lies (the denial of the existence of objective reality, the continued mutation of the past, and total ignorance about the real people of the other superstates) serving the interests of the powerful elite.

"War is Peace" is given a similar, devastating analysis. When it became clear that "an all-round increase in wealth threatened the destruction—indeed, in some sense was the destruction—of a hierarchical society," perpetual, potentially disastrous but never decisive imperialistic warfare evolved as a way of killing the expectation and reality of increased material well-being for the proletarian masses. By thus preventing revolutionary protest, it gave the party elites and most of the proles (outside the imperialistic battlegrounds) a kind of anxiety-full peace. Of the two central war aims of the party, neither was realistic; yet doublethink encouraged their passionate, self-contradictory pursuit. The first, the desire to conquer the entire earth, destroyed the surplus products of human labor; it was neither feasible nor based in any objective vital national interest other than elite perpetuation. The other, the extinguishing "once and for all of the possibility of independent thought," was mightily encouraged by "war hysteria," (producing something like Lasswell's chauvinistic "drastic redefinitions" of the objective conflict situation); it flew in the face of the need of party managers for rational assessment.

Finally, for "Freedom is Slavery," I offer my own, Orwellian reconstruction. This self-contradictory slogan ironically contradicts the major emancipatory thrust of Western civilization. That thrust might briefly be characterized as movement toward materially supported, life-serving, rationally redeemable, self-realizing, mutually supporting forms of individual and collective self-determination. Consistent with the political economic analysis of the previous paragraph, this thrust is being propagandistically equated with obsessive, compulsive adherence to an imposed ideal: such goals are to be given up by Oceanians, just as they have been given up by the collectivist death worshipers of *1984*'s Eastasia. *1984* for many of its less politicized readers is most importantly the totalitarian, statist destruction of Winston Smith's human identity by his forced renunciation of the intimate, idiosyncratic, intensely personal fulfillment, self-understanding and interpersonal commitment achieved through his love for Julia.

One might even take Orwell's irony one level higher: the party elite of Oceania is itself obsessively enslaved by the constant "necessity" of combatting the potential freedom of thought and action of those amongst or outside their numbers who might revolt against them. The "autonomy" which Oceania "enjoys" in perpetuating itself is at the same time the slavery of *all* its subjects. Like Hegel's lord-bondsman relationship, the "free" dominion of the master enslaves both the master and his serf.

In concluding this brief review of the generating principles of doublethink, we shall not list lots of contemporary examples of Oceania's obfuscating Newspeak. Any citizen of our society can, with care, fill in examples: limiting myself to the Reagan Administration, "Ignorance is Strength" vividly came to mind when Admiral Poindexter told millions of American citizens that there are important things about how their government is conducted "that they don't want to know," and "War is Peace" achieved renewed resonance when Secretary of Defense Weinberger called mass-murdering MX missiles "Peacemakers." That Soviet leaders practice similar deceptions is evident from the degree of misunderstanding Soviet citizens regularly exhibit concerning the "defensive" character of their own government's recent force buildup. It is worth quoting Crick's judgment of Orwell's transpartisan, intellectual consistency: "Orwell did not denounce intelligence or possibly intellectualism. . . . He was no anti-intellectual as such, only against most of the self-styled intellectuals of the 1930s vintage," whose loss of objectivity and critical independence he so viciously attacked.[28]

It is perhaps more surprising to discover that, at least in the last years of his life, Lasswell, too, found intellectuals to have been severely deficient, in particular with respect to the perpetuation of the power-oriented war system, sustained by and contributing to a continuing worldwide pattern of expectations of international violence. The most eloquent statement of these views, which can be found in several of his papers from the late 1960s, occurs in a paper given first to the American Psychological Association, entitled "Must Science Serve Political Power?"[29] Presumably Lasswell chose a nonpolitical science audience as more likely to be sympathetic to such views. Given that "science works for power," his explanatory focus is on the inner reward structure of knowledge institutions, those that cement parochial relationships of mutual interest within the societies where they reside. Scientists do not do much better than the "militantly competitive elites of the opulent and knowledgeable powers." On the basis of prototypical contextual considerations, he concludes that in the aggregate scientists "contribute more directly to the service of war and oligarchy than to world security and the welfare of the whole community."[30] In part, Orwell's tendencies have actually been realized.

BEYOND POWER-HUNGRY PERSONALITIES

The careful reader of this essay (and its footnotes) will recall a particularly problematical point in my attempted reconciliation of Orwell and Lasswell, on the basis of which I want to argue how problems of international hierarchy might fruitfully be studied. Like Goldstein's partly-fabricated theory of the eternal three classes and Burnham's analysis of politics as a perpetual swindle of the occasionally revolutionary masses, Lasswell's early Machiavellian political "realism" clearly conflicts with Orwell's belief in the possibility of democratic Socialism by personalities far different from those allowed to survive in garrison or totalitarian states.

Here, too, a remarkable essay on "Democratic Character" represents an evolution in Lasswell's perspective, one much more consistent with Orwell's most mature views.[31]

Lasswell's famous formula for political man,

$$p \} 1/2 \: d \} 1/2 \: r = P$$

suggests how private motives (p) are displaced onto public objects (d), following by rationalization (r) in terms of certain positions about the public interest.[32] His discussion of the structure of the democratic character is motivated by a long quotation from *The Authoritarian Personality,* the first part of which confirms this projective formula: "Thus a basically hierarchical, authoritarian, exploitive parent-child relationship is apt to carry over into a power-oriented, exploitively dependent attitude toward one's sex partner and one's God and may culminate in a political philosophy and social outlook which has no room for anything but a desperate clinging to what appears to be a strong and disdainful rejection of whatever is relegated to the bottom." The tendency toward rigid, convention-bound, dichotomous handling of ingroup-outgroup cleavages resonates with Lasswell's much earlier discussions of the chauvinistic consequences of war crises. But a more democratic alternative is also identified by the authors of *The Authoritarian Personality.* "There is a pattern characterized chiefly by affectionate, basically equalitarian, and permissive interpersonal relationships . . . encompassing attitudes within the family and toward the opposite sex, as well as an internationalization of religious and social values. Greater flexibility and the potentiality for more genuine satisfactions appear as results of this basic attitude."[33]

No longer is political man prototypically Machiavellian. Lasswell's extraordinarily creative and affirmative response to the preoccupation in American intellectual circles with the authoritarian personality is to formulate an empirically assessable democratic alternative and discuss the conditions affecting the likelihood of its emergence and persistence. Given a newly articulated commitment to human dignity defined operationally in terms of the wide sharing of many values, democratic character is now said to be "cast into relief" by its alternative, *homo politicus,* who relishes the pursuit of power by the use of power, which definitionally for Lasswell involves the capacity to invoke severe sanctions. "Since we understand that power relationships have, or are assumed by the participants to possess, the element of severe deprivation, it is apparent that the human being who is fascinated by power is out of harmony with our basic concept of human dignity."[34] The self-system of the democratic character, because it has not been crushed by pervasive experiences of low self-esteem, evidences "deep confidence in the benevolent potentialities of man." How antithetical to *1984!* Its value demands are multiple; it is "disposed to share rather than hoard or to monopolize."

Its "open ego" is "warm rather than frigid, inclusive and expanding rather than exclusive and constricting," capable of friendship and "unalienated from humanity." Its energy system is free from anxiety, having "at its disposal the energies of the unconscious part of the personality."[35] In his old age, Lasswell, too, seems to have become more democratic, more optimistic, even idealistic about the potentialities of his fellow man: "Can the violence system be changed into a nonviolent system? Can this transformation be brought about nonviolently? The answer, I submit, is yes."[36] Corresponding to Orwell's internationalism, Lasswell's old, idealistic search for a world-unifying myth and technique has been fulfilled.

POLITICAL COMMITMENTS: PATRIOTISM AND INTERNATIONALISM

Orwell considered himself a radical patriot; though a supporter of the British war effort, he saw World War II as a revolutionary socialist opportunity in England and steadfastly opposed British imperialism in India and Burma. He was an antinationalist, and therefore in some sense an internationalist. These terms are most fully defined and illustrated in his 1941 volume on "The Lion and the Unicorn: Socialism and the English Genius": and his 1945 essay "Notes on Nationalism." "By 'patriotism' I mean devotion to a particular place and a particular way of life, which one believes to be the best in the world but has no wish to force upon other people." "Nationalism" means "first of all the habit of assuming that human beings can be classified like insects and that whole blocks . . . of people can be confidently labelled 'good' or 'bad.'" Secondly, nationalism refers to "the habit of identifying oneself with a single nation or other unit, placing it beyond good and evil and recognizing no other duty than that of advancing its interests." Thus a "nationalist is one who thinks solely, or mainly in terms of competitive prestige." The "nationalist" is broadly defined; the concept is meant to refer as an overdrawn extreme type to neo-Toryism, Communism, pacifism, ethnic nationalisms, class feelings, etc. It has extremely negative connotations: "Nationalism is power hunger tempered by self-deception. Every nationalist is capable of the most flagrant dishonesty, but he is also—since he is conscious of serving something bigger than himself—unshakably certain of being in the right."[37] In extreme cases nationalism is characterized by high degrees of obsession with the superiority of one's own power unit, the instability of political loyalties to it, and indifference to belief-contradicting reality. Telling illustrations include the varying attitudes of different British intellectuals toward the political capacities, the economic performances, and the atrocities committed by Allied and enemy powers before and during World War II.

One is reminded of Lasswell's indictment of chauvinism, his critique of national imperialistic movements as driven in reality by the demand for supremacy.

In 1934 he characterized "modern national imperialism" as "a mass demand for permanent control over peoples of alien culture, to be attained by force if necessary, and justified by allegations of mutual advantage."[38] But Lasswell went further toward a communitarian internationalism than even Orwell. Distinguishing between a world *public order* sustained by potentially violent sanctions and a world *civic order* relying on nonviolent sanctions in support of concerted action, he called for a transnational World Community Association to foster "metroglobal community, meaning a world organized as voluntarily as possible among the emerging metropolitan centers of the globe." His varied set of economic, social, educational and political activities for this association he described as "the preparation of a new world within the framework of the old."[39] Proposing an attack on the war system, he attacked the world public order's nationalistic biases by advocating "the break up of national power monopolies by dividing the giant powers into small powers and consolidating an international organization strong enough to maintain at least minimum public order and to prevent barriers to the movement of persons and goods."[40]

Both Lasswell and Orwell patriotically supported their governments during World War II, Lasswell working for the Office of War Information and Orwell orchestrating broadcasts to India by the BBC. But as we have seen, their patriotism did not prevent them from taking, at one time or another, radically revisionist attitudes toward world order. Our Orwellian Lasswell sounds more like Richard Falk, their radical internationalist descendant, than Machiavelli, Vilfredo Pareto, or Henry Kissinger!

POLITICAL COMMITMENTS: DECENCY, DIGNITY, AND DEMOCRATIC SOCIALISM

Against power-hungry intellectuals Orwell regularly appealed to the decency and morality of the ordinary citizen. He made no secret of his political commitments. In the famous essay "Why I Write," which was written in 1946 and chosen to introduce his *Collected Essays,* Orwell states that "every line of serious work that I have written since 1936 has been written, directly or indirectly, *against* totalitarianism and *for* democratic Socialism, as I understand it."[41]

Lasswell, on the other hand, despite his democratic "repugnance and apprehension" toward the garrison state, did not to my knowledge identify himself as a Socialist. Moreover, his political commitments and his professional scientific work were argued to be rigorously separate. Thus he emphatically introduced his influential conceptualization of political analysis, *Power and Society* (1950), by first recognizing "the existence of two distinct components in political theory—the empirical propositions of political science and the value judgments of political doctrine." He then went on to state flatly that "only statements of the first kind are explicitly formulated in the present work."[42] If Lasswell were consistent across his writings, this would be a sharp difference in political and professional orientation between Orwell the journalist and Lasswell the political scientist. But Lasswell was not.

Orwell was active in the League for the Dignity and Rights of Man, which tried to define democracy in a multivalued way, going beyond nineteenth-century liberalism.[43] Lasswell's concern for the multivalued democratic character correlated with a new commitment of his own in the post-World War II era to the policy sciences of human dignity. Personality and culture were innerly dependent, often mutually reinforcing. Therefore, along with a commitment to democracy comes a commitment to a kind of personality most likely to realize and perpetuate such values. "A democratic community is one in which human dignity is realized in theory and fact. It is characterized by wide rather than narrow participation in the shaping and sharing of values."[44]

Notice what, operationally, these vague standards are supposed to mean. "Power is shared when in fact there is general participation in decision-making," when it is assumed that "office-holders can be criticized without fear of serious retaliation," and "there is a presumption against the use of power in great concentration, particularly in the form of regimentation, centralization, and militarization." Although there is to be a strong presumption of the widest possible scope for voluntary choice and privacy, the political myth of a democratic community "emphasizes the desirability of congenial human relationships."

In economic terms, both in expectation and reality, democracy means "security of basic income is guaranteed in theory and fact," that "opportunities are open to every capable person to earn more than the basic income. A balanced, graduated distribution of income is valued and realized, preventing a division of the community into 'rich' and 'poor.'" An expectation of continuing economic growth is also part of Lasswell's democratic myth. Although this may be associated in many minds with liberal "trickle down" rationalizations, it should be recalled that in *1984* these expectations were killed by wealth-consuming perpetual warfare; the consequence was the easier justification of a hierarchical society on the basis of a presumed scarcity of economic rewards.[45]

Orwell's democratic Socialism was non-Marxist and atheoretical. It allowed for altruistic, nonmaterial motivational elements in human nature. It connoted "liberty, equality and internationalism," or "political democracy, social equality and internationalism." In his famous phrase, "Liberty is the right to tell people what they do not want to hear."[46] Operationally speaking, with Lasswell's commitment to basic needs-oriented economics, and Orwell's distrust of centralized, bureaucratic socialism, are these two political commitments really very different after all?

One may still ask whether these remarkably similar value commitments extend fully into their professional attitudes toward political commitment. In his writing Lasswell at times seems, like most behavioral political scientists, to follow the model of value neutrality supposed to guide the scientist; Orwell clearly belongs in the tradition of the critical humanist. Even acknowledging the importance Orwell placed on logical argument (symbolically the absurdity of $2 + 2 = 5$ in *1984*, a slogan actually blazing forth from Moscow apartment buildings during the Stalin era) and an objective truth (which totalitarian ideologies tend to distort or deny), my "convergence" thesis seems in real trouble.

This difficulty disappears, however, when the Orwellian Lasswell speaks out movingly at the end of his powerful, affirmative essay on democratic character:

> To some extent descriptive probing into the processes of political life has been held back by inapplicable analogies from the natural sciences. It is insufficiently acknowledged that the role of scientific work in human relations is *freedom* rather than prediction. By freedom is meant the bringing into the focus of awareness of some feature of the personality which . . . has been operating 'automatically and compulsively.' The individual is now free to take the factor into consideration in the making of future choices. This enlargement of the scope of freedom is the most direct contribution of the study of interpersonal relations to democracy. Hence it is the growth of insight, not simply of the capacity of the observer to predict the future operation of an automatic compulsion, or of a non-personal factor, that represents the major contribution of the scientific study of interpersonal relations to policy. From the classical inheritance we have no static tradition, but a vast panorama of inspiration and suggestion for the reshaping of all civilizations and all cultures toward the goal of free men in a society at once universal and free.[47]

Lasswell may be more grandiose than Orwell; his prose may only approximate Orwell's eloquence on rare occasions. But Lasswell's political psychiatry is grounded in the same tradition of critical and constructive humanism as Orwell's. The deep emancipatory interest of both men in a world order transcending imperialistic power politics and diminishing the resulting hierarchical patterns of domination shines through their work.[48]

DEMOCRATIC POSSIBILITIES TODAY

Having established at least several noncontradictory identifications, expectations, and demands characteristic of the Orwellian Lasswell, I must now answer the question, "What does he have to say to us today?" Do not the preoccupations of World War II and its aftermath seem long out of date? Has not international political science progressed to the extent that the journalistic writing and psycho-analytically informed hypotheses of the 1930s and 1940s are obsolete? I hope the title of this concluding section does not suggest too narrowly partisan a view.[49]

An Orwellian Lasswell is a scholar committed to a world of greater human dignity, of wider value-sharing as an overriding objective of his or her political analysis, patriotic but internationalist. The oligarchic collectivism of swollen military establishments, the bureaucratically entrenched and corporate wealth has little attraction at home or abroad. Now that 1984 has come and gone, it is clear that Orwell's worst case of a hierarchical world of totalitarian garrison states of invulnerable, deeply hypocritical, war-based reproductive mechanisms had *not* been *fully* realized. For that we should be thankful.

Detailed discussion of the degree of movement toward or away from that conception are worth continuing analysis. Compared to 1941 or 1944, I believe we have moved back from that nightmare. Comparing 1984 and 1948, I am not so sure of the direction of movement, especially if we take the boundaries of Oceania for our comparisons: England plus the Americas.

Cold War hysteria is again alive and well. The terror used by elites to control the peripheries of these regions over the last several decades has been enormous. The partial demilitarization of the "Southern cone," ironically in part due to revanchist colonialism in Britain concerning Gibraltar and the Malvinas, is being compensated for by the Vietnamization of Central America. Cuba's export of doctors and educators is unfortunately matched by military assistance, not all (viz., Grenada) oriented strictly toward the increase of human dignity. A small fraction of the arms expenditures in the region since 1948 could have ended poverty there by 1984. Freedom of speech is still paid for with one's life, one's job, or personal independence in too many places.[50]

But an Orwellian Lasswell committed to real democracy has the right, indeed the obligation, to cry out: America, where has your commitment to human dignity, to decency gone? Right-wing authoritarians solicitous of the economic privacy of their richest supporters are not "dignified" by that respect for "freedom," which can mean virtual economic slavery for most of their fellow countrymen and women. Our foreign policies promote the same bimodalization of world income that we are seeing at home.[51] The Soviet Union avoids large redistributional aid programs by blaming all inequalities on capitalism, yet through its allies it competitively contributes to the militarization of Asia, Africa, and even (to a much lesser extent) Latin America. Compared even to the oil-rich Arab states, the United States gives less real developmental aid, and sells many more weapons. In perhaps half the receiving countries such "assistance" is not primarily justifiable by external threats to national security. Compared to 1960, militarization of the Third World has probably increased.[52] For too many rural poor, family sizes are still too large because development has stagnated. One of the few arenas of cooperation among the superpowers is in their fated attempt to limit the monopoly of nuclear terror to the great powers. Terrorism of the weak competes on unequal terms with the state terrorism of the strong. There are many more affronts to human equality and dignity that need to be criticized.

Surely an Orwellian Lasswell has something important to say as well about "realism" as an intellectual style of political analysis, especially when promoted nationalistically, as it often is by those whose preoccupation with power-prestige tends to make them argue that military self-help is a universal necessity. Let us accept that in the 1930s too many idealists ignored the ominous implications of the foreign policies of the United States, Britain, Japan, Italy, France, the Soviet Union, and Germany. But one who is moved to change a world political order that is in many ways a continuing affront to human dignity should not treat it merely as a natural phenomenon, a tragic necessity whose harmful effects might hopefully be minimized. Elite authoritarianism, "realist" national security priorities, and exploitive, systemic role-rule structures *inner-act,* more often in a mutually supportive than a self-contradictory way. By not recognizing the role realist foreign policy practices play in the legitimating of international domination, such scholars become apologists for the systemic status quo. The conditions for the reproduction of such systems need continually and contextually to be studied; practices that constructively undermine them need to be identified and explored.

An Orwellian Lasswell speaks as well to the fashioning of concepts we use to comprehend and steer ourselves through the often difficult and insecure world of international politics. Sanctioning power is an essential feature of world politics; economics can not be fully separated from politics. Using thought models from instrumentalist, utilitarian economics obscures the coercive underside of supposedly free and voluntary market exchanges. Their costs and benefits are more than economic; they include effects on the autonomy and dignity of national and subnational actors. Yet so many of our best modelers misunderstand themselves as riding starward the chariots of "high mathematical science" when what they are really doing might better be described as circling above congested unsafe airports, burning up precious fuel, going nowhere but up and down through clouds of ideological distortion, leaving many of their student passengers feeling more than a little queasy.

The narrative immediacy of Orwell, the configurative contextualism of Lasswell, and the systemic possibilism of my Orwellian Lasswell all suggest giving substantive names to contending possible sources of order in world politics. These names would be conceptually keyed to the varying recruitment, legitimation, and perpetuation practices of these candidate orders. Surely, the organizing principles of international actions by and through major states deserves special attention. Liberal conceptions of utilitarian action are likely to be inadequate and inappropriate in much of the modern world. The extent to which Communist, Fascist, "friendly Fascist," democratic nationalist, democratic Socialist, neo-imperialist, or totalitarian systems of practice are emerging, retreating and/or renewing themselves deserves special attention. As knowledgeable observers we must not be squeamish about criticism or rigidly parsimonious in the choice of conceptual equipment. We should look for winners *and* losers among contending world powers; see if together they make up a larger, coherent, extendable pattern of order; and go beyond the limiting grammar of utilitarian realism and the structuralism of power rankings in describing what is happening.

Nothing could be a more immediate reflection on the previous biographical construction than the urgency of orienting oneself, as concerned citizen or scholar, toward the emergent possibilities among the major contenders for world power. The extent to which these actors reflect, coproduce or reproduce newly emergent patterns of political practice is particularly noteworthy; the obsolescent, partial renewal of other concerted efforts, like nineteenth-century power balancing, must also be taken into account. Lenin used such a strategy in his brilliant, polemical, yet scientifically suggestive reconceptualization of turn-of-the-century imperialism. We have seen how hierarchical constructs like "oligarchic collectivism" and a world of "garrison states" were critically generalized reflections by Orwell and Lasswell of Communist double-dealing in Spain and the Stalin-Hitler pact of 1939. The same could be said of totalitarianism, a concept and practice used by the losing German General Staff at the end of World War I, and borrowed, with amplifications, by Mussolini and Hitler later on. Totalitarianism's genuine novelty and unpredictability have been less at the focus of attention of international relations scholars than modern comparativists. On the other hand, Hannah Arendt, among others, has argued that Khrushchev's reforms helped end totalitarianism as the dominant mode of political life in the Soviet Union;[53] if this argument is more valid in the Gorbachev era, then "nationalistic" we/they rhetoric about "freedom vs. totalitarianism" is particularly suspect. There is the possibility that a different kind of more authoritarian pluralism might be developing in world affairs.

Although mathematical modelers may have particular difficulties in paying attention to multiple, emergent-order possibilities, it is important to be able to empathize with the legitimating appeals of serious contenders without succumbing to them. Otherwise, all the biasing effects of nationalism (in Orwell's sense) will be at work. Neither are simple projections of short-term trends (like the non-aggression pact of Nazi Germany and Soviet Russia, or Germany's later advances in Russia that so impressed James Burnham, or the popularity of Reagan's foreign policy style) necessarily good indicators of longer-term trends. Orwell's writing had a peculiar cogency for ex-Communists and Socialists; his books were even highly sought after by certain elites within the Communist states of the Stalinist era. They helped play a crucial orienting role. Lasswell's treatments of the betrayal of Communist myths has more cogency for other leftists because of his acknowledgement of (and analysis of the reasons for) Marxism's enormous appeal. When he shows how democratic nationalism has helped restrict, and in turn been partially incorporated by, the international relations of the Soviet Bloc, Lasswell benefits from his previous, careful analyses of the ways National Socialism similarly restricted and reflected the more internationalist Soviet variant.

Patriotic political scientists are especially susceptible to the distorting temptations of national power or the fetishism of the state. After all, if we were not interested at least vicariously in the successes of the powerful and/or their supercession by the formerly powerless, we probably would not be very good at our jobs. But in an era riven by the expectation of violence, indeed the cataclysmic threat of aerial nuclear warfare, objectivity and decency are very hard to maintain. The "mental cheating" of doublethink is especially tempting in a jingoistic time.[54] But the self-righteous nostalgic hegemonism of imperial democracies, the rosy glow of Pax Britannica or Pax Americana, the superstate fetishism of English (and Russian) language international relations research have been serious problems for genuine self-understanding for a longer time than the language of the recent presidential campaign in the United States. They infect otherwise admirable scholarship. More academically speaking, self-serving theories and question-begging treatments of opponents—cheap putdowns directed toward those of alternative metatheoretical orientations—are too often the rule, especially toward the Marxist tradition of scholarship, which has much more scientific vigor in the First, Second, and Third Worlds than most behavioral "neo-realists" are willing to admit. Serious, uncoerced engagement with intellectuals from opposing and dominated states, as well as other traditions of interpretive scholarship, is both patriotic and scientifically defensible. Such activities can help finally correct such self-serving biases if only we come to realize that an international science of international politics oriented toward the universalization of human dignity is now possible. My Orwellian Lasswell, who tries to write and speak English that ordinary people can appreciate and understand, would argue that real freedom *transcends* slavery if by that we mean unending, proud nonimperialistic dedication to the cause of a more democratic world order.

NOTES

* *Revised version of "An Orwellian Lasswell for 1984," originally presented at the Annual Meeting of the American Political Science Association, Washington, D.C., 1984, as a theme paper on hierarchical aspects of international politics.*

[1] See Richard Ashley's undated "Section Description" for "Section 18: International Relations: Hierarchical Aspects of International Politics" of the 1984 American Political Science Association Program. I am responsible for my interpretations of these themes.

[2] Bernard Crick, *George Orwell: A Life* (Boston: Little, Brown and Company, 1980); William Steinhoff, *George Orwell and the Origins of 1984,* (Ann Arbor: University of Michigan Press, 1976). Any quotations or paraphrases from the text of Orwell's *1984* will be taken either from these studies or the New American Library edition, New York, 1983, without further acknowledgment.

[3] Crick, *George Orwell,* p. 406.

[4] Harold D. Lasswell, "The Garrison State," *American Journal of Sociology,* 46 (January 1941): 455–468.

[5] Harold D. Lasswell, *World Politics and Personal Insecurity,* reprinted in Harold D. Lasswell, Charles E. Merriam and T. V. Smith, *A Study of Power,* (Glencoe, IL: Free Press, 1950; originally published 1934).

At this point Orwell's rejection of the rather similar political "realism" of James Burnham should be noted as a potential stumbling block in my efforts to construct a consistent Orwellian Lasswell. In his essay/pamphlet "James Burnham and the Managerial Revolution," Orwell admits the impressive projective plausibility of Burnham's thesis of an increasingly oligarchic managerial revolution (neither Socialist nor Capitalist) leading at the international level to a world of three totalitarian superstates. But he rejects Burnham's Machiavellian political analysis, which we might paraphrase as: 1) Politics (the struggle for power) is essentially the same in all ages; 2) Power hunger is a natural instinct forever separating an unscrupulous ruling elite from an unpolitical, brainless mob of the ruled; 3) History is a series of swindles wherein elites lure masses into revolution with the false promise of Utopias, only to reenslave them after the revolt succeeds.

Orwell counters that the proper question is "Why does the lust for naked power become a major human motive exactly *now,* when the dominion of man over man is ceasing to be necessary?" He takes seriously the possibility "that the Machiavellian world of force, fraud, and tyranny may somehow come to an end," i. e., that democratic Socialism could happen. And he attributes to Burnham and many other intellectuals an unsavory and ultimately unrealistic form of power worship: "That a man of Burnham's gifts should have been able for a while to think of Nazism as something rather admirable, something that could and probably would build up a workable and durable social order, shows what damage is done to the sense of reality by the cultivation of what is not called 'realism.'" The essay is reprinted in Sonia Orwell and Ian Angus, editors, *The Collected Essays, Journalism and Letters of George Orwell,* 4 volumes (New York and London: Harcourt Brace Jovanovich, 1968), Volume 4, *In Front of Your Nose,* pp. 160–181. My paraphrasing and quotations are from pp. 176–181. The problem of reconciling this later view, which I agree with, and Lasswell's earlier "realism" will be addressed in the second section of this essay.

⁶ Lasswell, *World Politics and Personal Insecurity,* p. 3f.

⁷ Lasswell, "The Garrison State," p. 455.

⁸ Ibid.

⁹ Ibid., p. 466.

¹⁰ *World Politics and Personal Insecurity,* pp. 57, 74, 84.

¹¹ Harold D. Lasswell, *The World Revolution of Our Time,* reprinted and augmented as Chapter 2 of Harold D. Lasswell and Daniel Lerner, editors, *World Revolutionary Elites: Studies in Coercive Ideological Movements* (Cambridge, MA: M.I.T. Press, 1965; orig. pub. 1951), pp. 29–96. The citation is from p. 29 of this edition.

¹² George Orwell, "Red, White, and Brown," Review of *The Totalitarian Enemy* by Franz Borkenau, *Time and Tide,* 4 May 1940; cited by Steinhoff, p. 182. Crick is right to stress (on pp. 260–263 of his biography) the importance of "Inside the Whale" for understanding Orwell's gloomy views about the rise of totalitarianism, in part through the corruption of power-hungry, inexperienced intellectuals. That essay is reprinted in *The Collected Essays,* Volume 1, *An Age Like This, 1920–1940,* pp. 493–527.

¹³ George Orwell, "Marx and Russia," *Observer* (London), 15 February 1948; cited by Steinhoff, p. 182.

¹⁴ I am paraphrasing an Orwell quote given on p. 183 by Steinhoff, *George Orwell.*

¹⁵ Harold D. Lasswell, *World Politics and Personal Insecurity,* p. 129 is the source of the first quotation in this paragraph. The second, longer one, is from *The World Revolution of Our Time,* p. 29.

¹⁶ Ibid., p. 69f.

¹⁷ Both Crick, *George Orwell,* p. 395, and Steinhoff, *George Orwell,* p. 199, cite similar statements, offering interpretations similar to the one made here. To quote Orwell selectively from their citations: "Specifically the danger of the present trend toward a world like 1984 lies in the structure imposed on Socialist and on Liberal capitalist communities by the necessity to prepare for total war with the U.S.S.R. and the new weapons, of which of course the atomic bomb is the most painful and the most publicized." "I believe also that totalitarian ideas have taken root in the minds of intellectuals everywhere, and I have tried to draw these ideas out to their logical consequences. The scene of the book is laid in Britain in order to emphasize that the English-speaking races are not

innately better than anyone else and that totalitarianism, if not fought against, could triumph anywhere."

[18] Lasswell, *World Politics and Personal Insecurity,* p. 20.

[19] Lasswell, "The Garrison State," p. 467f.

[20] Lasswell, *The World Revolution of Our Time,* p. 92.

[21] This passage from Orwell's short, patriotic 1941 book *The Lion and the Unicorn: Socialism and the English Genius* is taken from a longer quotation in Crick, *George Orwell,* p. 276. The book itself is reprinted in the *Collected Essays,* Vol. 2, *My County Right or Left, 1940–1943,* pp. 56–108.

[22] "Review of *Russia Under Soviet Rule* by N. de Basily," reprinted in the *Collected Essays,* Vol. 1, pp. 378–381. Both Crick, *George Orwell* (p. 247f) and Steinhoff, *George Orwell* (p. 183f) cite and discuss this review.

[23] Orwell, *The Lion and the Unicorn,* p. 94. Quoted and discussed in Crick, *George Orwell,* p. 275.

[24] I accept Crick's judgment (p. 307) about Orwell's views concerning future post-war totalitarian possibilities; it correlates with numerous statements by Orwell, including his essay "Inside the Whale." (See quotations in note 17.)

[25] Lasswell, *The World Revolution of Our Time,* p. 85f.

[26] Ibid., p. 77.

[27] Orwell, "James Burnham and the Managerial Revolution," p. 179. An anonymous reviewer of this essay has suggested that Lasswell's commitments to 'value free,' empiricist social science reinforced his own "corruption as an intellectual," his empathetic, power-oriented complicity with the "treason of the clerks" that Julian Benda, Orwell, and, more recently, Noam Chomsky have so brilliantly and passionately criticized. Indeed, in Chomsky's *American Power and the New Mandarins* (New York: Pantheon, 1969) some of Lasswell's closest associates—Daniel Lerner, Ithiel Pool, and Lucian Pye—and Lasswell himself are effectively targeted. Accepting much of the force of such criticisms, my essay nonetheless attempts to suggest several ways Lasswell's own intellectual development, his historial sensitivity, and his uniquely influential disciplinary self-understanding may be seen as profound responses to them. There was, I believe, an underappreciated, gradually maturing Orwellian moralist inside Harold Lasswell as well.

[28] Crick, *George Orwell,* p. 274f.

[29] Harold D. Lasswell, "Must Science Serve Political Power?" Paper for the American Psychological Association, dated August 31, 1969; published without significant change in Harold D. Lasswell, Daniel Lerner, Hans Speier, editors, *Propaganda and Communication in World History,* Vol. III: *A Pluralizing World in Formation* (Honolulu: University Press of Hawaii, 1979), pp. 3–15. My page references are to the APA version.

[30] Ibid., p. 5.

[31] Harold D. Lasswell, "Democratic Character," in *The Political Writings of Harold Lasswell* (Glencoe, IL: Free Press, 1951), pp. 465–525.

[32] Lasswell, *World Politics and Personal Insecurity,* p. 39n, gives both this formula and earlier citations. At this point I must note that both Lasswell and Orwell regularly use the now outdated, and to my mind chauvinistic, linguistic convention where "man" refers to "man or woman." Because of the frequency of such quotations, in the present essay I have resisted giving "The last woman in Europe" and "political woman" their due.

[33] Lasswell, "Democratic Character," p. 508; his citation to T. W. Adorno et al., *The Authoritarian Personality,* published in 1950 by the American Jewish Committee as one of their "Studies in Prejudice," is to p. 971.

[34] Lasswell, "Democratic Character," p. 498.

[35] These summary descriptions paraphrase or quote the same article from pp. 495–514. The issue of the changing patterns of "determining factors which are currently moulding character" is raised explicitly on p. 514.

[36] Harold Lasswell, "Toward World Community Now," in *Alternatives to Violence: A Stimulus to Dialogue* (New York: Time-Life Books, 1968), pp. 118–126.

[37] Orwell, "Notes on Nationalism," in his *Collected Essays,* Vol. 3, *As I Please, 1943–1945,* pp. 361–380. The quotes in this paragraph are from this essay, p. 362f.

[38] Lasswell, *World Politics and Personal Insecurity,* titles Chapter VI as "Imperialistic Movements: The Demand for Supremacy." The quotation is from the first sentence of this chapter, p. 117.

[39] Lasswell, "Towards World Community Now," p. 122f.

[40] Harold D. Lasswell, "The Social and Economic Framework of War and Peace," unedited paper prepared for the Conference of Brain Research Institute, University of California Medical School, Los Angeles, November 17, 1965. The citation is to page 14 of this essay, which, along with the call for simultaneity in revolts against the war system suggests (p. 2) "the obvious hypothesis . . . that unless the war system were supported by the socio-economic system, and the socio-economic system were supported by the war system, the institution of war would long since have disappeared from human culture." A published version may be found in Carmine D. Clemente and Donald B. Lindsley, editors, *Aggression and Defense* (Berkeley: University of California Press, 1967), pp. 317–325.

[41] Orwell, "Why I Write," in his *Collected Essays,* Volume I, pp. 1–7. Citation is to page 5.

[42] These quotations from Lasswell and Abraham Kaplan, *Power and Society: A Framework for Political Inquiry* (New Haven: Yale University Press, 1950), p. xiii.

[43] Crick, *George Orwell,* p. 344f.

[44] Lasswell, "Democratic Character," p. 473f.

[45] Ibid., pp. 476–477.

[46] These quotes appear in Crick, *George Orwell,* on p. 306 and p. 362, and in Orwell's essay "James Burnham and the Managerial Revolution," p. 164.

[47] Lasswell, "Democratic Character," pp. 523–525.

[48] Emancipation is discussed as well in Lasswell's much earlier *World Politics and Personal Insecurity,* p. 98, where its "fullest psychological sense" is limited "to the achievement of release from an internalized symbol of authority." What a change some fifteen years later!

I am reminded of the curious convergence between the "iron cages" of Orwell and Weber. Nothing is a more powerful symbol of dehumanizing totalitarian terror in *1984.* Nothing is less value neutral and more powerfully antibureaucratic, antimaterialistic value-pleading than Weber's final remarks in *The Protestant Ethic and the Spirit of Capitalism* (New York: Scribner's, 1958), pp. 181–183:

> The Puritan wanted to work in a calling; we are forced to do so. . . . In Baxter's view the care for external goods should only lie on the shoulders of the 'saint like a light cloak. . . .' But fate decreed that the cloak should become an iron cage. . . . Victorious capitalism, since it rests on mechanical foundations, needs the support of religious asceticism no longer. The rosy blush of its laughing heir, the Enlightenment, seems also to be irretrievably fading, and the idea of duty in one's calling prowls about in our lives like the ghost of dead religious beliefs. . . . No one knows who will live in this cage in the future, or whether at the end of this tremendous development entirely new prophets will arise, or there will be a great rebirth of old ideas and ideals, or, if neither, mechanized petrification,

embellished with a sort of convulsive self-importance. For of the last stage of this cultural development, it might well be truly said: "Specialists without spirit, sensualists without heart; this nullity imagines that it has attained a level of civilization never before achieved."

[49] Independently of the present enterprise, I have been stimulated by the writing and the reading of two recent review articles on the state of international relations research in the United States: Hayward R. Alker, Jr., and Thomas Biersteker, "Dialectics of World Order," *International Studies Quarterly*, 28, 2 (1984): 121–142; and Richard Ashley, "The Poverty of Neorealism," *International Organization*, 38 (Spring, 1984): 225–286.

[50] See the publications of Ruth Sivard and of the Bariloche group for further relevant quantitative analyses, particularly Amílcar D. Herrera et al., *Catastrophe or New Society? A Latin American World Model* (Ottawa: International Development Research Centre, 1976).

On the more journalistic side, an excellent, informed critique of the "distortions, disingenuous statements, tortuous interpretations, half-truths" (and outright lies) of congressional testimony and public declarations by American policy makers concerning Central America, so reminiscent of Vietnam, is Raymond Bonner, *Weakness and Deceit: U.S. Policy and El Salvador* (New York: Times Books, 1984); the quotation is from p. 9. We learn how American Presidents have certified progress in human rights to have occurred even when Archbishop Oscar Arnulfo Romero is publicly assassinated with apparent impunity for such "communistic" views as the claim, surely consistent with human dignity, that "the root of all violence is institutional violence. The situation in the country is lamentable, particularly among peasants and slum dwellers. The rich are getting richer, the poor are getting poorer" (p. 43).

[51] The domestic evidence on bimodalization is assessed in Joshua Cohen and Joel Rogers, "After the Fall," *Boston Review*, 9 (August 1984): 18–20; and Thomas B. Edsall, *The New Politics of Inequality* (New York: Norton, 1985). Relevant international evidence is in the book cited in the previous note.

[52] See Richard Falk, *A World Order Perspective on Authoritarian Tendencies* (New York: Institute for World Order, 1981).

[53] Hannah Arendt, Preface to Volume 2 (*Totalitarianism*) of her *The Origins of Totalitarianism*, 3 volumes (New York: Harcourt, Brace and World, 1968).

[54] Alexander Zinoviev is the living political writer of my acquaintance who comes closest to continuing the Swift-Voltaire-Orwell tradition, see his *The Yawning Heights* and *The Radiant Future* (New York: 1979 and 1980). Two profound and provocative semiformal, dialectically inspired treatments of Soviet doublethink are Jon Elster's analysis of Zinoviev, "Negation Active et Negation Passive," *Archive for European Sociology*, Vol. XXI (1980); and Vladimir A. Lefebvre, *Algebra of Conscience: A Comparative Analysis of Western and Soviet Ethical Systems* (Dordrecht and Boston: Reidel, 1982). On the roots of American jingoism, see Michael Hunt's historical treatment in *Ideology and Foreign Policy* (New Haven: Yale University Press, 1987).

TOWARDS 2084

CONTINUING THE ORWELLIAN TRADITION

๛ *James Combs*

The year 1984 came and went without undue public consternation about the significance of the event. Orwell's year was characterized by attempts to ignore reflection on the meaning of the year, through efforts to enlist Orwell in the ranks of some contemporary political position, or to accuse others of misinterpreting Orwell for the sake of some currently fashionable political idea. Ironically enough, Orwell's name and year were reduced in significance by transformation into propaganda. Neoconservative polemicist Norman Podhoretz told *Reader's Digest* readers that Orwell's message was being twisted by the "new aristocracy" who control media and classroom into the opposite of what he meant.[1] But he also assured *Harper's* readers that if Orwell were alive today he would definitely be a neoconservative damning the orthodoxies and delusions of "the Left."[2] Similarly, Professor A. M. Eckstein of the University of Maryland attended an Orwell conference and concluded that the professoriate interpreting Orwell thought *1984* an allegory for contemporary America.[3] All told, a wide variety of journals of opinion as well as individual writers invoked the authority and sympathy of a man long dead. Such writers were like the medium in the ancient Japanese tale *Rashomon,* conjuring up Orwell's ghost so that he could testify as to what he really, really meant and how the conjuror-writer had truly represented his thoughts on the matter, since Orwell himself was regrettably absent. The polemical battle over custody of Orwell's corpse became nearly idolatrous, transforming a man *in absentia* who prided himself on fierce independence of thought into a propagandist for this and that political stance thirty-five years after his death. Some thought the academic cottage industry that sprang up around *1984* was a sort of Orwellian nightmare in itself, moving Leopold Labedz to remark, "Reading the unending stream of commentaries of Orwell and 'his' year, it is indeed obvious that, more often than not, he has been misunderstood and generally trivialized, and his insights willfully distorted."[4]

In a sense, such silly appropriation of the ghost of Orwell present demonstrated that Orwell had both succeeded and failed. He had succeeded in that he had drawn attention to a demonic political trend of the twentieth century in no uncertain terms. No serious reader of *1984* could fail to imagine what living in such a world meant for the individual. But Orwell seems to have failed in other ways. For one thing, his commitment to a more hopeful political trend that he wanted to triumph —democratic socialism—was quickly forgotten after his death. For another, his novel was pointed to as an anticommunist tract, used itself as proof of the ultimate goals of Soviet and Chinese Communism. The most disturbing political novel of the century was understood as propaganda immediately, as useful in the Western mobilization against the Soviet empire. No amount of pleading that he meant us, too, could free the book from its popular perception as a portrait of what Russia had become and wanted to do to us as well. Orwell's very warning about the reduction of literature into propaganda was ignored, and early on the book had taken on attributes the author did not intend. (To this day, you can buy paperback copies of *1984* in John Birch Society bookstores.) Not only was his message distorted, it was also trivialized. "1984" became a popular symbol for every innovation that smacked of regimentation, manipulation, and control. When Orwell's vision became popular, perhaps we should have suspected that the horror of his tale would be undermined. Since it was too grim to erase from consciousness, and too well known to deny, it was either casually applied to anything and everything or scoffed at as a prophecy that did not come true.

It was true in 1984 that the book was a best seller again, that there was a plethora of popular articles on Orwell, and even a new movie of the novel (which was not released until 1985 and was a box office failure). But the tone of much discussion was one of displacement: it may be happening to Them, but not to Us. Rather than a self-fulfilling prophecy, Orwell's cautionary tale was seen as a self-thwarting prophecy. He warned us, we heeded him, and the disaster was averted here, we smugly told ourselves. In the self-righteous atmosphere of the eighties, Orwell's ghost haunted not the American mansions and corridors of power. Interestingly enough, the problematics of *1984* entered the Presidential race that year only once, when Vice-President George Bush told graduating students at Texas A&M that Orwell's prophecy cannot happen here if we "stand together, firm and strong, in defense of our freedom." The meaning of the novel is strictly anti-Soviet: "Big Brother may be all-powerful in Havana, but the United States will not stand idly by while Big Brother tries to extend his power and influence over our freedom-loving neighbors in Central America." Bush's rhetorical misuse of Orwell should have been expected, as in a larger sense should the extent to which his message was ignored, and probably repressed, in the ethos of the 1984 election. Similarly, the press reported, and scoffed at, a Soviet political journal's attempt to characterize the real-life version of *1984* in the U.S. under a "Big Brother" named Ronald Reagan. The article in *New Times,* by Viktor Tsoppi, acknowledged that the West had tried to show it as a portrait of Soviet society, but concluded (along with the unnamed "new aristocracy" of Podhoretz and the Professor Pinko Q. Bedwetters that Eckstein saw at the Orwell conference) that Orwell intended his book as a warning of what the capitalist West would become someday. America, the Soviet writer contended, was now a society in which complete uniformity of view was possible. In Reagan's America, we now have a leader who claims to be the inexhaustible source of wisdom, happiness, and virtue. The FBI are the Thought Police; the networks present hate broadcasts that condition us into continuous frenzies of hatred of foreign devils; the American Ministry of Plenty presides over unemployment, homelessness, starvation, and bankruptcy; the American Ministry of Truth propagates lies and disinformation; and the American Ministry of Peace prepares for war and empire. But by 2084, with the triumph of communism, we will live in a world that will be lovely.[5]

It may well be the case that by 2084 both communism and capitalism have long been superseded by something else. But in 1984, both economic systems were so integral to the competing political ideologies of the rival superpowers that their defenders argued that they produced what was true, beautiful, and good and accused the other of producing all that was false, ugly, and evil. Both sides saw in the other system the seeds of the perfected totalitarianism of Orwell's nightmare. But as Nelson understood, we were dealing with the mythologic rather than the ideologic, with both sides projecting their own fears and fantasies on the Other through the imaginative prism of Orwell's familiar nightmare. Thus the most profoundly antipropaganda book of our time was enrolled from publication through its celebration as alternative propagandas; the book that pleaded so eloquently for truth and tolerance became a weapon in the political struggle of 1984 for the lies and intolerance of the endless war Orwell had predicted; the book that made the most heroic effort to face the political realities unraveling in the latter half of the twentieth century was used to deny the potential of those realities; the book by a man who saw hopefully a democratic socialism that could transcend the totalitarian tendencies of West and East was enlisted by both to prove the other more totalitarian. "In our time," Orwell wrote in his famous essay on politics and the English language, "political speech and writing are largely the defense of the indefensible." In the time of 1984, Orwell's very own political writing was used largely in the defense of the indefensible.

Outside the academy, then, Orwell's year was characterized either by a concerted effort to avoid critical reflection on the meaning of *1984,* or to mobilize that meaning into those political habits against which Orwell had so mightily struggled. And, as we have seen with Podhoretz and Eckstein, thought on Orwell within the academic circle was also attacked. But much the same thing happened there, too. A lot of what was said and written about *1984* did involve the very special pleading and intellectual overkill that Orwell might indeed have found distasteful. But he might well have also disliked intellectuals like Podhoretz and others in a semiofficial capacity telling the mass public to ignore the biased intellectuals of the ivory tower who have prejudged and altered Orwell's message and rather heed the "new aristocracy" of right-thinking intellectuals attached to the Reagan administration who will offer a correct interpretation. One may here ask, who's in the contemporary Ministry of Truth and who's not?

In any case, academic reflection on Orwell in 1984 was fortunately not limited to ideological rhetoric or diatribes against particular regimes or politics. Indeed, the editors of this volume read many worthwhile papers on Orwell that were either reprinted elsewhere or not reprinted here because of the limitations of space. The papers we did select are representative of the range of interests and applications serious scholars brought up in 1984 and suggest rather well the kind of questions that should be raised in the post-1984 world. For if Orwell and these essays mean anything, it is that we (and, yes, the Russians and Chinese) are not out of the historical woods yet. Orwell hit both an intellectual and a popular nerve so long ago because he articulated in bold and bleak terms what many thought or sensed we were becoming. These essays say one way or another that we should not have seen 1984 go with a sigh of relief or smug self-satisfaction. Although diverse in their foci, our authors are all implicitly saying that Orwell's nightmare vision is not a dream that is over because we are past "that year." Orwell saw not a year but a tendency, not a specific system but a fundamental and universal corruption, not a present elsewhere to be condemned but a future everywhere that might not be avoidable. For this reason, we want to extract an Orwellian propositional inventory that can be observed and tracked as we move all too quickly into the twenty-first century and towards 2084.

ORWELL'S WORLD

This volume comes forward on the assumption that Orwell's fictional future might not someday be a fiction. When he wrote the book, it had enough foundation in fact to be recognizable as a possibility. As Elie Weisel has said, the twentieth century is unique in that it can imagine the unimaginable. Nuclear annihilation and the systematic murder of millions are apocalyptic events that we can now imagine after Hiroshima and Auschwitz. But Orwell imagined something else hitherto unimaginable, something more insidious and permanent: the idea that the advanced technological societies of whatever ideology and political culture were inexorably changing into new tyrannies with powers and ambitions far beyond anything hitherto attempted. Apologists for both Communist and Western societies can point to countertrends they claim negate Orwell's thesis. But the historical stakes are too high to rest easy in such claims if we think Orwell anything more than an alarmist. Forecasting is an inexact science, and indeed Orwell was quite right to use political art as the best way to project his possible future. Here we must be content with some propositions, themes that run through the Orwellian literature, that it would be wise for us to watch for when and if they unfold in the future.

Orwell envisioned a future characterized by one overriding fact: *the decay of Western civilization and the rise and apparent triumph of a new and unprecedented civilization.* The Western world's political and social traditions will be, if Orwell is right, transformed sooner or later into a totalitarianism so complete, and so efficient, that it will not absorb the traditions of the West (as, say the early West absorbed Rome) but rather destroy them. Orwell sees a new Dark Age unleavened by the rise of a new faith that leads to the new civilization of Charlemagne and Alfred the Great. Rather it is a Dark Age that revels in its own permanent immunity from change and decay, and reforms only to make its powers of control all the more complete. There is no hope for a Renaissance that ends the long night of darkness.

The project of Orwell's future world-managers, if Promethean in scope, is perverted in purpose: they aim at nothing less than the *end of history.* Not only do they now believe they have the means to arrest change, they also think they can end history as a concept in both remembrance and as a cumulative discipline. History suggests a knowledge of process that invites comparison of past and present. But if the concept of history is destroyed, then the idea that there was anything else in the past that was better, and by extension anything better in the future, vanishes. This disconnection from any sense of history ends history. The individual and State live in an eternal present, an endless and stultifying cycle of enforced sameness that admits not the possibility of a past or a future. Time would still exist in the rhythmic sense of the passage of days, seasons, years, and generations, but it would be ahistorical. Time would be noncumulative, a world without history. The only infinity would be the eternal present.

The epistemological correlate of this project is equally bold. Orwell's world of tomorrow would *eliminate reality itself as a feasible hypothesis.* The common-sense notion that reality is a property of experience that in some sense gives us access to "the real world" would disappear. The notion of "reality as fact" is replaced by "reality as fiction." Reality is a property of political definition that does nothing less than deny facticity. Reality becomes a "collective solipsism," as O'Brien calls it, a delusional dream that serves to sustain the eternal present. Orwell seems to think that the malleability of mind is infinite, to the point of denying one's common sense experience of reality and affirming a pseudo-reality that is a creation of the political control of imagination. Rather than "radical empiricism," such a world is one of "radical illusionism." Power is ultimately rooted in the propagation of a fantasy world that supersedes the mundane and palpable. The psychic mechanisms of self-delusion—doublethink, crimestop, and so on—would be based in the ubiquity of infinite credulity. We will become permanent residents of Plato's Cave content with the political shadow-show that we think real.

In Orwell's future, the elimination of the concept of reality is accompanied by *the substitution of truth with propaganda.* The idea of truth as a value in itself becomes outmoded in favor of lying as a value in itself. Truth is replaced by "political truth," an expedient use of communication for purposes of deception and manipulation. Something is only "true" if it is useful for an immediate political purpose. Like the distinction between "good and evil" and "beauty and ugliness," "true and untrue" becomes a false dichotomy devoid of meaning. The principle of propaganda—that nothing is true, beautiful, or good unless it serves a political purpose—destroys such archaic and naive notions. Truth, like reality, would no longer have any inherent or commonsense value. In Orwell's polity, we would no longer speak truth to power; power would speak truth—their truth—to us. The future will have then completed the process of substituting truth with propaganda. We will not retain any more sense of the value or recognition of truth than we will the real.

Although truth will be a function of political orthodoxy, Orwell's future is *devoid of ideology.* The managers of the future, like O'Brien, will be technocrats interested in the logic of power not the logic of ideas. Theirs will be a power philosophy pure and simple, without forensic articulation of, or commitment to,

ideas. Ideology is a form of mystification. It is communicated as propaganda because that is all it is. The attitude of an Orwellian elite will be that ideology is an
"ignoble lie" in a future of no noble truths. In that spirit, the official doctrine of
such states will be closer to myth and folklore than ideology. The pseudo-war
and pseudo-conspiracy of Oceania are tales told for popular consumption and
control. The managers control a "drama of permanence" enacted over and over
again to demonstrate the efficacy of their political myths and propagate a political
folklore rather than an ideology centered around the lie of the tenacity of the
rulers, the "truth" of slogans, and the inspiration of tales of sacrifice and devotion. Ideology will be a political irrelevance.

In that way, Orwell's imagined future is curiously *bereft of political "isms."*
Not only is that world without the spectral ideologies that agitate the present, it is
also emptied of the enduring political temperaments that have been part of the
world political scene since the ancient world. Orwell's political world does not
invite political realism in the sense of a rational science of political conduct to
achieve good political ends. Quite the contrary, it is the perfect model of Max
Weber's "iron cage," the degenerate form of "crackpot realism" that expresses the
irrationality of total control. If Machiavellian realism can be said to aim at a rational economy of political power, then Orwellian pseudo-realism by contrast can
be said to aim at an irrational diseconomy of political power. Too, Orwell's state
is devoid of the temper of political romanticism. It discourages hope, enthusiasm,
even fanaticism, since emotion, like reason, can get out of control. Here, too, we
see a degenerate political form, a sort of pseudo-romanticism that affects vivacity
but cannot sustain it. Even Big Brother is a kind of substitute pseudo-charismatic
figure that is a controlled object of political feelings. Political emotion in Oceania
is as false as political reason. Finally, Orwell's dystopia is without the temper of
political classicism, the lessons of tradition. Devoid of classical models or historical precedent, the future state inherits nothing, learns nothing, and aims for
nothing. It has not the authority of rationality, charisma, or tradition. It is a
pseudo-authority ruling in a mindless void of its own making.

It is obvious enough that in Orwell's future freedom ends completely. So
completely that in a sense the State aims for the *omission of personal identity*. Personal identity in such a world would not be real or true. The concept of "self" as
a free and identifiable core of being would make no sense. The internal "thought
police" that eventually would make the external control-force largely superfluous
gains its power through psychic self-controls. The idea of a multidimensional
Protean self disappears in favor of a restrictive self. Psychic energy is blended into
a collective self, of which Big Brother serves as a palpable symbol. Not only will
we escape from freedom, we will also escape from identity. The "psychological

man" of the future will be trained to practice a strict economy of the inner life, identifying instead with an all-powerful and immortal political self. The technocratic managers of the future will conquer the last frontier, the mind and soul of man. As their power grows more subtle, the old crude methods of imposed external enslavement will be superseded by methods of induced self-enslavement. Like Winston Smith, we will all learn how to win the victory over ourselves. The masters of Orwell's world will then have not only severely circumscribed the bounds of thinkable thought but also the bounds of knowable self.

This is not to say, as Orwell understood, that the more direct and brutal forms of totalitarian domination will disappear. But Orwell was one of those dystopian writers who suggested that the ingenuity of such a state would be one of the expansion and perfection of the means of domination, including means not well understood before. This "political logic" of total domination we may term *omnipression.* An omnipressive state of the future mobilizes every social and psychic tool to perfect its control of its subjects. It will refine such means as suppression, oppression, and repression but not be confined to those. For example, Orwell understood the power of diversion through entertainment. One of the major forms of mystification is drawing people into the pseudo-drama of the state, diverting them from real problems by the vicarious delights of imaginary ones. For lack of a better term, this mode of domination we will call *supercession,* in which reality is superceded by fantasy, directing our attention toward, and inviting our obsession with, theatrical representations that substitute for the absence of contact with realities grounded in truth. Supercession is domination through entertainment, using political theater to dramatize the ritual drama of the State. The unending pseudo-war of Oceania against her enemies foreign and domestic may have been a bad melodrama, but it gave a theatrical rhythm and purpose to the political order that made the individual part of something larger than himself or herself. Such "projective identification" not only merges one's self with a larger-than-life collectivity but also submerges mundane evidence of the sinister power of the other forms of omnipression. In Orwell's dystopian world, we will amuse ourselves into self-enslavement. The cruder forms of omnipression would become all the less necessary as we absorb ourselves in the grand, and cyclically unending, drama of the State.

The stability of such a State is grounded on an *end to politics,* at least in the way Orwell's generation thought of it. For in Oceania politics is replaced by political *ritualism,* cyclical rituals of economic pseudo-dramas of production quotas and consumption promises; political pseudo-dramas of conspiracy, betrayal, exposure, and righteous revenge; and military pseudo-dramas of the clash of arms, victories, and plunder, and yet the eternal threat of new states and armies marching to destroy us. Orwell foresaw a political elite with the supercessive power to engineer periodic and universal cycles of wills-to-believe and to sustain forever the willing suspension of disbelief. The comfort of ritual drama is in the predictability of role and story, bearable and brief anxiety over the outcome climaxed by certain triumph, followed by the Sisyphean task of rebeginning and retelling the story all over again. Such an eternal recurrence might seem to us boring and stultifying, but perhaps that is the very point: the sense of a political eternity can be sustained in a timeless context of cyclical supercession. As long as the fundamental delusion can be perpetuated, the pseudo-drama of the State is as much a part of the natural order as the seasons.

If in the future politics is transformed into ritualism, this means that the role and function of politicians will be very different. Orwell was, we know, influenced by ideas about "the managerial revolution." The political elite of Oceania is indeed an organizational structure of psychic and social managers, functionaries in the fullest Kafkaesque sense of the word. But their job is not limited to obfuscatory mystification; their mission, in O'Brien's words, is to be "priests of power," to *transform organized power from an instrument into a metaphysic.* Orwell's future is in an odd way the obverse of Machiavelli: rather than use power for instrumental reasons that minimize political trouble and extended effort, the priests would use power to manufacture bogus political troubles and maximize at least the appearance of public effort in response. The doctrine "God is power" suggests that the rulers of that future rule as the keepers of an idolatrous political magic, the high priests of a phony religion, the tenets of which only they know. In the future, then, there will be no political science, rather there will be political magic, the illusions of the political shadow-show of the magic lantern projected for us by the stage manager-priests with powers unlimited by values external to its exercise. If this be megalomania, O'Brien seems to say, then make the most of it; we control the puppets, and know the outcome of the show: what could be more godlike?

Orwell was not a religious man, but his vision of negative power exercised by a cynical and untouchable caste of manager-priests is reminiscent of the legend of the Grand Inquisitor. In Fyodor Dostoevski's famous parable, Jesus returns to Earth and is immediately arrested by an ancient cardinal, the conductor of the Inquisition. The Grand Inquisitor explains to Christ in His cell that They (the rulers of the Church) had "corrected" His work, ruling in His stead with "miracle, mystery, and authority." Jesus should not have returned, since now He can only hinder the work of those who understand that mankind is incapable of freedom and willingly trades freedom and the knowledge which makes one free for the paternal embrace of the Inquisitor and the mysterious power he represents.

O'Brien resembles the Grand Inquisitor in many ways: his cynical and nihilistic stance above value; his paternalistic attitude towards his victim, as both father-punisher and guide-corrector; and his willingness to live with, and rule in, an existential vacuum without hope or meaning. O'Brien's candor is even more bold than the Grand Inquisitor: he makes no claim whatsoever to benevolence, even though both spare the great mass of men the uncomfortable truths that they cannot live with. For the ruling class of O'Brien's world, *power is totally demonic.* Power here has not even the modicum of pragmatic efficacy claimed by the Grand Inquisitor, necessitating a pact with Satan for the good of a weak and fearful mankind. In Orwell's nightmare there is no demonic pact, no Faustian bargain, for an earthly good. Rather, O'Brien's Inner Party is in itself the demonic force, bargaining with no external power, not even God and Satan. O'Brien's frank mendacity commits the State to an agenda that tests the demonic imagination. As Hannah Arendt once argued, the microcosmic model for O'Brien's perfected State could only be the death camp, an expanded necropolis whose ultimate triumph would be the mental and physical annihilation of anything resembling human life.

Winston Smith objected, we may recall, to the political logic of such an order. He thought it self-destructive, suicidal, a dead empire of demons ruling ghosts. The more demonic the expression of total power the less vitality. Such a system has a kind of built-in death wish, giving impetus to nothing save entropy. It would have no power to revitalize itself, given the inhuman commitment to the destruction of any form of authenticity. Its power would be the power of death, the political expression of a death culture. Without any power to create, it would have no other choice than the power to destroy. Since it has tried to destroy reality itself, its final nihilistic project would by its own logic *be the destruction of the source of any notions of reality, truth, or idea: consciousness.* "Orthodoxy means not thinking—not needing to think," Syme told Winston Smith, "Orthodoxy is unconsciousness." But even the ubiquity of external controls and the linguistic rigidities of Newspeak cannot insure complete orthodoxy of action and thought. The possibility of subversive thought exists even in Newspeak, and independence of action might persist because of aversion to pain. It may be, then, that the complete, and final, solution to the project of Orwell's dystopia would be the political act of self-induced destruction of consciousness. The completion of the power of such a State would be in its ability to convince its subjects that in the end the final orthodox act, the solution to the threat of consciousness, would be universal suicide. In that expression of total obedience, political power reaches both its zenith and nadir. The obliteration of the self solves the problem of orthodoxy. The true precursor of Orwell's future was Jonestown.

If this seems insane, it is not Orwell's fault for imagining the unimaginable. We here in this volume have tried to imagine the implications of Orwell's bleak vision. Orwell did not speak of the alternative form of universal self-destruction we have invented, nuclear war. But if our inference above is correct, Orwell was on the track not of nuclear winter but of psychic winter, the obliteration of the race through the obliteration of the self. At least in terms of the principles and logic of Oceania, such an obliteration is not only feasible but in the end desirable. We think that serious inquiry should be directed into the proposition that the major advanced technocratic states of the late twentieth and early twenty-first century are becoming *death cultures with an unspoken but insidious commitment to the principle of death.* This would be manifest not only in the expansion of the principle of death as the basis for military policy, expanding to the node of actual use the varied means of universal self-destruction; but also in policies and processes which transform humans into "robopaths" and kill off honest or humane thoughts and actions.[6] It would be a violation of the intellectual spirit we venerate in this volume if we did not think the bleakest thoughts in order to examine ways of avoiding what we are in the process of becoming. Like Orwell, we do not assume that good naturally prevails. If there is a fatal sickness unfolding in our time, those of us in the Orwellian tradition want to try to imagine what it is before it reaches the terminal stage of political death.

THE HUXLEYAN COMPLEMENT

Our use of the Orwellian perspective on the future should be complemented by that of another great dystopian novelist of our time, Aldous Huxley. His novel *Brave New World,* while more comic in its satire of the future, is no less bleak in its consequences. Huxley contended that, in the long run, the managers of the future will find modes of scientific manipulation and control so subtle that the brutal immediacies of *1984* would become superfluous. As we have seen, Orwell sees this too: Huxley's "brave new world" is Oceania far in the future. But the fundamental demon of control lurks there too. In a letter to Orwell after reading his book, Huxley saw their dystopian futures rooted in what he called the "philosophy of the ultimate revolution—the revolution which lies beyond politics and economics, and which aims at the total subversion of the individual's psychology and physiology—to be found in the Marquis de Sade, who regarded himself as the continuator, the consummator, of Robespierre and Babeuf." But, he contended, the sadism of the ruling Inner Party of Orwell's nightmare has inverted de Sade's demonic project: rather than sexual activism as the ultimate expression of political domination, the rulers of *1984* express "a sadism which has been carried to its logical conclusion by going beyond sex and denying it." Huxley thought that the sadistic lust for power of *1984* would evolve into the "scientific" controls of *Brave New World,* wherein "the lust for power can be just as completely satisfied by suggesting people into loving their servitude as by flogging and kicking them into obedience."[7]

The two authors are looking at two sides of the same historical impulse rooted in the ancient Grand Inquisitorial arrogance of power. Our dystopian writers see a reach for absolute power with a chance of approaching it. The Weberian "iron cage" can now for the first time really be created, because of the power of what Jacques Ellul calls *technique.* How it can be done will require "rationalization" of means. Orwell emphasizes the technologic of pain; Huxley emphasizes the technology of pleasure. "In *1984,*" wrote Huxley in *Brave New World Revisited,* "the lust for power is satisfied by inflicting pain; in *Brave New World,* by inflicting a hardly less humiliating pleasure."[8] Both pain and pleasure, denial and access, prohibition and license, punishment and reward, are merely the major techniques of control available to rational elites. However, both are agreed that power in such future worlds is a deception, and that control, whether overt or covert, and not freedom, is the agenda of the State. For example, both are agreed that the deception of diversion, what we have called supercession, is fundamental to absolute rule. Huxley in 1958 foresaw the power of the communications industry, ". . . concerned in the main neither with the true nor the false, but with the unreal, the more or less totally irrelevant. In a word, [we have] failed to take into account man's almost infinite appetite for distractions." In the future, "non-stop distractions . . . are deliberately used as instruments of policy; for the purpose of preventing people from paying too much attention to the realities of the social and political situation." People in the future will spend a great part of daily life "somewhere else," in the "irrelevant other worlds of sport and soap opera, of mythology and metaphysical fantasy" and thus will "find it hard to resist the encroachments of those who would manipulate and control" them.[9]

Perhaps what Huxley means here is not so much the unreal as the *surreal,* our vicarious entry into imaginary social worlds that supercede the confines and logic of mundane reality through the representation of fantastic imagery. The power of such future states will stem in large measure from their ability to control the play of imagination, restricting and channeling it into surreal worlds that make political use of our "infinite appetite" for distractions. We will ask the Grand Inquisitors of the future to take our freedom, but entertain us. Already it is thought that ". . . most Americans probably spend more time in artificial interactions [with media fantasy figures] than they do in real ones."[10] Television, argues another observer, has contained our consciousness to the point where we are now spectators to our own annihilation: "As you watch, there is no Big Brother out there watching you—not because there isn't a Big Brother, but because Big Brother is you, watching."[11] And Neil Postman thought that at the very time we were congratulating ourselves for avoiding Orwell, we were succumbing to Huxley: "What Orwell feared were those who would ban books. What Huxley feared was that there would be no reason to ban a book, for there would be no one who wanted to read one." "Big Brother," he says, "turns out to be Howdy Doody."[12] The future would then be not so much logocratic, concerned with the control of the word, as iconocratic, concerned with the control of the image. The ultimate consequence of the emergent "visual culture" would be in the political organization of the imagination. "Collective solipsism" would in that case be quite feasible.

Perhaps what we are talking about here is the emergence of a new kind of politics, the *politics of simulation.* The French thinker Jean Baudrillard has given impetus to the idea that in the still forming "postmodern" world, we are "substituting signs of the real for the real itself," since "the real is no longer real," and power itself "produces nothing but the signs of its resemblance." We now live in a psychotic world, in which "artifice is at the very heart of reality." It is the model that we substitute for the real, and the aesthetic simulation that we recognize and appreciate over the brute reality.[13] "Political theater," then, is not a set of histrionic devices with which we augment political conduct, rather theater is politics itself, an aesthetic simulation of what we in our imaginary "model worlds" conceive politics to be. If we take artifice to be reality, then reality is a property of play and not work, imagination and not tactility, communication and not objects, ritual magic and not brute empiricism, the power of aesthetic representation and not the power of the ideal, the inspiration, or even the boot in the face. The successful political actors of the future will rule imaginary states with simulated power. Like King Canute, their simulated power will derive from the quixotic heroism of commanding the waves, rather than their actual power to command them.

We may only speculate how long a state based on a simulated surreality can survive. Huxley's complement to the Orwellian vantage point is decidedly comic. His brave new world is awful but absurd, a dystopia whose allure is not its Orwellian embrace of pure evil, but rather its descent into silliness. Its science is not so much sinister as preposterous, reducing us not to the grim ghosts of *1984* but rather to cheerful and insipid servomechanisms with uniform and superficial desires and mindsets. Huxley's sugarcoated and smiling world is reminiscent of William James' reaction after a week in the nineteenth century's version of *Brave New World,* the Chautauqua: It was, he thought, too tame, too good, too stale, and unadventurous. Just as many found Skinner's *Walden II* later on, James was repelled by the "atrocious harmlessness of all things."[14] Huxley's world is a giant Chautauqua, peopled by smiling and empty mannequins living out their lives of administered happiness. Huxley may be right in that such a State might be perpetuated by the power of its own silliness. The sinister may well eventually collapse of its own weight, but not the preposterous. The preposterous has no weight and thus is sustained and lofted by the air of its own conceit.

Towards 2084

This volume exists because there was interest in Orwell's political perspicacity in the late twentieth century. The passage of 1984 should now, however, be the end of the story. For in a major sense Orwell's message is now all the more urgent in the wake of 1984 and the complacency that characterized that year. It will remain a major task of social science not only to forecast dangerous trends that might undermine human values in the future. The demon-of-control that writers like Orwell and Huxley discovered in the political heart of darkness of the twentieth century will still lurk out there in the future, and it will take all the talents of the bearers of civilization to defeat it. For this reason, social scientists would do well to continue the futuristic visions of poets and novelists and filmmakers. For example, Margaret Atwood's recent novel *The Handmaid's Tale* is clearly in the Orwellian vein, a grim view of a loveless American future ruled over by a quasi-religious order of men that enforces a regimented caste system in which one female caste, the "Handmaids," are designated to procreate to perpetuate the elite and offset the drastic decline in population.[15] The study of fantasy and science-fiction works should become one of the major concerns of social science. Such a task runs against the optimistic grain of the 1980s, but that should not dissuade us from the urgency of the task. It is the burden of those impressed with Orwell's achievement in imagining the "worst case" of a political future to keep alive his perspective, what we may term *the negative imagination*. The negative imagination does not envision political evil, bleakness, or silliness just to be negative, but rather for the moral purpose of negating the negation itself. Imagining the unimaginable in great flights of negative fancy lets us articulate the worst of what we might expect and the consequences of what still might happen.

In that spirit, this volume took advantage of the Orwellian moment to examine both hindsight and foresight. We looked with hindsight on the now symbolic figure of George Orwell and now must look with foresight towards a still potentially menacing future. Fortified by the example of Orwell, we must now ask, with all the imaginative powers at our command, what might the world of 2084 be like? If George Orwell were alive, it is likely that he would find that a most interesting question. Let us hope that those of us in the Orwellian tradition find it no less interesting.

NOTES

[1] "1984 is Here: Where is Big Brother?" *Readers Digest,* 124 (January, 1984): 33–38.

[2] "If Orwell Were Alive Today," *Harper's,* 266 (January, 1983): 29–37.

[3] "An Orwellian Nightmare Fulfilled: An Eyewitness's Account," *Chronicle of Higher Education,* 29 (October 17, 1984): 72.

[4] "Will George Orwell Survive 1984?" *Encounter,* 63 (June, 1984): 11.

[5] "Bush Says U.S. Can Avert '1984' If Allies Are Firm," *New York Times,* May 7, 1984, p. B8; "Soviet Says Orwell's Vision is Alive in the U.S.," *New York Times,* January 8, 1984, p. 8.

[6] Cf. Jules Henry, *Culture Against Man* (New York: Random House, 1963), pp. 475–476; Lewis Yablonsky, *Robopaths: People as Machines* (Baltimore: Penguin, 1972).

[7] Aldous Huxley, "Letter to George Orwell," in Irving Howe, editor, *Orwell's Nineteen Eighty-four: Text, Sources, Criticism* (New York: Harcourt Brace Jovanovich, 1983), pp. 373–374.

[8] *Brave New World Revisited* (New York: Perennial Library, 1958), p. 27.

[9] *Ibid.,* p. 37.

[10] John L. Caughey, "Artificial Social Relations in Modern America," *American Quarterly,* 30, 1 (1978): 73; see also Caughey, *Imaginary Social Worlds* (Lincoln: University of Nebraska Press, 1984).

[11] Mark Crispin Miller, "Big Brother Is You, Watching," *Georgia Review,* 38 (1984): 695–719; quote at p. 719.

[12] Neil Postman, *Amusing Ourselves to Death* (New York: Viking, 1986), p. 15.

[13] Jean Baudrillard, *Simulations* (New York: Semiotext, Inc., 1983).

[14] Cf. Robert E. Park and E. W. Burgess, *Introduction to the Science of Sociology* (Chicago: University of Chicago Press, 1924), pp. 598–599.

[15] Margaret Atwood, *The Handmaid's Tale* (New York: Houghton Mifflin, 1986).

LIST OF CONTRIBUTORS

HAYWARD R. ALKER, JR., has been a professor of political science at M.I.T. since 1968. Previously he taught at Yale, Flacso (Santiago, Chile), Geneva, and Michigan. He has authored or co-authored *Mathematics and Politics, The Global Interdependence,* and *Resolving Prisoners' Dilemmas.* He is currently at work with Tahir Amin, Thomas Biersteker, and Takashi Inoguchi on a study of *The Dialectics of World Order.* He teaches courses on theories of international relations, complex models of social systems, philosophies of social science, logic and arguments, and nuclear war.

GEORGE BISHOP is professor of political science and a senior research associate in the Behavioral Sciences Laboratory at the University of Cincinnati's Institute for Policy Research, where he directs the Greater Cincinnati Survey. He is also associate director of the Ohio Poll at the Institute. A past president of the Midwest Association for Public Opinion Research, he is an active participant in the American Association for Public Opinion Research and has published a number of articles on survey research in the *Public Opinion Quarterly.* His recent research has focused on how the results of public opinion polls can be affected by the way in which survey questions are worded, the form in which they are presented, and the order or context in which they are asked.

JAMES COMBS, a professor of political science at Valparaiso University, whose research interests have focused primarily upon political communication and manifestations in popular culture, has authored a number of books including *Polpop: Politics and Popular Culture in America* and has had articles appear in publications such as *Dimensions of Political Drama.* He received his Ph.D. from the University of Missouri.

THOMAS W. COOPER is assistant professor of communication at Emerson College and founding director of the Association for Responsible Communication. He has been an assistant speechwriter to former President Jimmy Carter and was an assistant to Marshall McLuhan for five years.

MARK E. CORY, professor of German at the University of Arkansas, studied at Dartmouth College, the Universities of Freiburg and Munich, and received his Ph.D. from Indiana University (1971). He has published a book on the contemporary German experimental radio play, as well as articles on post-war drama and fiction. He has served on the editorial boards of *Studies in Twentieth Century Literature* and *German Studies Review.* His current research projects involve the late novels of Günter Grass and Heinrich Böll, especially as they treat aspects of violence.

RICHARD L. JOHANNESEN (Ph.D., University of Kansas) is chair of the Communication Studies Department and adjunct graduate professor of English (rhetoric) at Northern Illinois University, DeKalb. He teaches courses in freedom and responsibility in communication, contemporary rhetorical theory, and contemporary speakers and speeches. He is author of *Ethics in Human Communication,* editor of *Contemporary Theories of Rhetoric* and of *Ethics and Persuasion,* and co-editor of *Contemporary American Speeches* and of *Language Is Sermonic: Richard M. Weaver on the Nature of Rhetoric.* Recent essays have focused on the ethicality of President Reagan's rhetoric (*Political Communication Yearbook 1984,* eds. K. R. Sanders et al.) and on the jeremiad genre in contemporary discourse (*Communication Monographs,* June 1985).

JOHN S. NELSON is professor of political theory and co-director of the Project on Rhetoric of Inquiry at the University of Iowa. He studied political science and philosophy at the University of Kentucky (BA) and the University of North Carolina at Chapel Hill (Ph.D.). His books include *The Rhetoric of the Human Sciences* (1987), *Tradition, Interpretation, and Science* (1986), and *What Should Political Theory Be Now?* (1983). His continuing interests embrace the interaction of myth, rhetoric, and theory in politics. He often studies the portrayals of cultural crisis and personal trouble that characterize much of our civilization. Among his current projects are essays on political mythmaking in science fiction, horror stories, and adult fantasies.

DAN NIMMO is professor at the Political Communication Center, Department of Communication, University of Oklahoma. He has published books and articles in the areas of communication studies, political communication, political persuasion, and campaigns and voting behavior.

ROBERT L. SAVAGE is professor of political science at the University of Arkansas-Fayetteville. Focusing primarily upon the roles of perception, communication, and culture in politics, he has authored or coauthored a number of works appearing in political science, communication, sociology, and economics publications.

MICHAEL ZUCKERT teaches political philosophy and constitutional law at Carleton College, Northfield, Minnesota. He has particular interest in the liberal tradition and alternatives to it, an interest which brought him to the study of Orwell.

INDEX